1900-1919

All-American Ads

PROBABLY no other area in the worl concentrated than the great entrar Over the elegant, agreeable, richly-c

PENNS
INTER
RUBBE

with which the floor is paved, the in many of the magnificent the or any other material would qu state, years of service can o this most durable floor cover

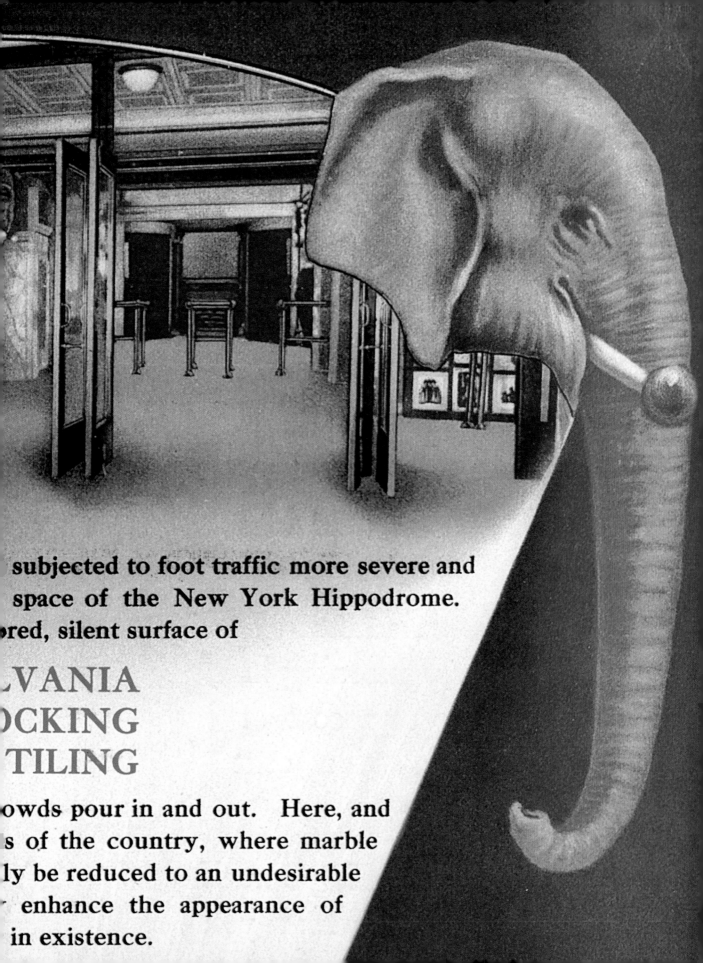

subjected to foot traffic more severe and
space of the New York Hippodrome.
red, silent surface of

LVANIA
OCKING
TILING

owds pour in and out. Here, and
s of the country, where marble
ly be reduced to an undesirable
enhance the appearance of
in existence.

Caruso Melba Schumann-Heink Martin McCormack Tetrazzini S

mbrich

Calvé   Eames   Scotti

Gadski   Homer   Farrar

AQUITANIA

Acknowledgements

This volume of historical material would never have been completed without the help of numerous individuals. Among them are Cindy Vance of Modern Art & Design who continues to labor on these massive volumes with her enthusiasm intact while infusing them with her design and image editing expertise; Nina Wiener who managed to keep this project and countless others at TASCHEN on track, in order and beautifully edited; Steven Heller for his impeccable and swift writing; and Andy Disl, Stefan Klatte, Florian Kobler, Kathrin Murr, Horst Neuzner, and the rest of TASCHEN staff in Cologne for their help and guidance in consistently producing a quality product. Special thanks in the L.A. office to Kate Soto and Morgan Slade, who swooped in to save the day and get this volume out; to intern Alison Clarke for her adventures in captions and fact-checking; and to interns Morgan Weatherford and Chris Evans for all the help organizing images.

As always, a tip of the hat is due to all of those who provided the magazines and material that eventually wound up in this book including Dan DePalma, Ralph Bowman,

Gary Fredericks, Jeff and Pat Carr, Gerry Aboud, Cindy and Steve Vance, Sherry Sonnet, and all the other dealers of paper ephemera. I couldn't have done it without you.

Finally, a big "Souci" thanks to Mr. Taschen for inspiring this important contribution to the visual arts.

Jim Heimann, Los Angeles

All images are from the Jim Heimann collection unless otherwise noted. Any omissions for copy or credit are unintentional and appropriate credit will be given in future editions if such copyright holders contact the publisher.

Cover: Cunard Cruise Line, 1914
Endpapers: Sherwin-Williams Paints, 1917
Page 1: Page-Davis Co., 1903
Pages 2–3: "Bull" Durham Tobacco, 1915
Pages 4–5: Milburn Light Electric, 1918
Pages 6–7: Pennsylvania Rubber Tiling, 1907
Pages 8–9: Old Dutch Cleanser, 1917
Pages 10–11: Victor Victrola Phonographs, 1911
Pages 12–13: Mennen's Borated Talcum, 1908
Pages 14–15: Life Savers Candy, 1917
Pages 16–17: Southern Pacific Steamships, 1910

Imprint

To stay informed about upcoming TASCHEN titles, please request our magazine at www.taschen.com or write to TASCHEN, Hohenzollernring 53, D–50672 Cologne, Germany, Fax: +49-221-254919. We will be happy to send you a free copy of our magazine which is filled with information about all of our books.

© 2005 TASCHEN GmbH
Hohenzollernring 53
D–50672 Köln
www.taschen.com

Art direction & design: Jim Heimann, Los Angeles
Digital composition & design: Cindy Vance, Modern Art & Design, Los Angeles
Cover design: Sense/Net, Andy Disl, Cologne
Production: Stefan Klatte, Cologne
Editorial coordination: Florian Kobler & Kathrin Murr, Cologne
English language editors: Nina Wiener & Kate Soto, Los Angeles
German translation: Anke Caroline Burger, Berlin
French translation: Lien, Amsterdam
Spanish translation: Gemma Deza Guil for LocTeam, S.L., Barcelona
Japanese translation: Hiromi Kakubari, Tokyo

Printed in Spain
ISBN 3-8228-2512-3

1900-1919

All-American Ads

Edited by Jim Heimann
with an introduction by Steven Heller

TASCHEN

KÖLN LONDON LOS ANGELES MADRID PARIS TOKYO

Steven Heller:

Alcohol &
Tobacco
42

Automobile
102

Business
& Industry
200

Consumer
Products
228

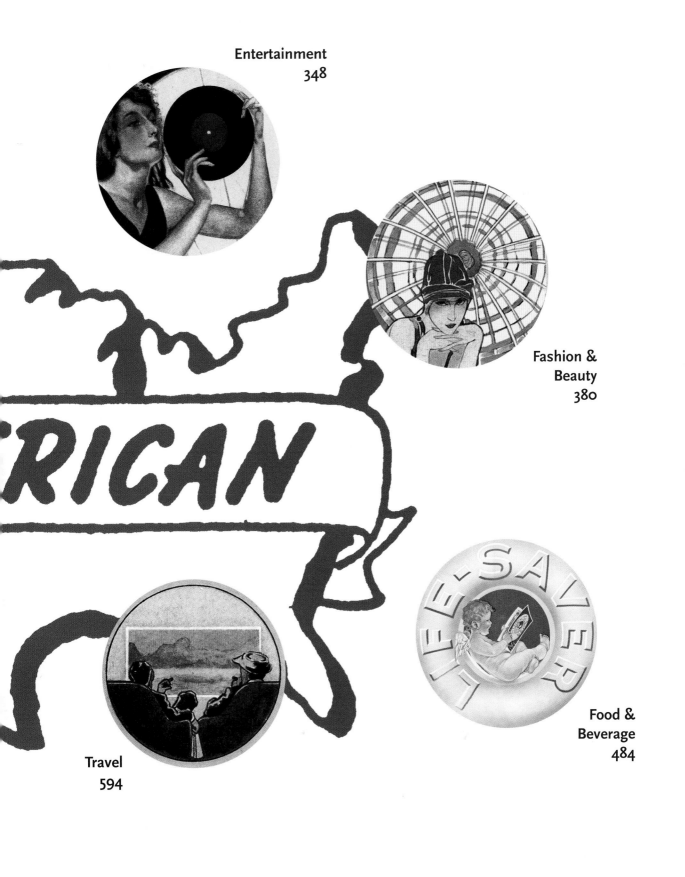

RICAN

1900–1919:
Seducing the New Consumer

by Steven Heller

A more innocent time

American advertising has never been more sumptuous than during the years between 1900 and 1919, when decorative typography and ornate compositions targeted a new consumer class caught in the vortex of twentieth-century progress. Advertising promoted product mythologies and pushed aesthetic ideals. Women emulated and men desired the post-Victorian beauties who sold everything from cameras to toilet powders, while art nouveau design, imported from France, injected a sense of elegance into the printed page.

Call it nostalgia for a more innocent time, before hawking and pitching became pseudo-sciences beholden to marketing Svengalis, trend spotters, and focus groups. This was an era when guileless persuasion and earnest salesmanship reigned supreme. Although graphic humor was a staple of many American popular magazines of the period, most ads, even ones featuring playful mascots like the Gold Medal® Flour clown (page 514), would never poke fun at consumers. Selling goods was no laughing matter.

A religious fervency underscored advertising images of latter-day gods and goddesses promoting the likes of Coca-Cola® and Warner's® Rust-Proof Corsets. Spiritual homilies were frequently sprinkled throughout the sales pitches, and the Gospel — in the form of catchy proverbs or "slogans" and lengthier chapter and verse tracts or "ad copy" — inveigled the mass consciousness. Magazine advertisements were not trying to save souls, however, but to foster capitalist dogma.

Woe be the unwashed

At the dawn of the century, personal hygiene was a secular virtue ripe for propagation. In fact, "cleanliness is next to godliness" was not a religious decree, but an advertising pitch that urged the dirty masses to consume. Soap was one of the first products sold nationally, and many brands quickly flooded the market. In order to differentiate the brands and trigger their sales, new social mores (and taboos) were created that demanded lifestyle changes. Take the example of Sapolio® soap: "The first step away from self-respect is lack of care in personal cleanliness...You can't be healthy, or pretty, or even good, unless you are clean." (page 426). Woe be the unwashed.

Other advertisements commanded consumers to eat packaged cereals, imbibe bottled soft drinks, play recorded music, use powdered cleansers, and even savor citrus fruits. Sunkist®'s earnest headline, "Oranges — what do they mean to you?" (page 563), hinted that this product was Eden's second most sacred fruit (and good for you, too). Consumers were also routinely offered various exotic gifts, like Watkins® Mulsified Cocoanut Oil (pages 386–387), a name that implied a refined degree of cleansing intensity derived from who-knows-where. Sanitas, Veribest, Luxite, Djer-Kiss®, Kiddie-Kar, Nashua Woolnap, CraniTonic, Egg-O-See, Mennen's Borated Talcum, Pro-phy-lac-tic, and Multigraph: hundreds of imaginatively coined ad-words contributed to brand mystique and triggered brand consciousness, which in turn demanded brand loyalty. When commanded to "Stop and think" (Hiawatha Spring Water, page 583), "Blow in on this one" (Prince Albert® tobacco, page 63), and "Be sure and get" (Waterman's® pens, page 327), consumer sales rose and national brands became household words.

No more snake oil

America had arrived as the largest commercial manufacturer in domestic and foreign markets. National magazines burgeoned to meet the new marketplace and became primary outlets for ad sales, com-

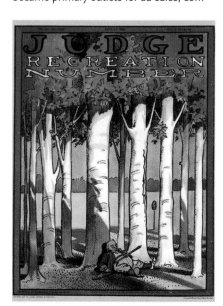

peting with and often overtaking newspapers for total ad linage sold. In 1825, there were fewer than a hundred magazines in the country, but by 1850 the number had swelled to six hundred. By 1900, there were more than five thousand magazines in the United States. Technological developments in printing and distribution also meant that the cover price of magazines dropped dramatically, while higher literacy rates made for increased readership. The new market was growing more sophisticated and now had many product choices. By 1908, over fifty percent of all magazine pages were advertisements. A new commuter class further gave rise to billboards and streetcar and train "car cards" as important advertising outlets.

Prior to 1900, print advertising had been mostly left to hucksters who bludgeoned readers with false claims and promises. Their ads were composed by newspaper and job printers and lacked artistic acuity. The new advertising followed the European tradition, however, (which from the late-nineteenth century was rooted in eye-catching posters) and often seduced its prey through style. The days of snake oil and patent medicine ads were long gone and striking designs and sophisticated pitches were in demand. Advertising had been transformed from an afterthought to an indispensable commercial art. In 1903, Walter Dill Scott published advertising's first official manual, *The Theory of Advertising*, offering templates for effective ad composition. At the same time leading advertising agencies in New York, Chicago, and Philadelphia, including J. Walter Thompson®, N. W. Ayer & Son, E. A. Wheatly, and Pettingill & Co., which originally bought space in newspapers, snapped up as many talented artists as possible to produce custom advertising for their growing client rosters.

For the love of pictures

Debates raged in the industry about what comprised an effective ad — was it purely word or mostly image, or was it a combination of both in seamless harmony? By the 1920s, the wordsmiths prevailed, but at the turn of the century image-makers held their own. The novelty of printing full-page images in four-color process was so alluring that large, stylish pictures were preferred over type alone. "A great many intelligent men disagree as to what constitutes a good advertisement," wrote contemporary adman H. C. Brown, in the trade journal *Art in Advertising*. "A good bright sketch will attract attention anywhere. Yet it should be reinforced by a concise statement in clear English covering the merits of the article. This combination is irresistible. And it is founded on a trait in human nature which is universal — the love of pictures." Furthermore, this was the golden age of illustration when America's best, N. C. Wyeth, Howard Pyle, Maxfield Parrish, C. Coles Phillips, the brothers J. C. and F. X. Leyendecker, and a young Norman Rockwell, created the highest quality commercial work.

They also fostered popular styles, iconic imagery and narrative tableaux that sold products while spinning elaborate visual tales. The ad for Luxite Hosiery (page 457) is a routinely straightforward depiction, but the vivid detail of the art presents the product with stark sensuality. The Autocrat Stationery ad (page 326) is a rococo, art nouveau, and Victorian stylistic mélange, proving that complexity is a virtue. While stylistically more consistent, the Mennen's Violet Talcum toilet powder ad (page 402) is overflowing with visually descriptive vignettes, presumably in case the viewer misses the point of the pitch. Djer-Kiss® (page 401) transports the viewer into a multifaceted fantasy world that resembles a children's book more than a magazine ad.

Usually, advertising illustrations were

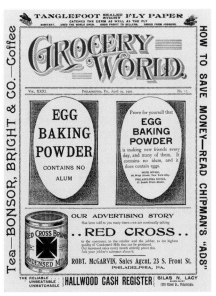

not totally integrated with typography — in fact, advertising today remains notorious for compartmentalizing the jobs of illustrators, writers, typographers, and layout artists. Yet the most effective ads were those that could have doubled as well-designed posters, like one for Fairy Soap (page 408), where the soap bar itself fits snugly into the "o" in the word. Visual economy is rare, but the few exceptions, such as the ads for Old Dutch Cleanser® (page 301), are powerful because the main illustrations are simple, set against a stark color field, with limited text. Likewise, the velvety Palmolive® Shampoo ad (page 431) showing a dramatically lit Cleopatra captures the eye without over-selling the product.

Magazine advertisements did not fight with editorial pages, which were usually text-heavy and tightly filled between small margins. Conversely, ads were afforded the license to do anything within reason, which meant a page could be composed in any quirky way. Indeed, most magazines welcomed the ads as respites from the bland. Although few advertisers wanted to pay good money for white space, the more adventuresome clients saw the visual equity in ads that allowed breathing room. Cream of Wheat®'s ads (pages 486–487) were captivating, in no small measure because the

reader's eye was focused in on a relatively small vignette in the center of the page — effectively a bull's-eye. Similarly, the al fresco scene of a golf picnic (page 576) for Coca-Cola® has a refreshingly light touch that contrasts nicely with the less exciting editorial pages sitting across from it. It is clear from these examples that there were numerous subtle ad variations, which still retained the overall graphic and stylistic impact of the times.

Fabricating reality

Most vexing however, is that the greatest mechanical engineering feat of the time, the automobile, was advertised in such conservative ways. The fact that advertising agents were cautious in springing novelty on the consumer, combined with the reality that most Detroit motorcars looked identical, made for some fairly staid ads. Basic black is black, and the boxy cab rarely offered artists inspiration. Convention dictated that cars should be seen lengthwise, often void of any driver. Marmon ads (pages 182–183) were the consistent exception to this rule, and among the most visually economic and eloquent. Each model was colorfully rendered as a still life without even the hint of a driver or passenger. Placed at the bottom of the

page, the rest of the ad is black framed by a white margin, and in the corner is a shield that contains brief descriptive copy, evocative of the German *sachplakat* (object poster).

Painted, drawn, and engraved pictures were standard fare because an artist could fabricate reality with ease. Occasionally, a photograph would be used — albeit manipulated — for dramatic purposes. The Warner Auto-Meter ad (page 160) is a stunning, though purposely cluttered, example of early photomontage (a form that reached its ascendancy in the 1930s). The Rexall® Hair Tonic ad (page 385), a classic application of hand-colored photography, was a common means of transforming bland black and white into chromatic joy. In this ad, color gives the beautiful model the air of a Pre-Raphaelite painting, given its comparative economy. Beautiful women also made frequent appearances in cigarette ads and on packages for Murad, Omar, and Fatima, though they were never shown with cigarettes in their mouths (at least not until the 1920s). Smoking was a solely male activity, just like airplane flying, fox hunting, and heroic warfare, which were featured as vignettes to capture the attention of tobacco hungry consumers.

Advertising is storytelling, and by 1900

many of the most popular commercial "folk tales" were being transcribed. A decade earlier, trade characters like Aunt Jemima®, the Cream of Wheat® man, Quaker Oats® pilgrim, and the Old Dutch Cleanser® girl — the symbolic embodiments and human faces of products — were introduced. The trade press of the day celebrated them as "housewives' best friends." They were also stars of domestic dramas that continued for decades. Cream of Wheat® ads, for instance, were serials, each one a building block in a larger narrative. Similarly, Kellogg's® ads for Toasted Corn Flakes (pages 508–511) chronicled a gaggle of children at the breakfast table. Actually, children were frequently the protagonists in ads for Jell-O®, Beech-Nut® Peanut Butter, and Ralston® Wheat and Barley.

What started in 1900 as guileless advertising had become resolutely premeditated, pseudo-scientific practice by 1920. Around World War I, sexuality crept into advertising formulas, starting a trend that has continued to this day. As suffrage and female liberation became more visible national issues, so did images of women smoking, drinking, and even showing some flesh, culminating in the Roaring Twenties. Advertising was quickly entering the mass culture as popular art. In the decade that followed, advertising became such an entrenched industry that, with exceptions, it was often too timid to take chances. 1900 to 1919 was an era when mannerisms and styles were being tested and tried; the result was lush, fresh, and smart.

Steven Heller is the art director of *The New York Times Book Review* and co-chair of MFA Design at the School of Visual Arts. He has edited or authored over eighty books on design and popular culture including *Merz to Emigre and Beyond: Avant-Garde Magazine Design of the 20th Century* and *Design Literacy Revised*.

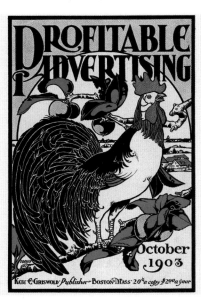

1900–1919:

Die Verführung der ersten Verbraucher

von Steven Heller

Eine Zeit der Unschuld

Die amerikanische Werbung war zu keiner Zeit üppiger und aufwändiger als in den Jahren zwischen 1900 und 1919, als verschnörkelte Typografie und reich verzierte Bildkompositionen die frisch gebackenen, im Sog des neuen, fortschrittlichen 20. Jahrhunderts mitgerissenen Verbraucher anzusprechen versuchten. Durch die Werbung wurden Produktmythologien geschaffen und Schönheitsideale verbreitet. Die spätviktorianischen Schönheiten, von Frauen verehrt und von Männern begehrt, bewarben alles, von Fotoapparaten bis hin zu Körperpuder, wobei der aus Frankreich übernommene Jugendstil der gedruckten Seite eine Aura der Eleganz verlieh.

Man kann es ruhig Nostalgie nach einer Zeit der Unschuld nennen, einer Zeit, bevor das Verhökern und Anpreisen von Waren eine Marketingstrategen, Trendscouts und Zielgruppenbefragern hörige Pseudowissenschaft wurde. Es war eine Ära, in der arglose Überzeugungsversuche und ernst gemeintes Verkaufsgeschick regierten. Obwohl die amerikanischen Zeitschriften voller Karikaturen waren, gestattete man sich in den meisten Anzeigen keine Späße, selbst wenn es um so verspielte Maskottchen wie den Clown des Gold Medal®-Mehls ging (S. 514). Das

Verkaufen von Waren war keine Sache, die man auf die leichte Schulter nehmen durfte.

Eine religiöse Eindringlichkeit beherrschte die neuen Göttinen und Götter der Reklamebilder, die Dinge wie Coca-Cola® und Warner's® rostfreie Korsetts anpriesen. Im Anzeigentext fanden sich regelmäßig Versatzstücke aus Kirchenpredigten und dem Neuen Testament – mit einprägsamen Sprüchen oder „Werbeslogans" und längeren Kapiteln und Verstraktaten (dem „Werbetext") wurde das Denkvermögen des Volkes eingelullt. Den Magazin-Annoncen ging es jedoch keineswegs um die Rettung von Seelen, sondern um die Verbreitung des kapitalistischen Glaubens.

Wehe den Ungewaschenen

Mit dem Aufbruch ins neue Jahrhundert wurde die Körperpflege zu einer der Verbreitung harrenden, religionsgleichen Tugend. Das damals wohl bekannte Motto: „Sauberkeit kommt direkt nach Frömmigkeit" war kein religiöses Gebot, sondern eine Schlagzeile aus den Inseraten, mit denen die schmutzigen Massen zum Konsumieren aufgefordert wurden. Seife war eines der ersten Produkte, das überregional verkauft wurde, diverse Namen überschwemmten schnell den Markt. Um die Marken voneinander ab-

zuheben und den Verkauf anzukurbeln, wurden neue soziale Maßregeln (und Tabus) geschaffen, die Änderungen des Lebenswandels notwendig machten. Man nehme nur das Beispiel der Sapolio®-Seife: „Der erste Schritt zum Verlust der Selbstachtung ist mangelnde Sorgfalt bei der Sauberkeit … Man kann nicht gesund oder hübsch, nicht einmal gut sein, wenn man nicht sauber ist." (S. 426). Wehe den Ungewaschenen!

Andere Annoncen befahlen den Verbrauchern, abgepackte Haferflocken zu essen, in Flaschen abgefüllte Limonade zu trinken, Musik von Schallplatten zu hören, Scheuerpulver zu benutzen und Zitrusfrüchte lecker zu finden. Die ernst gemeinte Sunkist®-Schlagzeile: „Orangen – was bedeuten sie Ihnen?" (S. 563) weist darauf hin, dass dieses Produkt die zweitheiligste Frucht des Garten Eden sei (und obendrein gesund). Den Verbrauchern wurden regelmäßig exotische Luxusartikel angeboten, so zum Beispiel Watkins® Mulsified Cocoanut Oil (S. 386–387), ein Name, der auf einen höchst verfeinerten Grad der Körperreinigung hinwies, von Gott weiß wo stammend. Sanitas, Veribest, Luxite, Djer-Kiss®, Kiddie-Kar, Nashua Woolnap, CraniTonic, Egg-O-See, Mennen's Borated Talcum, Pro-phy-lac-tic und Multigraph: Hunderte kreativer Produktnamen gaben den Marken eine Aura und ließen ein

Markenbewusstsein entstehen, das zur Markentreue anhielt. Wenn die Verbraucher die Aufforderung erhielten: „Denken Sie erst nach!" (Hiawatha Tafelwasser, S. 583), „Blasen Sie hier hinein" (Prince Albert® Tabak, S. 63) und „Kaufen Sie ausschließlich" (Waterman's® Füllfederhalter, S. 327) stiegen die Verkaufszahlen, große Markennamen gingen in die Alltagssprache ein.

Keine leeren Versprechungen mehr

Amerika war auf den heimischen und ausländischen Märkten bereits der größte Hersteller kommerzieller Produkte. Als Reaktion auf den neuen Markt entstanden viele überregionale Zeitschriften, die zum wichtigsten Medium für Anzeigen wurden und die Zeitungen bald in der Gesamtzeilenzahl der Annoncen überholten. 1825 gab es weniger als hundert Zeitschriften im ganzen Land, 1850 war die Zahl auf sechshundert angeschwollen. Im Jahr 1900 gab es über fünftausend Zeitschriften in den Vereinigten Staaten. Technische Fortschritte bei Druckverfahren und Vertrieb führten dazu, dass der Verkaufspreis sich drastisch verringerte, während eine niedrigere Analphabetenrate die Leserschaft vergrößerte. Die neue Marktwirtschaft wurde anspruchsvoller, man konnte bereits zwischen vielen verschiedenen Produkten auswählen. 1908 bestand über die Hälfte aller Zeitschriftenseiten aus Werbung. Für die neue Angestelltenschicht, die zur Arbeit fuhr, wurden Plakatwände und Anzeigetafeln in Straßen- und U-Bahnen als wichtige neue Werbeträger erfunden.

Vor 1900 waren Inserate ein Feld, das Bauernfängern vorbehalten war, die Leser mit leeren Versprechungen hinters Licht zu führen versuchten. Die Anzeigen wurden von den Druckern gestaltet und besaßen keinerlei künstlerischen Biss. Die neue Art der Werbung hingegen orientierte sich an europäischen Vorbildern (die seit dem ausgehenden neunzehnten Jahrhundert auffällig gestaltete Plakate zeigten) und verführte ihre Opfer durch Stil. Die Tage der Annoncen für Quacksalberprodukte und Wundermittel waren vorbei und anspruchsvolle Werbestrategien stark gefragt. Die Werbung hatte sich von einem nachträglichen Einfall zu einer unentbehrlichen Form der Gebrauchskunst entwickelt. 1903 veröffentlichte Walter Dill Scott das erste offizielle Handbuch der Werbung, *The Theory of Advertising*, das Vorlagen für die Komposition wirksamer Anzeigen enthielt. Gleichzeitig sicherten sich die führenden Werbeagenturen in New York, Chicago und Philadelphia, zu denen J. Walter Thompson®, N. W. Ayer & Son, E. A. Wheatly und Pettingill & Co. zählten, so viele talentierte Zeichner wie möglich, da sie den Anzeigenplatz selbst kauften und maßgeschneiderte Inserate für ihre wachsende Zahl von Kunden produzierten.

Die Liebe zum Bild

In der Branche tobte damals die Debatte, was eine wirksame Anzeige ausmachte – waren es nur die Worte oder eher das Bild, oder war es doch die Kombination von beidem in nahtloser Harmonie? 1920 siegten die Wortschmiede, aber um die Jahrhundertwende konnten sich die Bildproduzenten noch austoben. Der Neuheitswert von ganzseitigen, im Vierfarbdruck hergestellten Illustrationen war so hoch, dass große, stilvolle Bilder reinem Text vorgezogen wurden. „Viele intelligente Männer können sich nicht darauf einigen, was ein gutes Inserat ausmacht", schrieb der Werbemann H. C. Brown in der Fachzeitschrift *Art in Advertising*. „Eine gute, fröhliche Zeichnung wird überall Aufmerksamkeit erwecken. Sie sollte jedoch durch eine knappe Aussage in klaren Worten verstärkt werden, welche die Vorzüge des Artikels bespricht. Diese Kombination ist unwiderstehlich. Und sie gründet sich auf einen universellen menschlichen Charakterzug – die Liebe zum Bild." Diese Jahre waren außerdem das goldene Zeitalter amerikani-

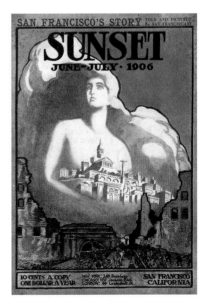

scher Illustratoren, in dem die besten Zeichner, N. C. Wyeth, Howard Pyle, Maxfield Parrish, C. Coles Phillips, die Gebrüder J. C. und F. X. Leyendecker und der junge Norman Rockwell, kommerzielle Arbeiten auf höchstem Niveau schufen.

Sie trugen zur Entstehung populärer Stile und unvergesslicher Bilder bei, die halfen Produkte zu verkaufen und gleichzeitig raffinierte Bildgeschichten erzählten. Die Anzeige für Luxite Strumpfwaren (S. 457) enthält eine bodenständige Abbildung, aber die lebendigen Einzelheiten der Illustration statten das Produkt mit einer großen Sinnlichkeit aus. Die Annonce für Autocrat Briefpapier (S. 326) ist eine Mischung aus Rokoko, Jugendstil und viktorianischem Stil, die beweist, dass Vielschichtigkeit eine Tugend ist. Die Werbung für Mennen's Veilchen-Talkumpuder (S. 402) ist vollgepfropft mit illustrierenden Vignetten, nur für den Fall, dass dem Betrachter die Botschaft entgangen sein sollte. Djer-Kiss® (S. 401) versetzt den Leser in eine bunte Fantasiewelt, die eher einem Kinderbuch als einer Anzeige entsprungen zu sein scheint.

Die Typografie war meist nicht vollständig auf die Illustrationen abgestimmt – selbst heute herrscht in der Werbebranche noch das Problem, dass die Aufgaben von Zeichnern, Textern, Typografen und Layoutsetzern zu stark voneinander getrennt sind. Doch die effektivsten Inserate waren solche, die auch als gut gestaltete Plakate durchgegangen wären, wie z.B. die Werbung für Fairy Soap (S. 408), bei der das Stück Seife perfekt in das „o" des Wortes passte. Visuelle Sparsamkeit ist selten, aber die wenigen Ausnahmen wie die Anzeige für Old Dutch Cleanser® (S. 301) sind besonders wirkungsvoll, weil die Illustrationen einfach gehalten sind, sich von einem einfarbigen Farbfeld klar abheben und die Textmenge begrenzt ist. Genauso zieht die samtige Palmolive® Shampoo-Werbung (S. 431) mit einer dramatisch beleuchteten Kleopatra den Blick magisch an, ohne das Produkt aufzudrängen.

Die Werbung in den Zeitschriften stand nicht im Konflikt mit den Textseiten, die meist zwischen schmalen Rändern eng mit Buchstaben vollgeschrieben waren. Anzeigen durften sich im Gegensatz dazu innerhalb vernünftiger Grenzen jede Freiheit herausnehmen, was bedeutete, dass eine Seite sehr merkwürdig aufgebaut sein konnte. Die meisten Zeitschriften begrüßten die Anzeigen als Abwechslung von der eintönigen Bleiwüste. Auch wenn nur wenige Werbekunden ihr gutes Geld in weiße Ränder stecken wollten, erkannten die fortschrittlichen Firmen doch den visuellen Wert von Annoncen, die etwas Raum zum Atmen ließen. Die Werbung für Cream of Wheat® (S. 486–487) war in erster Linie deshalb so aufsehenerregend, weil sich das Auge des Lesers auf eine relativ kleine Vignette in der Mitte der Seite konzentrieren konnte – von der Wirkung her wie das Schwarze einer Zielscheibe! Die Szene eines Picknicks auf dem Golfplatz (S. 576) in einer Werbung für Coca-Cola® zeugte von einer ähnlich erfrischend leichten Herangehensweise, was einen erfreulichen Kontrast zu der weit weniger aufregenden Textseite gegenüber darstellt. An diesen Beispielen wird klar, dass es eine Vielzahl subtiler Nuancen in der Werbung gab, die dennoch alle den grafischen und stilistischen Stempel der Zeit trugen.

Die fabrizierte Realität

Wirklich verstörend ist jedoch, dass die größte Ingenieursleistung der Zeit, das gerade erfundene Automobil, auf solch konservative Art beworben wurde. Die Werbeagenten waren bei der Versorgung der Verbraucher mit Neuheiten zurückhaltend; das entsprach der Tatsache, dass die meisten Kraftwagen aus Detroit schrecklich gleich aussahen – langweilige Inserate waren die Folge. Die Wagen waren einfach nur schwarz, die eckige Fahrerkabine bot den Zeichnern ebenfalls wenig Inspiration. Die Konvention

verlangte, dass Autos in Längsansicht und oft ohne Fahrer abgebildet wurden. Marmon-Anzeigen (S. 182–183) stellten immer wieder die Ausnahme von der Regel dar und waren optisch am sparsamsten und ausdrucksstärksten. Jedes Modell ist als farbiges Stillleben angelegt, es befindet sich unten auf der Seite, und der Rest der Anzeige ist schwarz, umgeben von einem weißen Rahmen. In der Ecke ist ein Schild mit einem kurzen, beschreibenden Text – das Ganze erinnert an das deutsche Sachplakat.

Gemalte Bilder, Zeichnungen, Stiche und Radierungen waren damals die Norm, weil ein Illustrator die Realität problemlos fabrizieren konnte. Nur selten wurde ein Foto verwendet, und auch das war dann manipuliert. Die Anzeige für den Warner Auto-Meter (S. 160) ist ein beeindruckendes, absichtlich übertriebenes Beispiel früher Fotomontage (eine Form, die ihren Höhepunkt in den Dreißigerjahren erlebte). Die Rexall®-Haarwasser-Werbung (S. 385), klassisches Beispiel einer handkolorierten Fotografie, zeigt eine verbreitete Methode zur Verwandlung von langweiligem Schwarz-Weiß: durch die Kolorierung erhält das schöne Mannequin mit relativ einfachen Mitteln das Antlitz eines präraffaelitischen Gemäldes. Schöne Frauen sind regelmäßig in Zigarettenwerbungen und auf den Verpackungen von

Murad, Omar und Fatima zu sehen, auch wenn sie nie mit einer Zigarette im Mund abgebildet wurden (das kam erst in den 20er Jahren auf). Rauchen war noch eine rein männliche Betätigung, genau wie das Steuern von Flugzeugen, die Fuchsjagd und der Kampf auf dem Schlachtfeld, als Vignetten abgebildet, um die Aufmerksamkeit der tabakhungrigen Verbraucher zu erregen.

Werben heißt Geschichten Erzählen, und um 1900 wurden viele der beliebtesten „Volksmärchen" der Werbewirtschaft aufgezeichnet. Zehn Jahre zuvor waren bereits Produktcharaktere wie Aunt Jemima®, der Cream of Wheat®-Mann, der Quaker Oats®-Pilgervater und das Old Dutch Cleanser®-Mädchen erfunden worden – die menschlichen Gesichter der Produkte. Die Presse feierte sie als „die besten Freunde der Hausfrau." Sie waren außerdem die Hauptdarsteller von Serien, die jahrzehntelang weitergingen. Die Cream of Wheat®-Anzeigen waren zum Beispiel Folgen einer Reihe und jede davon diente als Baustein einer größeren Geschichte. Ähnlich verfolgten die Kellogg's®-Annoncen (S. 508–511) für „Toasted Corn Flakes" die Entwicklung einer Schar von Kindern am Frühstückstisch. Kinder waren häufig die Hauptpersonen in Werbung für Jell-O®, Beech-Nut® Peanut Butter und Ralston® -Weizen- und Gerstenbrei.

Was 1900 als arglose Werbung angefangen hatte, war 1920 zu einer gnadenlos kalkulierten, pseudowissenschaftlichen Praxis geworden. Zur Zeit des Ersten Weltkriegs schlich sich die Sexualität in die Werbung und prägte damit einen bis heute vorhaltenden Trend. Als Frauenwahlrecht und –emanzipation zu wichtigeren Anliegen wurden, verbreiteten sich auch die Bilder von rauchenden, trinkenden Frauen, die manchmal sogar Haut zeigten, ein Trend, der in den wilden Zwanzigern seinen Höhepunkt fand. Die Adelung von Werbung als populäre Kunst setzte sich in der Massenkultur schnell durch. In dem folgenden Jahrzehnt wurde die Werbung zu einer so festgefahrenen Branche, dass sie, von Ausnahmen abgesehen, keinerlei Risiken mehr einging. 1900 bis 1919 hingegen war eine Ära, in der Manierismen und Stile ausprobiert wurden. Das Ergebnis war sinnlich, frisch und ansprechend.

Steven Heller ist Artdirector der *New York Times Book Review* und Vorsitzender der Fakultät Gestaltung (MFA/Design) an der School of Visual Arts in New York. Er ist außerdem Autor und Herausgeber von mehr als 80 Büchern über Grafikdesign und Populärkultur, u. a. *Merz to Emigre and Beyond: Avant-Garde Magazine Design of the 20th Century* und *Design Literacy Revised*.

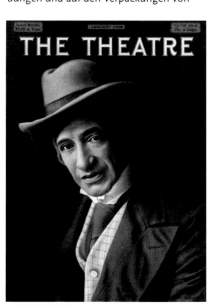

1900–1919:
Séduire le nouveau consommateur

par Steven Heller

Une époque plus innocente

C'est entre 1900 et 1919 que la publicité en Amérique a été la plus riche, une période où la typographie décorative et les illustrations luxuriantes visaient une nouvelle classe de consommateurs emportée dans le tourbillon de la course au progrès du XXe siècle. La publicité créait toute une mythologie autour des produits et imposait des idéaux esthétiques. Les beautés de l'époque post-victorienne, imitées par les femmes et désirées par les hommes, vendaient de tout, de l'appareil photo à la poudre de talc, tandis que l'Art nouveau, venu de France, insufflait le sens de l'élégance à la page imprimée.

Appelez ça de la nostalgie pour une époque plus innocente, l'époque où la vente et la harangue n'étaient pas encore devenues des pseudo-sciences réservées au marketing des marchands d'illusions, aux observateurs de tendances et aux groupes cibles. C'était l'époque où l'argumentation honnête et le sérieux professionnel régnaient en maîtres. Bien que l'humour graphique soit déjà abondamment utilisé dans de nombreux magazines populaires américains contemporains, les annonces publicitaires, même celles qui arboraient des mascottes joyeuses comme le clown de la farine *Gold Medal*® (page 514), ne se seraient jamais permis de se moquer du consommateur. Vendre était une affaire sérieuse.

Il y avait de la ferveur religieuse dans la représentation graphique de ces nouveaux dieux et déesses proposant des produits comme le Coca-Cola® et les corsets inoxydables Warner®. Les boniments étaient émaillés de sermons moralisateurs et l'Evangile – sous la forme de petites phrases accrocheuses ou « slogans » et de longs chapitres et versets appelés « textes publicitaires » – était instillé dans la conscience collective. La publicité de la presse écrite ne visait pas à sauver les âmes, mais à renforcer le dogme du capitalisme.

Honte à ceux qui ne se lavent pas !

A l'aube du XXe siècle, l'hygiène personnelle était une vertu laïque promise à un bel avenir. En fait, « la propreté est proche de la sainteté » n'était pas une ordonnance de l'Eglise, mais un argument publicitaire pour pousser les masses pas très propres à la consommation. Le savon fut l'un des premiers produits à être vendu au niveau national et de nombreuses marques inondèrent rapidement le marché. Pour différencier les marques et augmenter les ventes, de nouvelles valeurs morales – et des tabous – furent inventés, ce qui nécessitait un change-ment de style de vie. Prenez par exemple le savon Sapolio® : « La première entorse à l'estime de soi, c'est le manque d'hygiène personnelle... La santé, la beauté et même la bonté passent d'abord par la propreté ». (page 426) Honte à ceux qui ne se lavent pas !

D'autres publicités exigeaient du consommateur qu'il se nourrisse de céréales en boîtes, qu'il ingurgite des boissons non alcoolisées, qu'il écoute de la musique enregistrée, qu'il utilise des lessives en poudre et même qu'il aime les agrumes. Le fameux slogan de Sunkist® – « Oranges – what do they mean to you? » (page 563) – vous rappelait que ce produit était le second fruit le plus sacré du Paradis (et qu'il était bon pour vous). Les consommateurs se voyaient aussi régulièrement offrir divers produits exotiques, tel que Watkins® Mulsified Cocoanut Oil (pages 386–387), un nom qui suggérait un raffinement dans le pouvoir nettoyant venu d'on ne sait trop où. Sanitas, Veribest, Luxite, Djer-Kiss®, Kiddie-Kar, Nashua Woolnap, CraniTonic, Egg-O-See, Mennen's Borated Talcum, Pro-phy-lac-tic et Multigraph : autant de noms bien trouvés qui ont contribué à la mystique publicitaire et favorisé la prise de conscience des marques, qui à son tour exigea la fidélité aux marques. Quand les slogans « Stop and think » (l'eau de

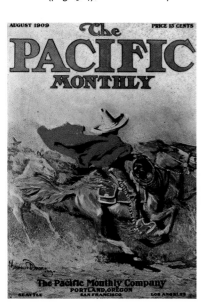

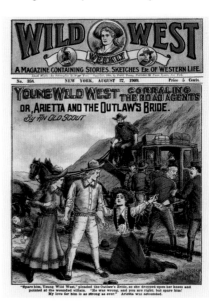

source Hiawatha, page 583), « Blow in on this one » (le tabac Prince Albert®, page 63) et « Be sure and get » (les stylos Waterman®, page 327) furent lancés, les ventes augmentèrent et les noms des grandes marques devinrent des noms communs.

La fin des remèdes miracle

L'Amérique était devenue le plus grand fabricant de produits de consommation sur le marché national et à l'étranger. De nombreux magazines apparurent un peu partout dans le pays pour combler les besoins des nouveaux marchés et, en devenant ainsi les principaux supports de publicité, ils faisaient concurrence aux quotidiens et les surpassaient souvent en termes de quantité d'espace publicitaire vendu. En 1825, il y avait moins de cent magazines dans tout le pays, mais en 1850, leur nombre était passé à six cents. En 1900, il y avait plus de cinq mille magazines aux Etats-Unis. Les progrès de la technique dans l'imprimerie et la distribution provoquèrent aussi une forte baisse du prix au numéro tandis que l'augmentation du taux d'alphabétisation entraîna une augmentation du nombre de lecteurs. Le nouveau marché devenait de plus en plus complexe et offrait de multiples choix. En 1908, les magazines contenaient plus de cinquante pour cent de pages publicitaires. Par la suite, apparurent de nouveaux supports publicitaires, comme les panneaux d'affichages, les affiches dans les trains et les transports publics, destinés à une nouvelle classe de consommateurs : les banlieusards.

Avant 1900, la publicité avait surtout été le domaine des charlatans qui bombardaient les lecteurs de fausses allégations et de fausses promesses. Leurs annonces étaient composées par les imprimeurs des journaux et manquaient de finesse artistique. Mais la nouvelle vague publicitaire s'inspirait de la tradition européenne (connue pour ses affiches attrayantes depuis la fin du XIXe siècle) et séduisait souvent sa proie par son style. Les beaux jours de la réclame pour la poudre de perlimpinpin et les remèdes miracle étaient bien révolus, cédant la place aux images percutantes et aux arguments sophistiqués. La publicité était passée de l'accessoire à un art commercial indispensable. En 1903, Walter Dill Scott publiait le premier guide officiel de publicité, *The Theory of Advertising*, qui proposait des modèles de composition pour des publicités performantes. Au même moment, les plus grandes agences de New York, Chicago et Philadelphie, dont J. Walter Thompson®, N. W. Ayer & Son, E. A. Wheatly et Pettingill & Co., qui initialement achetaient de l'es-

pace dans les journaux, recrutaient un maximum d'artistes de talent pour fabriquer des annonces sur mesure pour le nombre grandissant de leurs clients.

L'amour des images

Les débats faisaient rage dans la profession sur ce qui était le plus important dans une bonne publicité – était-ce le texte, les illustrations, ou un mélange harmonieux des deux ? En 1920, les partisans du texte prédominaient mais au tout début du siècle c'étaient les fabricants d'images qui l'emportaient. Les nouvelles illustrations en pleine page, imprimées en quadrichromie, étaient si attrayantes qu'elles l'emportaient sur le simple texte. « Un grand nombre d'hommes intelligents n'arrivent pas à tomber d'accord sur ce qui constitue une bonne publicité », écrivait H.C. Brown, publiciste contemporain dans le journal de la profession *Art in Advertising*. « Un dessin brillant attirera toujours l'attention où qu'il se trouve. Et pourtant, il devrait toujours être accompagné d'un texte vantant les mérites de l'article. C'est un mélange irrésistible. Et basé sur une qualité inhérente à la nature humaine : l'amour des images. » De plus, c'était l'Age d'or des illustrateurs, l'époque où la fine fleur américaine, comme N. C. Wyeth,

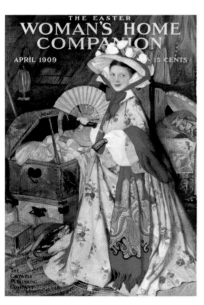

Howard Pyle, Maxfield Parrish, C. Coles Phillips, les frères J. C. et F. X. Leyendecker et le jeune Norman Rockwell, réalisaient des publicités de la plus haute qualité.

Ils ont aussi encouragé les styles populaires, les icônes et les tableaux narratifs qui servaient à faire vendre les produits grâce à des histoires visuelles détaillées. La publicité pour Luxite Hosiery (page 457) est un exemple typique assez simple, mais l'art dans les détails y ajoute une brutale sensualité. L'annonce d'Autocrat Stationery (page 326) mélange les styles rococo, Art nouveau et victorien, ce qui prouve que la diversité est un atout. Bien qu'elle soit d'un style plus homogène, l'annonce de Mennen's Violet Talcum (page 402) est couverte de vignettes visuellement descriptives, probablement pour le cas où le lecteur ne serait pas totalement convaincu en lisant le texte. L'annonce de Djer-Kiss® (page 401) transporte le spectateur dans un monde fantaisiste à multiples facettes et ressemble plus à une illustration pour un livre d'enfants qu'à une publicité de magazine.

En général, les illustrations n'étaient pas complètement assimilées à la typographie – en fait, le monde publicitaire d'aujourd'hui est connu pour compartimenter le travail entre les écrivains, les typographes et les illustrateurs. Pourtant, les annonces les plus parlantes étaient celles qui auraient pu servir

d'affiches, comme celle de Fairy Soap® (page 408) dans laquelle le savon se niche dans le « o » du nom. L'économie visuelle est rare, mais les quelques exceptions, comme la publicité pour Old Dutch Cleanser® (page 301), sont éloquentes parce que les principales illustrations sont simples, sur un fond de couleur violente avec un minimum de texte. De même, l'annonce pour le shampooing onctueux de Palmolive® (page 431), présentant Cléopâtre dans une lumière dramatique, retient l'attention sans être excessive.

Les annonces publicitaires ne concurrençaient pas les pages éditoriales, habituellement couvertes de texte entre des marges étroites. En revanche, la publicité pouvait tout se permettre dans la limite du raisonnable, ce qui signifiait que la composition d'une page était laissée à l'imagination. En effet, la plupart des magazines considéraient les annonces publicitaires comme une diversion à la monotonie. Bien que peu d'annonceurs soient prêts à dépenser de l'argent pour de l'espace blanc, les clients les plus audacieux comprenaient que l'équilibre visuel créait un style plus aéré. Les annonces de Cream of Wheat® (pages 486–487) fascinaient, c'est le cas de le dire, parce que l'œil du lecteur ne voyait que la vignette, relativement petite, placée au centre de la page,

comme le centre d'une cible. De même, la scène *al fresco* d'un pique-nique de golf (page 576) pour Coca-Cola® forme un agréable contraste avec la page opposée recouverte de texte. Ces exemples montrent clairement que les annonces différaient par de subtiles variations tout en gardant un style et un graphisme caractéristiques de l'époque.

Fabriquer la réalité

Mais le plus frustrant était que l'exploit mécanique de l'époque, l'automobile, soit présenté d'une manière si conventionnelle. Le fait que les annonceurs faisaient preuve de prudence en confrontant le consommateur aux dernières nouveautés, ajouté au fait que la majorité des voitures fabriquées à Detroit étaient presque identiques, ont donné des annonces assez formelles. Le noir classique est noir, et la forme carrée de la carrosserie inspirait rarement les artistes. La convention dictait que les voitures devaient être vues dans le sens de la longueur, le plus souvent sans conducteur. Les publicités Marmon (pages 182–183) faisaient exception à la règle et comptaient parmi les plus dépouillées et les plus éloquentes. Chaque modèle était pittoresquement représenté comme une nature morte sans la moindre

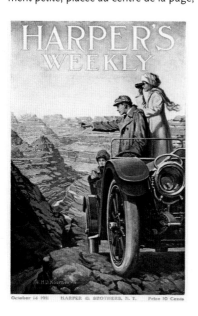

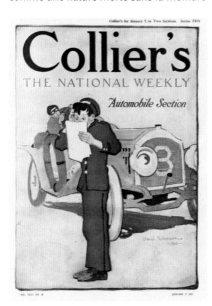

indication d'un conducteur ou d'un passager. Au bas de la page, le reste de l'annonce était en noir encadré d'un liséré blanc, avec au coin un encart contenant un court texte explicatif, rappelant un *sachplakat* (affiche objet) allemand.

Les images étaient généralement peintes, dessinées ou gravées de façon à ce que l'artiste puisse facilement fabriquer la réalité. Parfois, on utilisait une photographie – retouchée – pour des effets dramatiques. La publicité Warner Auto-Meter (page 160), bien qu'elle soit volontairement très chargée, est le parfait exemple de l'un des premiers photomontages (un style qui culminera dans les années 1930). L'annonce de Rexall® Hair Tonic (page 385) est l'exemple classique d'une photographie coloriée à la main, méthode habituellement utilisée pour transformer le fade noir et blanc en un régal de couleurs. Sur cette annonce, la couleur donne au splendide modèle un air de peinture préraphaélite, tout en étant relativement économique. Les publicités pour les cigarettes et les paquets de Murad, Omar et Fatima affichaient souvent de très belles femmes, même si on ne les voyait jamais une cigarette à la bouche (du moins jusque dans les années 1920). Fumer était une activité exclusivement masculine – comme l'aviation, la chasse à courre et l'héroïsme guerrier – présentée en vignettes pour attirer l'attention des utilisateurs de tabac.

Chaque publicité raconte une histoire et, en 1900, les « histoires publicitaires » les plus connues avaient été transposées. L'introduction de personnages comme Aunt Jemima®, l'homme de Cream of Wheat®, le pèlerin de Quaker Oats® et la demoiselle de Old Dutch Cleanser® – la personnification symbolique ct lc visage des produits – avait été faite dix ans auparavant. La publicité de l'époque les appelait les « amis de la ménagère ». Ils ont aussi été les vedettes de drames domestiques pendant des décennies. Les publicités Cream of Wheat®, par exemple, se suivaient, chacune d'elle étant un épisode d'une longue histoire. De même, les annonces Kellogg® (pages 508–511) pour des flocons de maïs grillés racontaient les aventures d'un groupe d'enfants autour de la table du petit-déjeuner. En fait, les enfants étaient fréquemment les protagonistes dans les publicités de Jell-O®, le beurre de cacahuète Beech-Nut® et le porridge Ralston®.

Ce qui avait commencé comme de la simple réclame en 1900 était finalement devenu une technique planifiée et pseudo-scientifique en 1920. À l'époque de la Première Guerre mondiale, la sexualité commença à infiltrer la publicité, inaugurant un genre toujours d'actualité. Au moment où les questions sur le droit de vote et la libération des femmes prenaient de l'importance au niveau national, apparaissaient des images de femmes fumant, buvant et même laissant voir de la peau, un style qui culmina dans les Années Folles. La publicité s'intégrait rapidement à la culture en tant qu'art populaire. Dans la décennie suivante, l'industrie publicitaire sera tellement repliée sur elle-même que, à part quelques exceptions, elle sera trop timide pour innover. La période entre 1900 et 1919 a été une époque où l'on expérimentait avec les manières et les styles ; le résultat était luxuriant, rafraîchissant et plein d'esprit.

Steven Heller est directeur artistique de *The New York Times Book Review* et codirecteur de la section de MFA Design à la School of Visual Arts. Il est également l'auteur et l'éditeur de plus de quatre-vingts livres sur le graphisme et la culture populaire, dont *Merz to Emigre and Beyond: Avant-Garde Magazine Design of the 20th Century* et *Design Literacy Revised*.

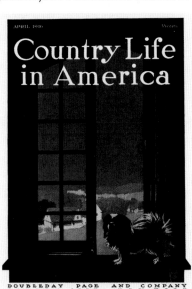

1900–1919:
Seduciendo al nuevo consumidor

por Steven Heller

Una época más inocente

La publicidad estadounidense nunca ha sido más suntuosa que en los años comprendidos entre 1900 y 1919, cuando la tipografía decorativa y las composiciones ornamentadas se dirigían a una nueva clase de consumidores atrapada en el torbellino de progresos del siglo xx. La publicidad envolvía los productos en mitología e imponía ideales estéticos. Las mujeres imitaban (y los hombres deseaban) a las bellezas postvictorianas que vendían desde cámaras hasta polvos de talco, mientras que el diseño *art nouveau*, importado de Francia, inyectaba elegancia en la página impresa.

La nostalgia por un tiempo más inocente imperó en una época en la que el vocerío y las campañas agresivas aún no se habían convertido en las pseudociencias publicitarias basadas en los conceptos del mentor y el protegido, los cazadores de tendencias y los grupos objetivo. Esta fue una era en la que la persuasión sin malicia y el arte serio de vender reinaron por encima de todas las cosas. Aunque el humor gráfico era un gancho que usaban todas las revistas populares en Estados Unidos por entonces, la mayoría de los anuncios, incluso los que contaban con mascotas divertidas, como el payaso de la harina Gold Medal® Flour (p. 514), nunca

se burlaron de los consumidores. Vender productos no era un asunto de risa.

Un fervor religioso recuperó imágenes publicitarias de dioses y diosas de antaño, con los que se vendieron marcas como Coca-Cola® y corsés inoxidables Warner's®. Los lanzamientos de ventas estaban tachonados con homilías espirituales, y el gospel –ya fuera en forma de proverbios pegadizos o «eslóganes», o de extractos más largos con capítulo y versículo, es decir, con «texto creativo»– engatusaba la conciencia de las masas. Con todo, los anuncios en revistas no intentaban salvar almas, sino impulsar el dogma capitalista.

¡Pobres de los sucios!

A principios de siglo, la higiene personal era una virtud secular lista para propagarse. De hecho, «el aseo personal sigue a la devoción» no era un decreto religioso, sino un eslogan publicitario que urgía a la sucia plebe a consumir. El jabón fue uno de los productos que primero se comercializó en el ámbito nacional, y el mercado no tardó en verse invadido por nuevas marcas. Para diferenciarlas y disparar sus ventas se crearon nuevas costumbres sociales (y tabúes) que requerían cambios en el estilo de vida. Pongamos por ejemplo el caso del jabón Sapolio®:

«La falta de aseo personal es el primer síntoma de la falta de amor propio... Para contar con salud y belleza, lo primero es la limpieza» (p. 426). ¡Pobres de los sucios!

Otros anuncios alentaban a los consumidores a comer cereales envasados, a beber refrescos embotellados, a reproducir música grabada, a usar detergentes en polvo e incluso a saborear cítricos. El atractivo eslogan de Sunkist®, «Naranjas, ¿qué significan para usted?» (p. 563), insinuaba que este producto era la segunda fruta más sagrada del Paraíso (y buena para cualquiera, claro). También se ofrecía a los consumidores varios presentes exóticos, como el aceite de coco emulsificado Watkins® (pp. 386–387), un nombre que indicaba un grado más refinado de intensidad en la limpieza derivado de dios sabe dónde. Sanitas, Veribest, Luxite, Djer-Kiss®, Kiddie-Kar, Nashua Woolnap, CraniTonic, Egg-O-See, Mennen's Borated Talcum, Prophy-lac-tic y Multigraph: cientos de anuncios con un texto imaginativo contribuyeron a conferir a los productos un aura de misterio y dispararon la conciencia de marca entre los consumidores, que a su vez dio pie a la fidelización de clientes. Cuando se exhortaba con frases como: «Párese a pensar» (agua con gas Hiawatha, p. 583), «Dele una calada» (tabaco Prince Albert®, p. 63) o «No olvide hacerse con una» (plumas

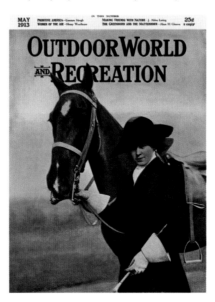

Waterman's®, p. 327), las ventas aumentaban y las marcas nacionales se incorporaban al vocabulario de la vida cotidiana.

No más aceite de serpiente

Estados Unidos se había impuesto como el mayor fabricante comercial tanto en el mercado interior como en el exterior. Las revistas nacionales florecían para satisfacer las nuevas demandas y se convertían en los principales puntos para las ventas de anuncios, compitiendo (y en ocasiones aventajando) con los periódicos en número de líneas publicitarias vendidas. En 1825, el número de revistas en circulación en el país no llegaba a cien; para 1850 esa cifra había ascendido a seiscientas. Y en 1900 había más de cinco mil revistas en circulación en Estados Unidos. Los avances en la tecnología de impresión y distribución suponían un descenso notable del precio de las revistas, al tiempo que la alfabetización creciente de la población generaba un número cada vez mayor de lectores. El nuevo mercado ganaba en sofisticación y ofrecía un número creciente de productos entre los que escoger. En 1908, más del cincuenta por ciento de las páginas de las revistas se dedicaba a publicidad. Una nueva clase de consumidores dio pie a la aparición de las vallas publicitarias y al uso de los trenes y tranvías como importantes soportes donde anunciar productos.

Antes de 1900, la publicidad impresa la realizaban en gran parte charlatanes que coaccionaban a los lectores con sus falsas promesas. Sus anuncios los componían los propios impresores de los diarios y carecían de toda agudeza artística. En cambio, la nueva publicidad seguía la tradición europea (que a partir del siglo XIX se basaba en carteles atractivos) y a menudo seducía a sus presas gracias a su estilo. Los días del aceite de serpiente y los ungüentos milagrosos habían tocado a su fin; la demanda de diseños sorprendentes y lemas sofisticados iba en aumento. La publicidad había pasado de ser una idea de último momento a ser un arte comercial indispensable. En 1903, Walter Dill Scott publicó el primer manual oficial sobre publicidad, titulado *The Theory of Advertising*, en el que incluía plantillas para una composición de anuncio efectiva. Paralelamente, las principales agencias publicitarias de Nueva York, Chicago y Filadelfia, incluidas entre ellas J. Walter Thompson®, N. W. Ayer & Son, E. A. Wheatly y Pettingill & Co., que antaño se dedicaban a adquirir espacios en diarios, atrapaban en sus redes a tantos artistas de talento como podían para producir anuncios personalizados para sus carteras de clientes, cada vez más abultadas.

Por amor a las imágenes

El sector debatía encarnizadamente en qué consistía un anuncio eficaz. ¿Debía constar solo de texto o basarse sobre todo en una imagen? ¿O tal vez había que lograr una combinación de ambas cosas en perfecta armonía? En la década de 1920 aún prevalecían los artífices de la palabra, si bien con el cambio de siglo los creadores de imágenes habían empezado a ampliar su mercado. La novedad de las imágenes impresas a toda página en cuatricromía era tan seductora que la mayoría prefería las fotografías e ilustraciones elegantes de gran formato a los anuncios de solo texto. «Muchos hombres inteligentes se muestran en desacuerdo sobre qué constituye un buen anuncio –escribió el publicista contemporáneo H. C. Brown en el diario especializado *Art in Advertising*–. Un buen dibujo siempre atrae la atención, si bien debería estar reforzado por un lema conciso, en un lenguaje claro, que satisficiera los méritos del artículo. Esta combinación es irresistible. Y se fundamenta en un rasgo de la naturaleza humana que es universal: el amor por las imágenes.» A ello cabe añadir que aquella fue la época dorada de la ilustración, durante la cual los mejores ilustradores de Estados Unidos, N. C. Wyeth, Howard Pyle, Maxfield Parrish, C. Coles Phillips, los

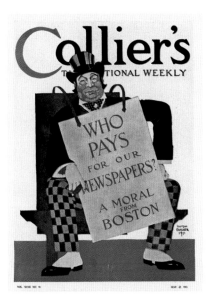

hermanos J. C. y F. X. Leyendecker, y un jovencísimo Norman Rockwell, crearon la obra comercial de más calidad de todos los tiempos.

También fomentaron la creación de estilos populares, imágenes icónicas y retablos narrativos que vendían los productos al tiempo que hilaban complejos relatos visuales. El anuncio de calcetería de Luxite Hosiery (p. 457) ofrece una descripción normal y corriente, pero el vivo detalle de la ilustración presenta un producto cargado de sensualidad. El anuncio de papelería de Autocrat Stationery (p. 326) es una mezcla de rococó, *art nouveau* y estilo victoriano en la que se demuestra que la complejidad es una virtud. Por su parte, el anuncio de polvos de talco Mennen's Violet Talcum (p. 402), más coherente estilísticamente, incluye profusión de viñetas visualmente descriptivas, tal vez por si el espectador no entiende el eslogan. Djer-Kiss® (p. 401) transporta al lector a un mundo de fantasía polifacético en lo que parece más un libro infantil que un anuncio para una revista.

Por lo común, las ilustraciones publicitarias no estaban totalmente integradas con la tipografía; de hecho, la publicidad actual sigue siendo notoria por compartimentar los trabajos de los ilustradores, redactores, tipógrafos y maquetistas. No obstante, los anuncios más efectivos eran aquellos que podrían haberse considerado también carteles bien diseñados,

como el del detergente Fairy (p. 408), en el que la propia barra de jabón se ensambla perfectamente en la «o» del texto. La economía visual no es frecuente, pero existen excepciones, como los anuncios de Old Dutch Cleanser® (p. 301), cuya fuerza radica en que las principales ilustraciones son simples y están recortadas sobre un campo de color austero con un texto breve. Del mismo modo, el aterciopelado anuncio de champú Palmolive® (p. 431), en el que se muestra a una Cleopatra iluminada por una luz teatral, captura la mirada sin intentar imponer el producto.

En las revistas, la publicidad no luchaba con las páginas editoriales, habitualmente atiborradas de texto y con escaso margen. Por el contrario, a los publicistas se les permitía tomarse la licencia de hacer lo que quisieran, siempre y cuando fuera razonable, lo cual suponía que una página podía componerse de un modo bastante estrafalario. Más aún, la mayoría de las revistas veían en los anuncios un respiro con el que romper la monotonía del desabrido texto. Aunque pocos anunciantes estaban dispuestos a pagar grandes sumas por un espacio en blanco, los clientes más atrevidos apreciaban la calidad visual de los anuncios que dejaban aire para respirar en la página. Los anuncios de Cream of Wheat® (pp. 486–487) resultaban cautivadores y, al lograr que el ojo del lector se concentrara en

una estampa relativamente pequeña centrada en la página, constituían una diana de diez puntos. Del mismo modo, la escena al fresco de un picnic en un campo de golf presentada por Coca-Cola® (p. 576) tiene un toque ligeramente refrescante que contrasta de forma agradable con las aburridas páginas editoriales entre las que se inserta. Estos ejemplos dejan claro que había multitud de variaciones publicitarias sutiles en las que, no obstante, se conservaba todo el impacto gráfico y estilístico de la época.

Fábrica de realidad

Sin embargo, lo más desconcertante es que el hito de la ingeniería más importante de la época, el automóvil, se anunciara de un modo tan conservador. El hecho de que las agencias publicitarias se mostraran cautas a la hora de vender aquella novedad al consumidor, combinado con la realidad de que la mayoría de automóviles de Detroit eran casi idénticos, creó una ristra de anuncios bastante sobrios y aburridos. El básico vehículo en negro de la época no servía de fuente de inspiración a los artistas. Las convenciones dictaban que los automóviles debían mostrarse a lo largo y siguiendo un estilo estrictamente representativo. La excepción a esta regla eran los anuncios de Marmon

(pp. 182–183), que se contaban entre los más elocuentes y económicos visualmente. Cada modelo se presentaba como una colorida naturaleza muerta sin el más mínimo rastro de conductor o pasajeros. En la parte inferior de la página, el resto del anuncio consta de negro enmarcado por un margen blanco, y en la esquina se incluye un destacado con un breve eslogan descriptivo, con evocaciones del *sachplakat* (póster objeto) alemán.

Las imágenes pintadas, dibujadas y grabadas eran un recurso estándar, porque un artista podía fabricar la realidad fácilmente. De tanto en cuando se usaba una fotografía (siempre manipulada) para crear un efecto más llamativo. El anuncio de Warner Auto-Meter (p. 160) constituye un ejemplo asombroso, y abarrotado a propósito, de los primeros fotomontajes, un recurso compositivo que alcanzó su punto álgido en los años treinta. El anuncio del tónico capilar Rexall® Hair Tonic (p. 385), el clásico ejemplo de una fotografía coloreada a mano, era un modo habitual de transformar una imagen en blanco y negro sin gancho en una atractiva escena colorida. En este anuncio, el color confiere a la bella modelo el aura de una pintura prerrafaelita, por su economía en comparativa. Las mujeres bellas poblaban también los anuncios de tabaco y los paquetes de las marcas Murad, Omar y Fatima, si bien nunca

se las mostraba con un cigarrillo en los labios (al menos hasta los años veinte). Fumar era una actividad exclusivamente masculina, como volar en aviones, cazar zorros y librar batallas heroicas, escenas que se representaban en viñetas para captar la atención de los consumidores ávidos de fumar.

La publicidad consiste en contar historias y hacia 1900 muchos de los «cuentos populares» comerciales se transcribían en los anuncios. Una década antes empezaron a crearse personajes publicitarios como Aunt Jemima®, el hombre de Cream of Wheat®, el peregrino de Quaker Oats® y la joven de Old Dutch Cleanser®, personificaciones simbólicas y rostros humanos de productos. La prensa de la época los celebraba como «los mejores amigos del ama de casa». Aquellos personajes se convirtieron en estrellas de series domésticas que se prolongaron durante épocas. Los anuncios de Cream of Wheat®, por ejemplo, eran bloques constructores de una historia, y los anuncios de cereales de Kellogg's® (pp. 508–511) presentaban a unos niños sentados a la mesa del desayuno. En realidad, los niños solían ser los protagonistas en los anuncios de Jell-O®, la mantequilla de cacahuete Beech-Nut® y los desayunos Ralston® a base de trigo y cebada.

Hacia 1920, lo que había comenzado en 1900 como una publicidad sin malicia había

dado paso a una práctica premeditada y pseudocientífica. Más o menos cuando estalló la Primera Guerra Mundial, la sexualidad empezó a abrirse camino en las fórmulas publicitarias, iniciando una tendencia que se ha perpetuado hasta nuestros días. A medida que la liberación y el sufragio femeninos devinieron temas nacionales más patentes, empezaron a mostrarse imágenes de mujeres fumando, bebiendo e incluso enseñando algo de carne, imágenes que prepararon el terreno para el estallido de «los locos años veinte». La publicidad se adentraba rápidamente en la cultura de masas como si de un arte popular se tratara. En la década que siguió, la publicidad se convirtió en una industria afianzada que, salvo en contadas excepciones, se mostró demasiado tímida para asumir riesgos. Los años comprendidos entre 1900 y 1919 sirvieron para probar gestos y estilos. El resultado de aquellos experimentos fueron anuncios exuberantes, frescos e inteligentes.

Steven Heller es director de arte del *New York Times Book Review* y codirector del Máster de Diseño en la School of Visual Arts. Ha editado y escrito más de ochenta libros sobre diseño y cultura popular, entre los que se cuentan *Merz to Emigre and Beyond: Avant-Garde Magazine Design of the 20th Century* y *Design Literacy Revised*.

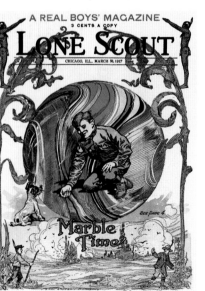

1900 – 1919：新しい消費者への誘惑

スティーヴン・ヘラー

さらなる無垢な時代

アメリカの広告が、装飾的な印刷術や凝った文章が20世紀の進歩の渦中に捉えられた新しい消費者階級をターゲットとした、1900年から1919年の間の年月ほど贅沢になったことはないだろう。広告は商品神話を助長し、審美的な理想を推し進めた。フランスから輸入されたアールヌーボーのデザインが印刷広告にエレガンスの感覚を注ぎ込むとともに、カメラから化粧パウダーまで何でも売り込む後期ビクトリア風の美女達に対し、女性は競争心を、男達は欲望を燃やした。

呼び売りや宣伝がマーケティング上のスヴェンガリ（訳者注：ドゥ・モーリアの小説に登場する催眠術師・人を邪悪な動機で操る者の意）やトレンドハンターやあるいはフォーカスグループ（訳者注：商品開発に有用な情報を得るため市場から抽出された消費者グループ）のせいで、えせ科学となってしまう前の、さらなる無垢な時代に懐古の念が思い起こされる。それは正直な説得とまじめなセールスマン精神がこの上なく勢力をふるった時代であった。この頃グラフィック的なユーモアは多くのアメリカ大衆誌の中心的要素ではあったが、ほとんどの広告は、たとえ Gold Medal® 小麦粉のピエロのように

陽気なマスコットをフィーチャーしたようなものであっても、決して消費者をからかったりはしなかった。物を売ることは笑い事ではなかったのである。

宗教的な熱情が、Coca-Cola® や Warner's® 防錆コルセットのようなものまで売り込む当世の神や女神の広告イメージに力を与えた。崇高な説教が宣伝文句の中にひんぱんに散りばめられ、人の心を捉える教訓もしくは "スローガン" や、くだくだしい聖書の詩行もしくは "広告コピー" 形式のゴスペルが大衆意識を誘い込んだ。雑誌広告は魂を救う気はなかったが、しかしながら資本主義的な教義は促進しようとした。

洗わざるものに災いあれ

この世紀初頭、身体衛生は非宗教的な美徳として宣伝にうってつけだった。事実、「きれい好きは敬神に近い」ということわざは宗教的な教令ではなく、よごれた庶民達を消費へと駆り立てる広告文句だった。石鹸は全国的に売られた最初の商品のひとつで、たくさんのブランドが市場に急速にあふれた。他のブランドから差別化し売上を誘引するため、生活様式の変更が要求されるような新しい社会的習慣（そして禁忌）が作り出された。Sapolio® 石鹸を

例に挙げてみよう：「自尊から遠ざかる第1歩は、清潔な身体に対する意識不足です。清潔でなければ、健康にも綺麗にも、善き人間にもなれません」（CP_00_Sapolio）洗わざるもの（訳者注：下層民たち）に災いあれ。

その他の広告は消費者達にパック詰めされたシリアルを食べ、瓶入りの清涼飲料水を飲み、レコード音楽をかけ、粉せっけんを使い、さらには柑橘類を賞味するように命令した。Sunkist® の大真面目な見出し「オレンジーあなたにとってどういう意味を持ちますか？」（F_16_8）は、この品物がエデンの園で2番目に神聖なフルーツである（そしてもちろんあなたにも良い）とほのめかしている。消費者達はまた、洗浄力の強さの程度の強化を暗示させ、どこだかわからないような所から由来して名付けられた Watkins® 乳化ココナツオイル（CP_19_9）のような様々な異国風のお買い得品を日々提供された。Sanitas、Veribest、Luxite、Djer-Kiss®、Kiddie-Kar、Nashua Woolnap、CraniTonic、Egg-O-See、Mennen's Borated Talcum、Pro-phy-lac-tic、そして Multigraph：何百もの想像力に富んだ広告新造語が、ブランドの神秘感に貢献し、ブランド意識を誘発し、やがてブランドへの忠誠心を要求

した。「立ち止まって考えて」（Hiawatha Spring Water）（F_07_X_Hiawatha 飲料水）、「こいつを吸って」（Prince Albert® タバコ）「確かめて買って」（Waterman's® ペン）（CP_07_4）、と命令されるとき、消費売上は伸び全国的ブランドは日常的な言葉となった。

スネークオイルはもういらない

アメリカは対国内・国外共に最大の商業生産者となった。全国誌が新しい市場に対応して急速に発展し、トータルでの原稿料では新聞と競い合いしばしば打ち勝って広告の主要な売上先となった。1825年、国内には100誌未満の雑誌しか無かったが、1850年には600誌に膨れ上がった。1900年には、合衆国に5000誌以上の雑誌があった。より高くなった読み書きの能力が読者数を増加させると同時に、印刷と物流システムの技術的な進歩が雑誌の定価を劇的に下げさせることとなった。この新しい市場はさらに洗練されていき、今や多くの商品選択が可能となっていた。1908年までに、全雑誌ページの50%以上が広告となった。新しい通勤者層が、重要な広告売上先としての屋外広告板や路面電車や電車の "車内ポスター" の発生を促進した。

1900年以前、印刷広告は不誠実な主張と保証で読者をだます宣伝業者にほとんど任されていた。広告は新聞社と印刷業者によって作成され、芸術的感覚の鋭敏さに欠けていた。新しい広告は（19世紀後期から人目を引くポスター形式に定着していた）ヨーロッパの伝統に従ってはいたが、しかし、しばしばその人をカモにするようなスタイルはやめるようになっていた。スネークオイルと新案特許薬（訳者注：両方ともインチキくさいまがい物の意）の広告の日々は絶えて去り、目立つデザインと洗練された売り込み文句が必要とされていた。広告は後から付け足すものから不可欠な商業芸術へと変わっていった。

1903年に、ウォルター・ディル・スコットが、効果的な広告文案を載せた最初の広告公式マニュアル「The Theory of Advertising」を出版した。同時期に、最初に新聞紙上に広告スペースを購入したJ. Walter Thompson®、N. W. Ayer & Son、E. A. Wheatly、Pettingill & Co.らを含むニューヨーク・シカゴ・フィラデルフィアの有力な広告代理店が、彼等の増える顧客リストのため注文制作の広告作りをするために、可能な限り大勢の才能ある芸術家を我先にと手に入れていった。

美しいものへの愛のために

何が効果的な広告を形成するのかという論争が業界で大流行した—純粋に言葉だけなのかそれとも大方が画像によるものか、はたまた双方の継ぎ目のない調和による組み合わせなのか？

1920年代までに言葉の細工師が優勢になったが、世紀の変わり目頃は画像の作成者も負けてはいなかった。四色印刷法のフルページ画像の真新しさがあまりに魅力的であったため、大きくスタイリッシュな画が活字だけよりも好まれた。「非常に多くの知的な人間が、何が良い広告を構成するかという点について意見を異にしている」と同時代の広告マンH. C.ブラウンは業界誌 Art in Advertising に書いている。「見事な、色彩あざやかなスケッチはどこでも注意を惹き付ける。さらにそれは冴えた英語で品物の長所を記述した簡明な記事によって増強されるのである。このコンビネーションには抵抗できない。これは普遍的な人間の本質—美しいものへの愛という特徴に基いている」さらに、この時アメリカの最高峰、N. C.ワイエス、ハワード・パイル、マックスフィールド・パリッシュ、C. コールス・フィリップス、J. C. と F. X.ライヤンデッカー兄弟、そして若いノーマン・ロックウェルらが最高品質の商業

作品を創造したイラストレーションの黄金時代でも
あった。

　彼等はまた、精巧に作り上げた長い物語の中の
偶像イメージや物語の場面などが商品を売り上げる
という流行のスタイルを育て上げた。Luxite 靴下
（FB_18_4）の広告は率直な日常の描写であるが、
飾りの無い官能で商品を表現した躍動的なアートで
もある。Autocrat 文房具（CP_06_Autocrat）の
広告はロココとアールヌーボーとビクトリア朝風文
体の混合であり、複雑さは効果的であるということ
を証明している。Mennen's Violet Talcum 化粧
パウダー（CP_13_7）の広告は、文体上さらに首尾
一貫し、恐らく見た者が広告文句のポイントを見逃
した場合に備えて、視覚的に訴えるように描写した
絵であふれている。Djer-Kiss®（FB_18_2_）は、
単なる雑誌広告と言うより児童文学に似て見た者
を多面性を持つ幻想世界へと連れ去る。

　一般的に、広告イラストは印刷物としてはまっ
たく完成されていなかった。事実、今日残る広告は
イラストレーター・ライター・印刷工・レイアウト
アーティストらの仕事を細分化している点で悪評高
い。しかし最も効果ある広告とは、石鹸の棒そのも
の自体が文字の「o」にぴったりとはまって上手にデ

ザインされた Fairy 石鹸（CP_15_）のポスターの
ように効果が倍増された広告である。視覚的に効果
の高いものは稀であるが、しかし Old Dutch
Cleanser®（CP_19_3_）（CP_19_5_）の広告の
ように、主たるイラストがくっきりとしたバックに数
少ない言葉と共に配された、シンプルであるが故に
力強い例はわずかにある。同様に、劇的に光に照
らされたクレオパトラを表わした Palmolive® シャ
ンプー（FB_18_5）の柔らかみのある広告は商品
を過大評価することなく人目を捉えている。

　雑誌広告は、一般に文字でいっぱいで小さな欄
にぎっちり詰め込まれた論説ページとは争わな
かった。逆に言えば、広告は常識の範囲内ではどん
なことでもする自由があり、つまり広告欄はどんな
風変わりな手法ででも作成することができた。実際、
ほとんどの雑誌は味気無さから脱却するために広
告を歓迎した。わずかな広告主が余白スペースに大
金を払い、さらに大胆な顧客は広告に余地を与える
視覚的な公正さに気付いた。Cream of Wheat®
（F_15_）（F_10_1）の広告は少なからず魅惑的であ
るが、それは読者の目をページの真中の比較的小さ
な画─雄牛の目に効果的に焦点を合わせているた
めである。同様に、Coca-Cola® のゴルフピクニッ

クの戸外のシーン（F_17_5_15）は、反対側にある
面白味の無い論説ページと見事に対照をなす爽や
かな軽いタッチを持っている。これらの例からも明
らかなように、絵画及び文体的にも時代に影響を
与えたたくさんの巧みな広告バリエーションが存在
した。

でっち上げの現実

　最もうるさい、しかしこの時代の最も偉大な機
械工学の功績である自動車はかなり保守的な手法
で広告されていた。広告代理店が消費者に対して真
新しさを持ち出す事に慎重であったという事実が、
デトロイトの殆どの自動車が同一に見えるという現
実と相まって非常にまじめな広告を促進した。根本
的に黒は黒であり、箱型のタクシーは芸術家達にほ
とんどインスピレーションを与えなかった。慣習は
車は長く見えるべきだと要求し、そしてしばしば運
転者は全く描かれていなかった。時々、Overland
（A_17_6_Overland_a）のような広告がかろうじ
て車全体を見せたが、運転者と乗客はむしろ牧歌的
な風景の中でのドライブを楽しんでいる。なかでも
Marmon（A_17_Marmon 34）の広告は最も視
覚的に効果的で雄弁である。それぞれの車種は運

転者や乗客を暗示すらさせずに色彩豊かに静物として描写されている。車は紙面の下部に配置され、残りの部分は白い緑で囲まれた黒で、隅には簡潔で記述的なコピーを含む盾型のコンテンツがあり、ドイツのsachplakat（製品が主のポスター）を喚起させる。

　彩色画・線描画・銅版画などは芸術家がたやすく事実をでっち上げることができるため一般的な手法だった。時たま、写真－修正されてはいても－が劇的な効果をあげるため使われた。 Warner Auto-Meter (A_14_1) の広告は意図的に乱雑化されているが、初期のモンタージュ写真（1930年代に優勢になった広告形式）のサンプルとしてすばらしい。Rexall®ヘアトニック (CP_06_) の広告は、手細工で彩色した写真の応用の傑作で、白黒写真を多彩な喜びへと変換させる一般的な手法である。この広告で、色彩は美しいモデルに前ラファエロ的な絵画の雰囲気を与え、かなりの効果をあげている。美しい女性達はまた（少なくとも1920年代までは）その口にタバコをくわえたことすら無いにもかかわらず、Murad、Omar、そしてFatimaのタバコの広告とパッケージにひんぱんに現れている。喫煙は、タバコに飢えた消費者の注意を惹きつけるための

画として呼び物にした飛行機操縦やきつね狩りや英雄的な戦争のように、純粋に男性だけの活動だった。

　広告は物語作りが巧みで、1900年までに、たくさんの宣伝用の人気ある"家族のお話"が著された。その10年ほど前、Aunt Jemima®、the Cream of Wheat® man、Quaker Oats® pilgrim、the Old Dutch Cleanser® girlなどの商標キャラクター－象徴の有形化であり商品の人間化である－が紹介された。当時の業界紙は彼等を「主婦の最良の友人」と褒め称えた。また彼等は何十年も続いた家庭ドラマの主人公でもあった。Cream of Wheat®の広告は、例えば、一つ一つの話がさらに長い物語を構成するシリーズ物になっていた。同様に、Kellogg's® (F_15_Kellogs_A) のこんがり焼いたコーンフレークの広告は子供達の朝食の食卓シーンを記録している。実際、子供達はひんぱんにJell-O®、Beech-Nut®ピーナツバター、Ralston®小麦/大麦オートミールの広告の主人公となっている。

　1920年までには正直な広告がきちんと計画され始めながらも、1900年に始まったのは、えせ科学的なやり方だった。第一次世界大戦の頃、次第に広告形式に性的なものが現れ始め、今日まで続く流行

となった。参政権と女性解放運動がより一層目に見えて全国的な問題となるにつれて、"狂騒の1920年代"の中で、女性の喫煙や飲酒やさらには身体を露出することに対するイメージさえもが頂点に達した。すぐに広告は国民の芸術として大衆文化に加わった。それに続く10年間で、しばしば臆病過ぎてチャンスをものにできなかった例外を除き、広告は大変に確立された産業となった。1900年から1919年は、マンネリズムと様式がためされ試みられた、結果として豪華で新鮮で洗練された時代であった。

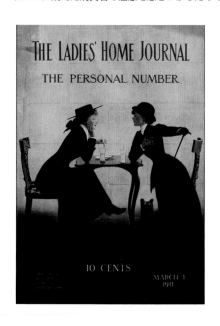

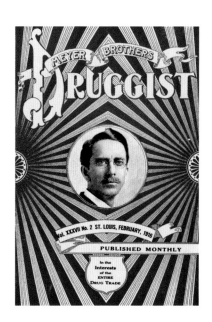

The Evening Glass of Cheer

Pabst
Blue Ribbon
The Beer of Quality

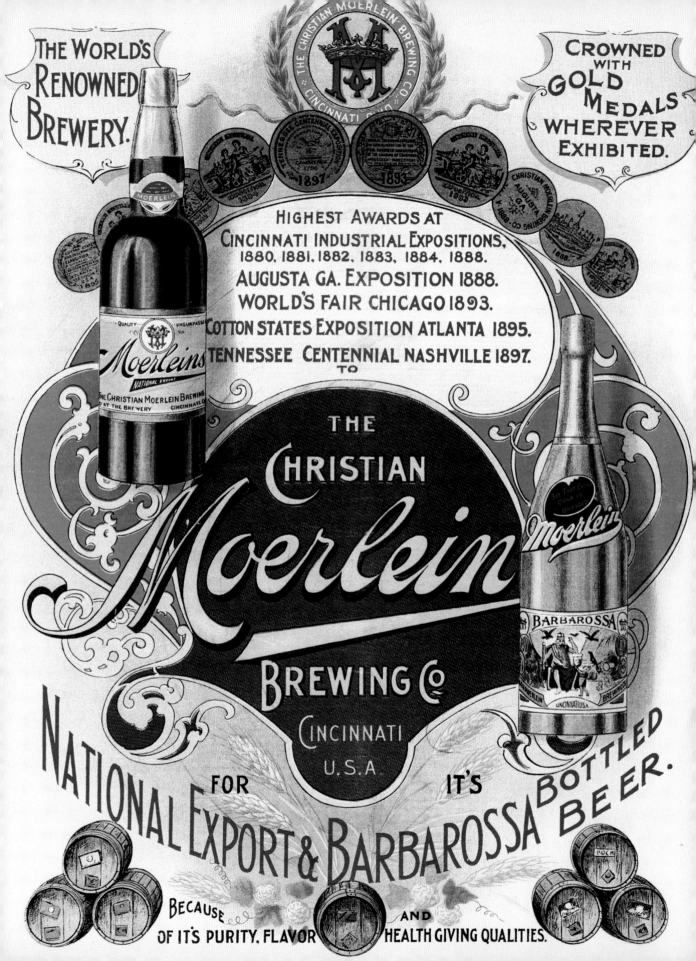

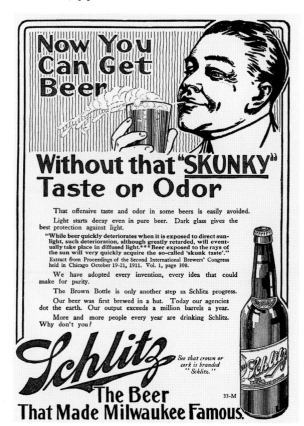

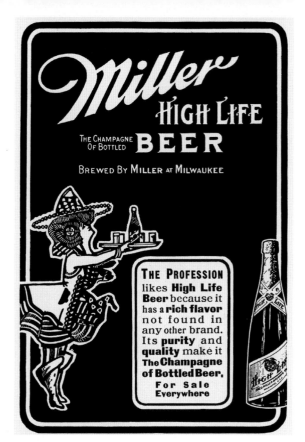

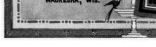

Budweiser Beer, 1905

Miller Beer, 1909

Moerlein Beer, 1901 ◀   Schlitz Beer, 1913

Clysmic Bottled Water, 1913

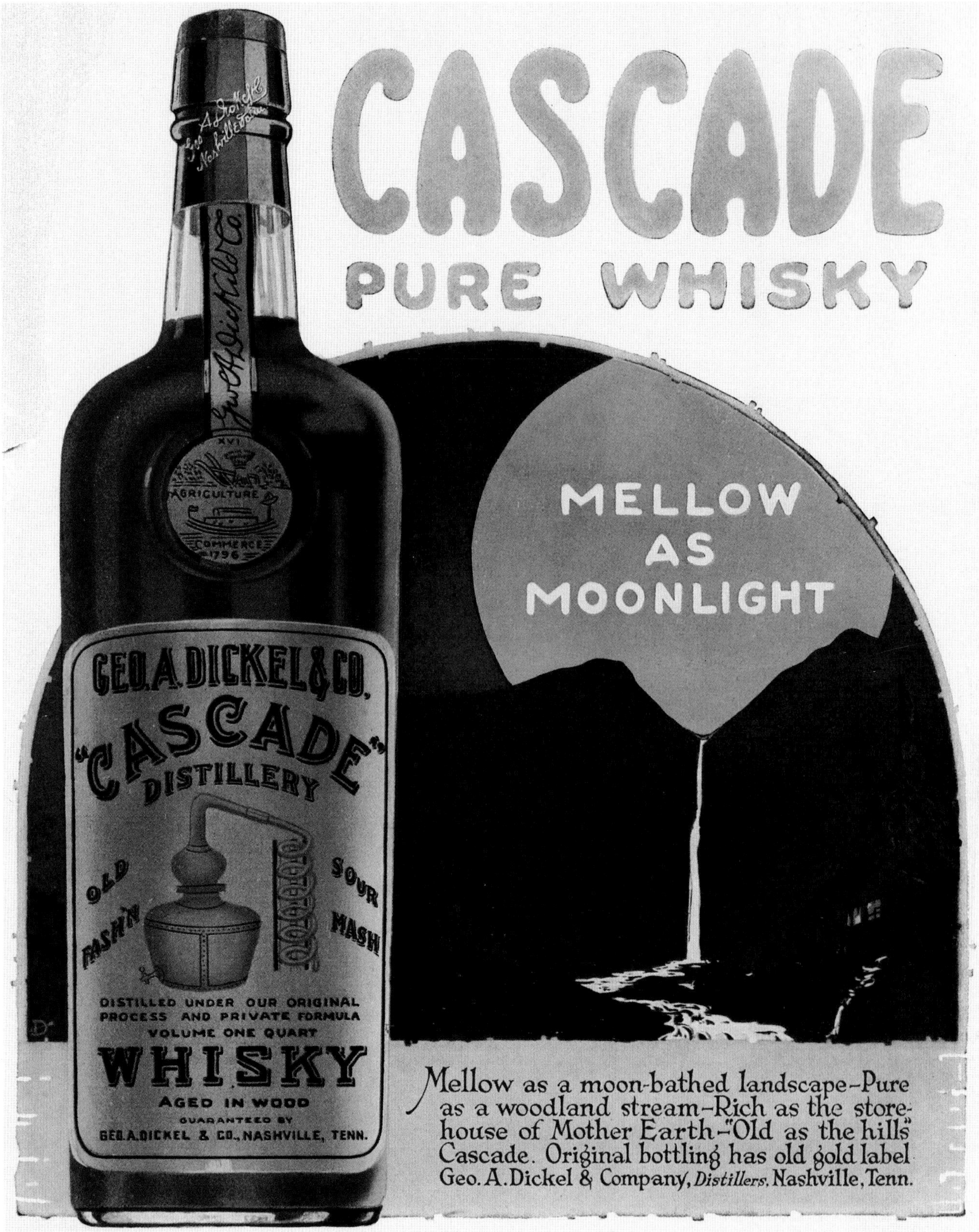

Cascade Whisky, 1916

▸ *Club Cocktails, 1912*

Green River Whiskey, 1917

Wilson Whiskey, 1913

Pabst Blue Ribbon Beer, 1912

Red Top Rye Whiskey, 1902

Underberg Bitters, 1910

White Rock Bottled Water, 1912

The world is moving and learning—a few years more it will be

Gibson's

Rye Whiskey Everywhere !

To-day the favored whiskey of those who appreciate purity, character, flavor and bouquet.

Gibson's Rye Whiskey, 1908

From the very beginning the success of the Christmas feast has depended on Cooks. You may depend upon Cook's Imperial for purity-life-bouquet-flavor. Grace your feast with it.
Sold Everywhere------Served Everywhere.
American Wine Company. St. Louis, U.S.A.

COOK'S
Imperial
Extra Dry

Cook's Champagne, 1916

Johnnie Walker Scotch, 1913

Wilson Whiskey, 1901

E. La Montagne's Sons Wines, 1913

Gordon Sloe Gin, 1914

Gordon Gin, 1912

Gordon Gin, 1916

Gordon Gin, 1913

A Gordon Gin Daisy For Hot Days

DIRECTIONS
PONY GORDON GIN — JUICE OF A LIME — 1 SLICE OF ORANGE — AERATED WATER
PONY RASPBERRY SYRUP — OR 1/2 LEMON — CRACKED ICE — LARGE GLASS

Gordon Gin, 1914

Great Western Champagne, 1914

Moët & Chandon Champagne, 1902

Cook's Champagne, 1914

Cook's Champagne, 1913

Tobacco Redeemer, 1916

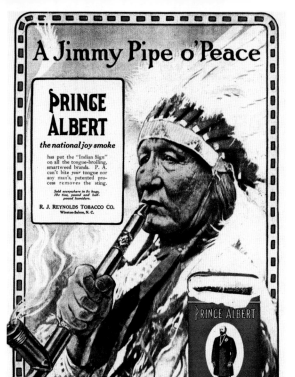

Prince Albert Tobacco, 1913

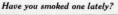

El Principe De Gales Cigars, 1912

United Cigar Stores, 1906

Stag Tobacco, 1913

Cuban Splits Cigars, 1901

Stag Tobacco, 1913

Prince Albert Tobacco, 1915

Velvet Tobacco, 1917

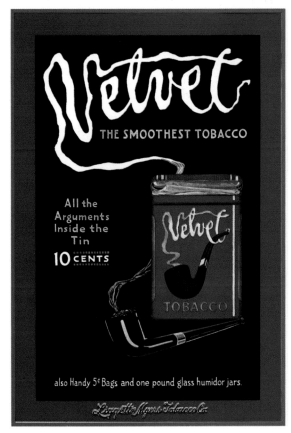

Velvet Tobacco, 1912

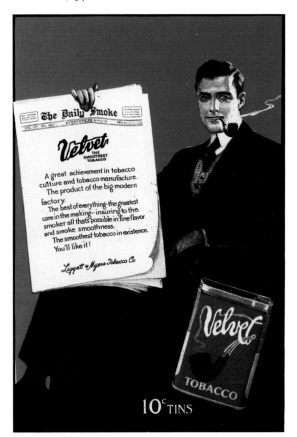

Velvet Tobacco, 1913

Pall Mall Cigarettes, 1916

Pall Mall Cigarettes, 1912

Pall Mall Cigarettes, 1914

Vafiadis Cigarettes, 1916

"Bull" Durham Tobacco, 1915

Egyptian Deities Cigarettes, 1914

Old English Tobacco, 1908

Pall Mall Cigarettes, 1915

Pall Mall Cigarettes, 1916

Pall Mall Cigarettes, 1918

Pall Mall Cigarettes, 1919

Pall Mall Cigarettes, 1918

Pall Mall Cigarettes, 1918

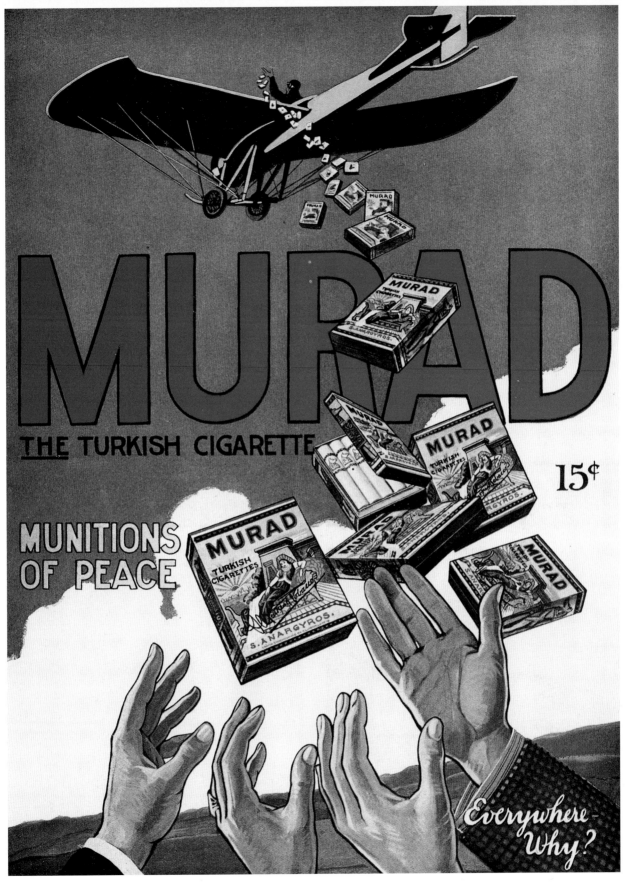

Murad Cigarettes, 1916

Pall Mall Cigarettes, 1918

Pall Mall Cigarettes, 1918

Murad Cigarettes, 1918

Murad Cigarettes, 1915

Murad Cigarettes, 1918

Prince Albert Tobacco, 1913

Prince Albert Tobacco, 1912

Murad Cigarettes, 1919

Murad Cigarettes, 1916

Murad Cigarettes, 1919

Murad Cigarettes, ca. 1917

Murad Cigarettes, 1917

Murad Cigarettes, 1917

Murad Cigarettes, 1917

Murad Cigarettes, 1917

Murad Cigarettes, 1917

Murad Cigarettes, 1918

Murad Cigarettes, 1914

Murad Cigarettes, 1911

Murad Cigarettes, 1919

Murad Cigarettes, 1916

Murad Cigarettes, 1919

Murad Cigarettes, 1919　　　　▸ *Murad Cigarettes, 1919*

Murad Cigarettes, 1918

Murad Cigarettes, 1917

Fatima Cigarettes, 1913

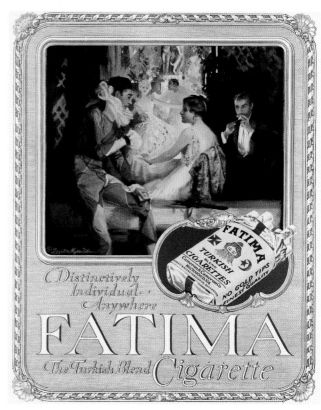

Fatima Cigarettes, 1915

Fatima Cigarettes, 1913

Fatima Cigarettes, 1914

Fatima Cigarettes, 1913

Murad Cigarettes, 1910

Fatima Cigarettes, 1915

Omar Cigarettes, 1917

Omar Cigarettes, 1915

Omar Cigarettes, 1918

Omar Cigarettes, 1918

Omar Cigarettes, 1916

EGYPTIAN
DEITIES

"The Utmost in Cigarettes"

Plain or Cork Tip

You can half see
in their smoke
the sunlight on the
spears of the fight-
ing men, the laugh-
ter in the eyes
of the dancing girls.

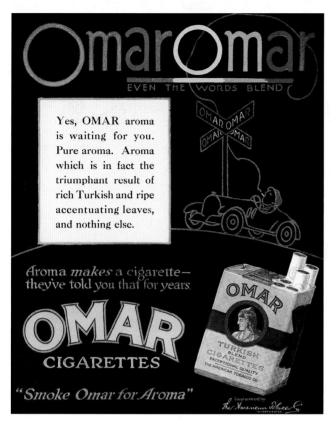

Omar Cigarettes, 1917

Omar Cigarettes, 1918

Egyptian Deities Cigarettes, 1913 ◀   Rameses Cigarettes, 1917

Mecca Cigarettes, 1915

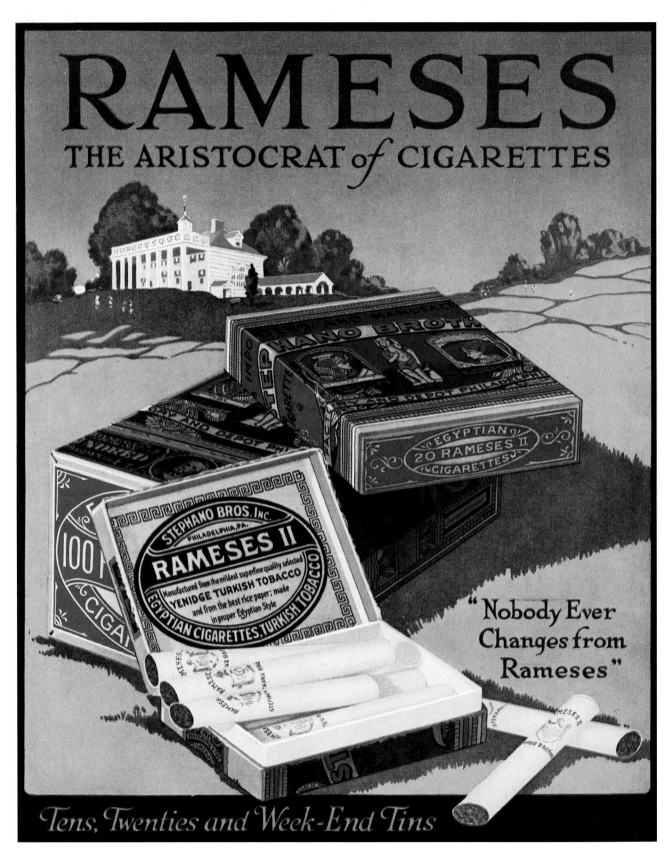

Rameses Cigarettes, 1919

Chesterfield Cigarettes, 1919

La Marquise Cigarettes, 1911

Chesterfield Cigarettes, 1917

Rameses Cigarettes, 1918

Helmar Cigarettes, 1918

Camel Cigarettes, 1919

Camel Cigarettes, 1919

Piper Heidsieck Chewing Tobacco, 1919

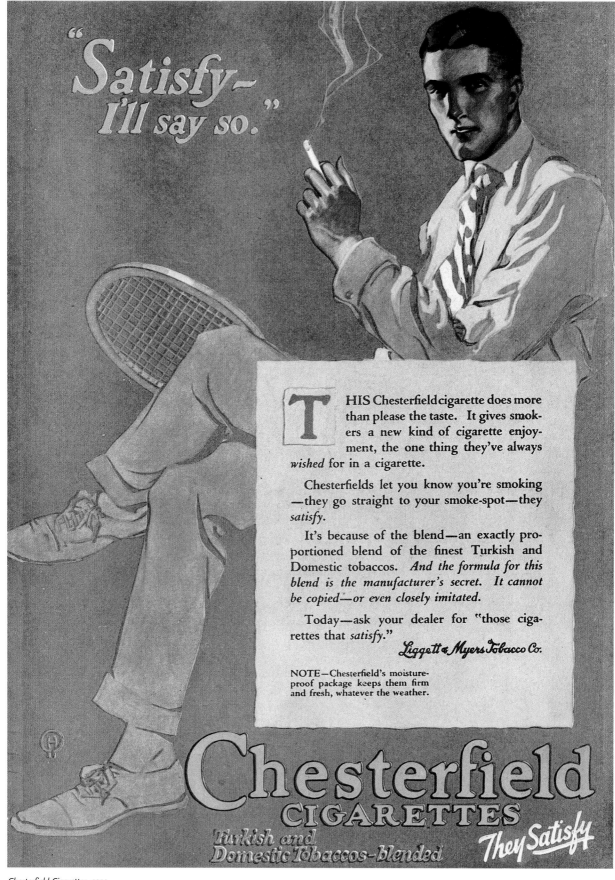

"Satisfy— I'll say so."

THIS Chesterfield cigarette does more than please the taste. It gives smokers a new kind of cigarette enjoyment, the one thing they've always *wished* for in a cigarette.

Chesterfields let you know you're smoking —they go straight to your smoke-spot—they *satisfy.*

It's because of the blend—an exactly proportioned blend of the finest Turkish and Domestic tobaccos. *And the formula for this blend is the manufacturer's secret. It cannot be copied—or even closely imitated.*

Today—ask your dealer for "those cigarettes that *satisfy.*"

Liggett & Myers Tobacco Co.

NOTE—Chesterfield's moisture-proof package keeps them firm and fresh, whatever the weather.

Chesterfield
CIGARETTES

Turkish and Domestic Tobaccos-blended

They Satisfy

Chesterfield Cigarettes, 1919

London Life Cigarettes, 1914

And the winner is...

Smoke Signals

The image of an Indian chief advertising tobacco reflects a time when Native Americans were still a visible presence in American culture and an acceptable marketing icon, especially when it came to smoking. The headline reinforces a prevailing stereotype of the period, that of the Native American as a backward, pidgin-English speaking misfit, while the copy invokes a classic appeal to masculinity, urging "real men" to keep smoking all day long.

Rauchzeichen

Das Bild eines Indianerhäuptlings, der für Tabak wirbt, verweist auf eine Zeit, in der Indianer noch sichtbarer Bestandteil der amerikanischen Kultur waren; wenn's ums Rauchen ging, waren sie in der Werbung noch akzeptiert. Mit der Überschrift wird das herrschende Vorurteil der Zeit bestätigt: Der Indianer ist ein rückständiger, vermurkstes Englisch sprechender, primitiver Eingeborener. Der Text appelliert dafür an das klassische Männerideal: „Echte Männer" rauchen den ganzen Tag wie ein Schlot.

Signaux de fumée

L'image d'un chef indien sur une publicité pour le tabac rappelle l'époque où les Amérindiens étaient encore visuellement présents dans la culture américaine et appropriés comme symbole publicitaire, surtout lorsqu'il s'agissait de fumer. Le titre souligne le stéréotype, largement répandu à l'époque, des Amérindiens considérés comme des asociaux arriérés parlant mal l'anglais, tandis que le texte fait typiquement appel à la masculinité, en poussant les « vrais hommes » à fumer toute la journée.

Señales de humo

La imagen de un jefe indio anunciando tabaco es el reflejo de una época en la que los indios americanos seguían teniendo una presencia visible en la cultura estadounidense y aún eran un icono de marketing aceptable, sobre todo para anunciar tabaco. El titular refuerza un estereotipo preponderante en aquellos tiempos, el de que los indios americanos eran unos inadaptados y atrasados que hablaban un inglés chapucero, mientras que el texto invoca un llamamiento clásico a la masculinidad e insta a los «hombres de verdad» a fumar todo el día.

狼煙（のろし）

インディアンの酋長がタバコを広告している絵は、アメリカ文化の中でネイティブアメリカンがまだ目に見える存在であり、とりわけ喫煙においてはマーケティングの偶像として受け入れられていた時代を反映している。ピジン英語を話し時代に遅れ適合できないネイティブアメリカンという、当時ごく普通であった固定観念を強化するヘッドラインが、コピーにより古典的な男らしさを訴えているのと共に、「真の男」に一日中タバコを吸い続けるよう主張している。

Here's
Heap Big Smoke Joy

Here *is* the big smoke joy with the real flavor and get-up-and-get in every whiff. Makes no difference, men, *how* you smoke it—jam it into a jimmy pipe, or roll it into a cigarette after breakfast—and you'll get the top-o-the-morning feeling into your system for all day. Yes, sir, P. A. is the one real biteless and stingless tobacco bet and it *keeps* men smoking it once they start.

PRINCE ALBERT
the national joy smoke

has the bite taken out by an exclusive, patented process. It never nipped anyone. It *can't* bite. You can smoke P. A. all day and until bedtime, without your tongue being any the wiser. P. A. won't parch your throat. It *is* the heap big smoke joy, for sure. You go and swap the change for a helping and know real tobacco. The cost is only 10c for the tidy red tin or 5c for the toppy red bag—also in pound and half-pound humidors.

Sold everywhere, so buy aplenty where stores are far apart.

R. J. REYNOLDS TOBACCO CO.
Winston-Salem, N. C.

Copyright 1914 by
R. J. Reynolds Tobacco Co.

PRINCE ALBERT

CRIMP CUT
LONG BURNING PIPE AND
CIGARETTE TOBACCO

Prince Albert Tobacco, 1914

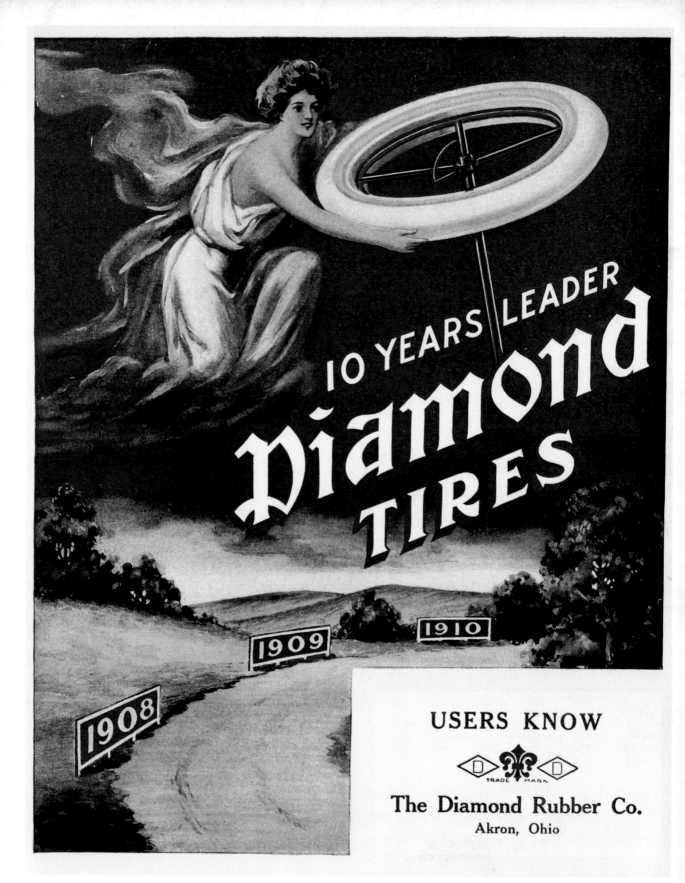

10 YEARS LEADER

Diamond TIRES

1910

1909

1908

USERS KNOW

The Diamond Rubber Co.
Akron, Ohio

Milburn Light Electric, 1918 ◀ *Diamond Tires, 1910*

▶ *Diamond Tires, 1909*

Diamond WRAPPED TREAD

Ten Years
in Ascendency
Its Lead
Will Be Increased
This Year

THE DIAMOND RUBBER CO.
AKRON, OHIO

Republic Tires, 1911

Michelin Tires, 1907

Hartford Tires, 1909

Goodrich Tires, 1918

Baker Electric Vehicles, 1909

Travel Tire Care Free!

The foundation of peace of mind when motoring is the foundation of your car—its tires. An insecure foundation destroys confidence—and may even provoke disaster as well as annoyance. Those who roll along on

GOODRICH TIRES

are supported by the best rolling stock that American skill can produce, from the cream of the world's cotton and rubber markets. A Goodrich equipment, consisting of selected fabric, woven and laid together according to our specifications, covered with the toughest tread in existence, forms a shock-resisting and almost impenetrable unit. Best on heavy closed cars, for city use, as they are best for long distance touring—under all conditions

Best in the Long Run

The B. F. GOODRICH Company
Akron, Ohio
Largest in the World

Branches in the
Principal Cities

Wholesale Tire
Depots Everywhere

Goodrich Tires, 1911

Time to Re-tire?
(Buy Fisk)

Faithful Service
Lasting Friendship

YOUR goodwill is of greatest value to us.

When you buy our product, you get more than tires. Every purchase includes our intention faithfully to fulfill our part of the contract.

Good tires, the will and the effort to see that your pleasure in them is such as to make you a satisfied and permanent Fisk user, *is our obligation*. We are meeting that obligation squarely and successfully with our thousands of satisfied users.

THE FISK RUBBER COMPANY
Factory and Home Office, Chicopee Falls, Mass.
18,000 Dealers and Fisk Branches in Principal Cities

Fisk Tires, 1914

Goodrich Tires, 1918

Fisk Tire Sundries, 1917

Diamond Tires, 1911

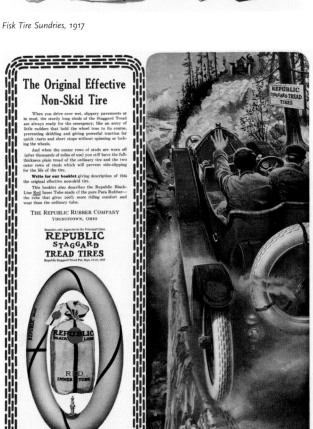

Republic Tires, 1912

Pennsylvania Tires, 1913

There is only one genuine

RED TOP

TRADE MARK REG U S PAT OFF

and that is **FISK**

It completely supplies the requisites of perfect tire equipment—attractiveness, correct style, real safety and remarkable mileage.

Fisk Tire Service in more than one hundred and twenty-five Fisk Branches is rendered without charge or obligation.

Fisk Red Top Tires, 1917

FISK
RED TOP
Trade Mark Registered U. S. Pat. Off.

THE SMARTEST runabout and the most luxurious limousine assume an added air of distinction and dignity when equipped with Fisk RED TOP Tires.

The motorist realizes, too, that there is not a happier combination of tire beauty and efficiency. Fisk Service, in more than One Hundred Direct Branches, is an important feature of the Fisk Policy.

JUNE—The Month of Weddings

Fisk Red Top Tires, 1916

FALLS
CORD
CASINGS

SOLID MERIT

LONG LIFE

COSTELLO-LANG COMPANY

A. J. (Gus) COSTELLO   A. J. (Bob) LANG

556 GOLDEN GATE AVE.   DISTRIBUTORS   SAN FRANCISCO, CALIF.

THE FALLS RUBBER CO., CUYAHOGA FALLS, OHIO

Falls Tires, 1918

Kelly Tires, 1919

RED CROWN TOPS THEM ALL

Up hill or down dale, anywhere your car may go

RED CROWN

"The Gasoline of Quality"

puts the full horse-power of your engine always at your command.
It does this because Red Crown is straight-distilled. It has the full
and complete chain of boiling points necessary for full-powered and
complete combustion of the gas under all motoring conditions.
For Dependable Power use Red Crown gasoline. Look
for the Red Crown sign before you fill.

STANDARD OIL COMPANY
(CALIFORNIA)

Red Crown Gasoline, 1917

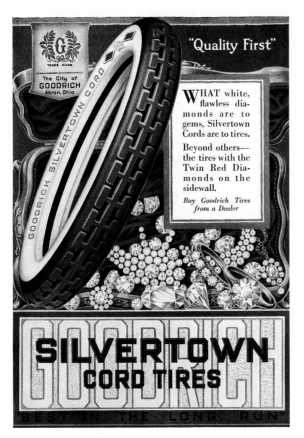

Goodrich Silvertown Tires, 1919

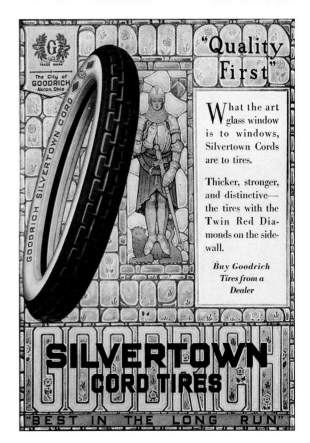

Goodrich Silvertown Tires, 1919

Michelin Tires, 1919

Johnson's Carbon Remover, 1918

FISK
RED TOP
Reg. U.S. Pat. Off.

HARRISON CADY

THE Tire
for Spring Driving

STUNNING! Of rugged construction and liberal mileage, with distinctive red non-skid tread and contrasting sidewall—the final touch to the perfectly appointed car.

Fisk Service Is Different

CHANGES, inspection, instruction, <u>absolutely free</u> in more than 100 Fisk Branches, regardless of the make of tire used. Consult Telephone Directory for Nearest Branch Address.

Fisk Red Top Tires, 1917

A Reproduction of
an original painting
made for The Fisk
Rubber Company
by Maxfield Parrish

FISK TIRES
The Modern Magic Shoes

Fisk Tires, 1917

ANYONE can spot trouble after it starts. But the Boyce Moto-Meter is 10 minutes ahead of your eyes, your ears and your nose put together."

THE MOTO-METER COMPANY, Inc
Long Island City, New York

THE MOTO-METER CO OF CANADA, Limited
Hamilton, Ontario

BOYCE MOTO METER

For sale by dealers everywhere

"*The Most Necessary Instrument on the Car*"

Boyce Moto Meter, 1919

▶ *Zerolene Oil, 1918*

ZEROLENE

in 15-gallon iron barrels, in the familiar 1- and 5-gallon tins, or in whatever quantity you stipulate when you fill at a Standard Oil Service Station. Zerolene is the oil for your car — it means long life for the engine, because it gives correct and complete lubrication. It's the popular motor oil, because it meets requirements. If you have any doubts, talk with users of

ZEROLENE

Truffault-Hartford Shock Absorber, 1911

Indian Motocycle, 1918

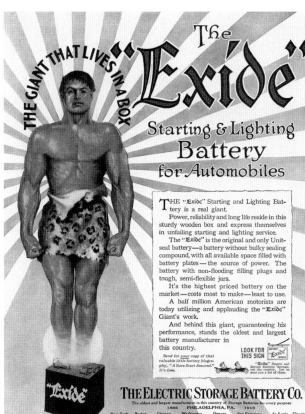

The "Exide" Battery, 1916

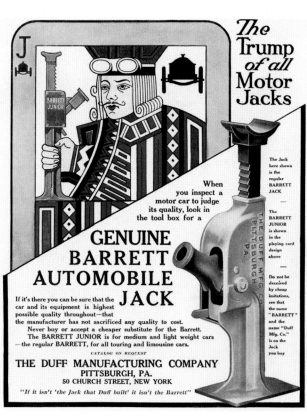

Barrett Automobile Jack, 1910

Approximately 20% of all motor trucks in the United States are Smith Form-a-Trucks giving the lowest hauling cost in the world
$350.00 and a Ford. Maxwell. Chevrolet. F.O.B. Chicago
Smith Motor Truck Corporation
Michigan Ave. at 16th Street
Chicago, Ill.
Smith
Form-a-Truck

Smith Form-A-Truck, 1913

Scandinavian Fur And Leather Co., 1907

Klaxon Auto Horn, 1910

Interstate Electric Steer Warms, 1918

Mezger Automatic Windshield, 1910   ▸ *Chase Motor Car Robes, ca. 1914*

Franklin, 1904

Oldsmobile, 1902

Haynes-Apperson, 1902

Ford, 1902

Decauville, 1904

Oldsmobile, 1903

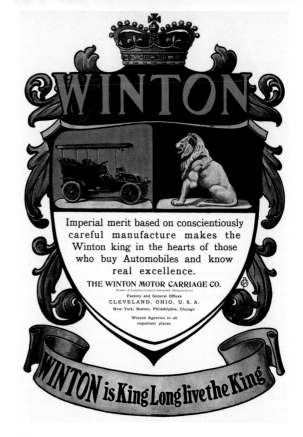

Winton, 1904

Cadillac, 1904

Knox, 1905

▸ *Blomstrom Queen, 1905*

The Queen

BE SURE TO SEE THIS WONDERFUL INNOVATION
IN FOUR CYLINDER CONSTRUCTION

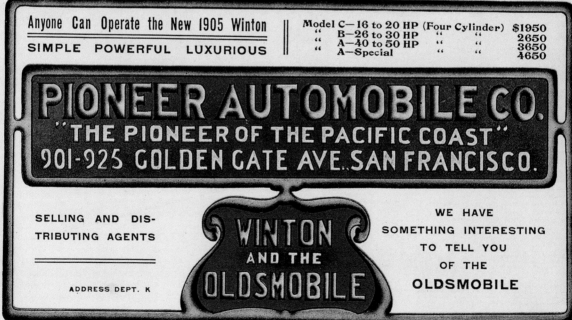

Anyone Can Operate the New 1905 Winton

SIMPLE POWERFUL LUXURIOUS

Model C—16 to 20 HP (Four Cylinder)	$1950
" B—26 to 30 HP " "	2650
" A—40 to 50 HP " "	3650
" A—Special	4650

PIONEER AUTOMOBILE CO.
"THE PIONEER OF THE PACIFIC COAST"
901-925 GOLDEN GATE AVE. SAN FRANCISCO.

SELLING AND DIS-
TRIBUTING AGENTS

ADDRESS DEPT. K

WINTON
AND THE
OLDSMOBILE

WE HAVE
SOMETHING INTERESTING
TO TELL YOU
OF THE
OLDSMOBILE

Winton, 1905

The Autocar

The Autocar 1907 Touring Type $3000
Five passengers — large, roomy tonneau   111-inch wheel base

Four-cylinder vertical motor. 30 horse-power. Direct shaft drive. Sliding-gear, roller-bearing transmission. Three speeds and reverse. Three-point suspension of motor, fly wheel, clutch and transmission as a unit. Extra long springs. The well-known Autocar clutch. Pressed steel frame. I-beam front axle. Autocar Control.

Reliability in every detail of construction and in every phase of performance *assured* by the most comprehensive system of factory tests employed anywhere in the world.

The Autocar will be exhibited in New York at the Madison Square Garden Show—Space 24, January 12 to 19, 1907. In Chicago at the Coliseum and First Regiment Armory Show, Space B 2, February 2 to 9, 1907.

The Autocar Company [Established 1897] 17th Street Ardmore, Pa.
Member: Association Licensed Automobile Manufacturers

Write for The Autocar Book, illustrating and describing the 1907 models,—and explaining the system of factory tests assuring Autocar Reliability.

Reliability

Autocar, 1906

LICENSED UNDER SELDEN PATENT

Matheson

GUARANTEED ONE YEAR

TOURING CARS, 50 H. P., $5,500

The Matheson is standardized. The few changes for 1908 are unimportant refinements. As a matter of fact, most of these were incorporated in mid-season, in our '07 cars. This is the Matheson policy. We do not "save up" new features till the beginning of a new selling season. We neither expect nor desire Matheson owners to buy a new car every year, nor every other year.

We are building today 1908 Mathesons, 1909, 1910, 1912 Mathesons and he who invests will have, years hence, a car which will, after the hardest use, be running as strongly, as reliably, giving as efficient and as economical road service as any high class car then offered for sale. A 1906 Matheson stock touring car still holds the world's record for having carried seven passengers a mile in 50 1-5 seconds. Most cars are bought; Matheson cars are invested in.

The salient Matheson features are those of the greatest foreign cars. The Matheson differs from these in one important respect—it's better. The great string of Matheson victories during the past season, its new speed records, hill-climbing records, endurance records, its perfect scores galore in reliability contests, made, not only without need of repairs, but without even adjustments; all these have repeatedly proven to us that there is no room for improvement in the Matheson. We have sought in vain for records of performance that would direct the improvement of a single feature. Feature for feature through the world's output of high-powered cars, not excepting the best of the foreign makes, there is nothing that can compare with the Matheson for performance over American roads.

Write for our new booklet, "I Drove My Matheson," by Matheson owners, some of whom have made thousands of miles without even an adjustment, some of whom have gone through an entire season with a repair bill of nearly five cents. Better still, visit our exhibit, Space No. 25, in the gallery at the Madison Square Garden Show. The Matheson sets a standard by which you may judge other high powered cars.

The Palmer & Singer Manufacturing Co., 1610 Broadway, N. Y.
Formerly Matheson Co. of N. Y.

Matheson, 1907

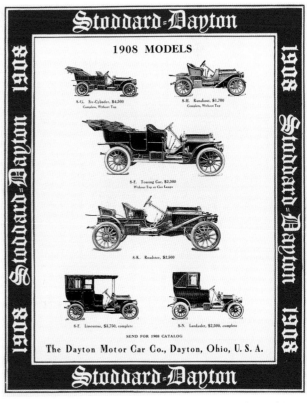

Stoddard-Dayton

1908 MODELS

8-G. Six-Cylinder, $4,500
Complete, Without Top

8-H. Runabout, $1,700
Complete, Without Top

8-F. Touring Car, $2,500
Without Top or Gas Lamps

8-K. Roadster, $2,500

8-E. Limousine, $3,750, complete

8-N. Landaulet, $2,500, complete

SEND FOR 1908 CATALOG

The Dayton Motor Car Co., Dayton, Ohio, U. S. A.

Stoddard-Dayton

Stoddard-Dayton, 1907

▶ Thomas-Flyer, 1907

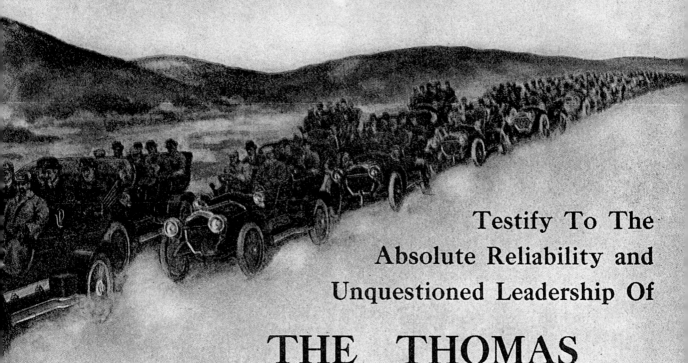

Peerless, 1909

OLDSMOBILE

The Flowing Road

The joys of the flowing road are not confined to athletes and owners who employ chauffeurs. The simplicity and **roadability** of the Oldsmobile put the real pleasure of motoring within the reach of everyone. More money buys nothing better than the Oldsmobile, since your car has all the luxury and style of the most expensive car, plus the roadability, which is lacking in some of the complicated products manufactured for the reckless rich. That is what makes the Oldsmobile appeal to all ages and all classes who want ease of riding, substantial construction, stylish appearance and the one and only roadability that everybody concedes to the Oldsmobile. If you enjoy the pleasures of the open road you should examine the simple Oldsmobile. Duplicates of its most famous cars on sale at all agencies. There is but one quality and one performance in the Oldsmobile.

Member Association Licensed
Automobile Manufacturers

OLDS MOTOR WORKS
Lansing, Mich., U. S. A.

Canadian Trade Supplied from
Canadian Factory. Address Fred-
erick Sager, St. Catherines, Ont.

Oldsmobile, 1907

English Daimler
Best of England

The Car of the King of England
and the Car de Luxe of the World

30 H.P. English Daimler Limousine seating 5 passengers inside. Complete equipment. Price $9,00

The English Daimler, long the standard car of England where it is endorsed and used by King Edward the VIIth, has gradually extended its popularity throughout the entire world. Not until 1906 did it reach the United States. Its great success on the rough roads and bad hills of the British Colonies suggested it as the ideal car for America where travel is hard, fast, and far.

The English Daimler Frame is a peculiar point of excellence. Constructed of pressed steel, it is unusually low, thus greatly facilitating entrance to and exit from the carriage. Yet the motor is so raised from the frame as to give eleven inches road clearance.

Long springs and a silent motor ensure pleasure and comfort. Fast as it is, the English Daimler may be driven through traffic as slowly and quietly as any electric. Hill climbing ability proved at every contest held in the East during the last year. English Daimler engineers have done their work on the road rather than at the drawing board; their ideas have been worked out in the best equipped automobile factory in the world. The result is a car that makes touring a real pleasure and not a game of chance.

English Daimler Co., 1743 Broadway, New York

Agents for

C. G. V. the best of FRANCE   STEARNS the best of AMERICA   FRANKLIN the best light car of the WORLD
ENGLISH DAIMLER best of ENGLAND   BABCOCK the best electric in the WORLD

Wyckoff, Church & Partridge
BROADWAY AT 56TH STREET

English Daimler, 1907

Peerless
All That The Name Implies

1909

Silence
Comfort

*Write to-day for our catalogue "J" which
fully describes the 1909 Peerless Models*

The Peerless Motor Car Co., 2435 Oakdale Av., Cleveland, O.
Member A. L. A. M.

Peerless, 1908

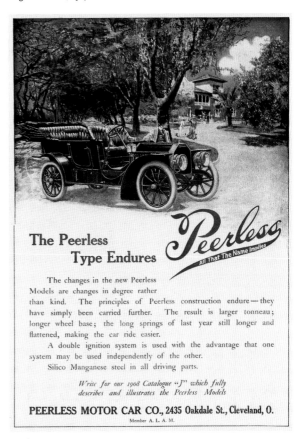

The Peerless
Type Endures

Peerless
All That The Name Implies

The changes in the new Peerless Models are changes in degree rather than kind. The principles of Peerless construction endure — they have simply been carried further. The result is larger tonneau; longer wheel base; the long springs of last year still longer and flattened, making the car ride easier.

A double ignition system is used with the advantage that one system may be used independently of the other.

Silico Manganese steel in all driving parts.

*Write for our 1908 Catalogue "J" which fully
describes and illustrates the Peerless Models*

PEERLESS MOTOR CAR CO., 2435 Oakdale St., Cleveland, O.
Member A. L. A. M.

Peerless, 1908

EVERY Pierce Arrow Car for 1910 is six cylinder. Experience shows that only the smooth operation of the six-cylinder engine gives that real luxury of power which harmonizes with the other equipments of the Pierce Arrow.

THE PIERCE-ARROW MOTOR CAR CO., BUFFALO, N. Y.
Members Association Licensed Automobile Manufacturers

THE THEATRE, SEPTEMBER 1909

Pierce Arrow, 1909

The Pierce Arrow

Pierce Arrow, 1909

The Pierce Arrow

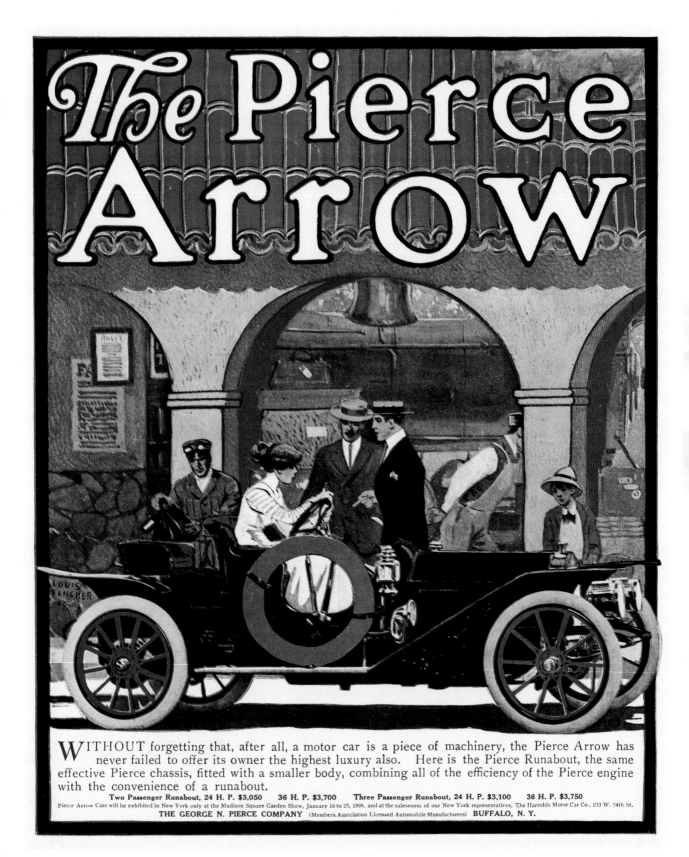

The Pierce Arrow

WITHOUT forgetting that, after all, a motor car is a piece of machinery, the Pierce Arrow has never failed to offer its owner the highest luxury also. Here is the Pierce Runabout, the same effective Pierce chassis, fitted with a smaller body, combining all of the efficiency of the Pierce engine with the convenience of a runabout.

Two Passenger Runabout, 24 H. P. $3,050   36 H. P. $3,700   Three Passenger Runabout, 24 H. P. $3,100   36 H. P. $3,750

Pierce Arrow Cars will be exhibited in New York only at the Madison Square Garden Show, January 16 to 23, 1909, and at the salesroom of our New York representatives, The Harrolds Motor Car Co., 233 W. 54th St.

THE GEORGE N. PIERCE COMPANY (Members Association Licensed Automobile Manufacturers) BUFFALO, N. Y.

Pierce Arrow, 1909 ◀ *Pierce Arrow, 1909*

The Social Prestige of a Baker Electric

is the result of years of refined usage by women who want and will pay for the best. Its graceful design gives the car a marked distinction. Its noiseless shaft drive and luxurious ease of riding fit it pre-eminently for social uses.

Equipped with either lead or Edison batteries (50 cells A4 or 40 cells A6), whichever purchaser may prefer.

1911 Models now being delivered. See them in salesroom of our agents in your city, or write for illustrated catalogue.

THE BAKER MOTOR VEHICLE COMPANY
39 West 80th Street :: CLEVELAND, OHIO, U. S. A.
Agencies in the Principal Cities

Baker Electrics, 1910

▶ *Pierce Arrow, 1910*

The PierceArrow

Peerless, 1910

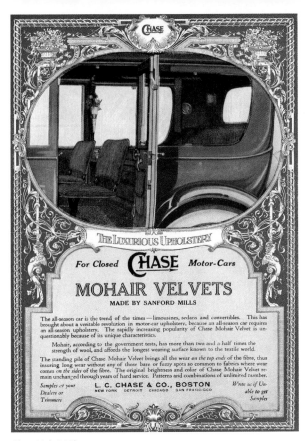

Chase Mohair Velvets, 1919

Baker Electrics, 1910

Brush Runabout, 1910

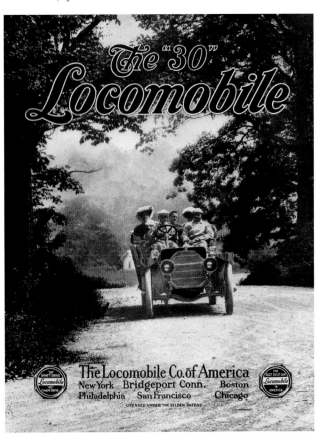

Locomobile "30," 1910

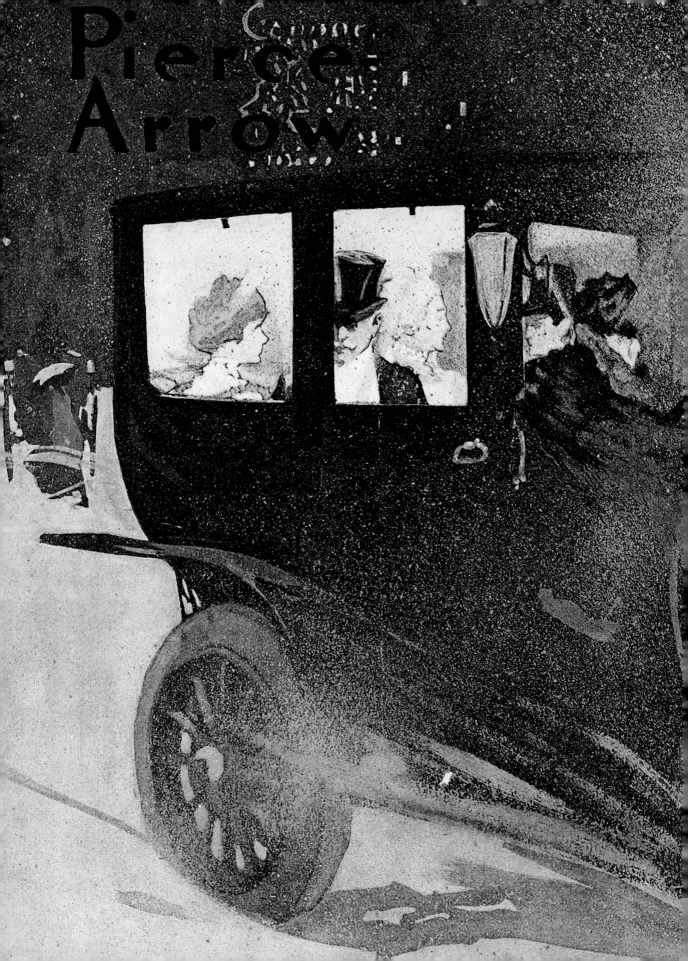

[*Shopping with the Pierce-Arrow*]

T HE PIERCE-ARROW CAR is particularly adapted to shopping, theatre and town use, where the traffic is great, because it can be started or stopped without any perceptible jar. Compare, for instance, the annoying experience of stopping and starting in the ordinary Taxicab.

THE PIERCE-ARROW MOTOR CAR COMPANY, BUFFALO, N. Y.
Licensed under Selden Patent

Firestone Tires

MOST MILES PER DOLLAR

STRENGTH for the e
gency, with the res
power and endurance the
insure a long life of full
ice, that is the comfort
confident feeling that
longs to those who ride
Firestone Tires.

In every country the r
Firestone has come to r
tire satisfaction and econ
And now the standar
raised to even a higher p
by the remarkable servi
Firestone Cord Tires.

With Firestone enginee
ability applied to Cord T
motorists expect more.
they get more. The Fires
design, the Firestone st
ards of quality and car
materials, workmanship
inspection produce not
the safe, carefree, luxur
ride, but Most Miles per
lar. Your dealer and
nearby Firestone Branch
to give you prompt, ecoi
ical service.

FIRESTONE TIRE & RUE
COMPANY, AKRON, C
Branches and Dealers Everyw

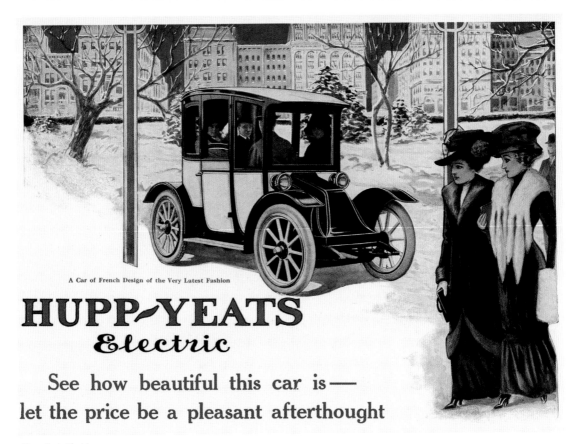

A Car of French Design of the Very Latest Fashion

HUPP·YEATS
Electric

See how beautiful this car is—
let the price be a pleasant afterthought

Hupp-Yeats Electric, 1911

Oldsmobile
12th Year

The four and six-cylinder Oldsmobiles have set a new standard of luxury in motoring. Graceful and finely finished as any yacht,—and the absolute reliability of their mechanism makes them independent of road or weather conditions.

Two types of chassis, each with four styles of body. 36 and 42 inch Tires

OLDS MOTOR WORKS LANSING MICHIGAN
LICENSED UNDER SELDEN PATENT

CORBIN
Never Wears Out

Model 40—Five or Seven Passenger Touring Car

If you only knew the Corbin Car as I know it you would decide in its favor mighty quick

THAT is what a Corbin owner said to a friend who had asked for an opinion. You too, will find upon investigation that the strongest advocates of the Corbin Car are those who have selected them over any other car on the market.

Perhaps you are putting off buying—from day to day—because you are a little skeptical as to the "cost of maintenance" or the "real practical value."

Make a mental note—right now—that you will either call or write one of our distributors—making an appointment for a demonstration.

The moment you are seated in a Corbin Car you will be convinced of the stability, durability, simplicity of operation, abundance of power, ease of control —all of which is positive proof of low cost of maintenance.

As you glide along comfortably and noiselessly you could not dispute the fact that if you owned a Corbin Car you could get to and from your office —night and morning—quicker, cleaner and in a better mood.

Then again, if you happen to be a physician, a contractor, a salesman, or if your business keeps you out around to any extent, you could make more calls—get around more conveniently—and the thought would occur to you that you are really losing time and money by not owning a Corbin Car.

Surely you could not overlook the fact that a Corbin Car would enable you to take the family out on little week-end trips, thus taking advantage of the pure, fresh, open air—exhilarating, invigorating—which means health and happiness —that pays good dividends.

The 1911 Corbin 40, $3000 also includes, please remember, as regular equipment—Imported Magneto, Top with full set of Curtains, Adjustable Rain Vision Wind Shield, Warner Speedometer, Prest-O-Lite Gas Tank, Headlights, Combination Oil and Electric Dash and Tail Lamps, Storage Battery, Firestone Q. D. Demountable Rims, Tire Holders, Trunk Rack and full set of tools, etc.

Let us give you more reasons why you should buy a Corbin Car—either for business or pleasure. A postal will bring our beautifully illustrated catalogue and name of nearest dealer.

CORBIN MOTOR VEHICLE CORPORATION, NEW BRITAIN, CONN.
Licensed Under Selden Patent

Firestone Tires, 1917 ◄ *Oldsmobile, 1910*

Corbin, 1911

The car of today—and tomorrow

At the automobile shows, or in any one of two hundred and fifty salesrooms, you are invited to pass judgment on the latest product of one of the oldest automobile factories—the Oldsmobile for 1911.

Your verdict on any car is generally based on present appearance and performance, but before purchasing assure yourself that the excellence of to-day will be permanent in after years. The soundest advice to the purchaser of a motor car is: buy your car for "tomorrow."

Nearly thirteen years of constant improvement, culminating in the 1911 Oldsmobile, assures the owner of all that is best today—and furthermore, of a substantial return on his investment for years to come.

THE SPECIAL	THE AUTOCRAT	THE LIMITED
Four-cylinder; Bore, 4¾"; Stroke, 4¾"; 36 inch Tires.	—shown above— Four-cylinder; Bore, 5"; Stroke, 6"; 38 inch Tires.	Six-cylinder; Bore, 5"; Stroke, 6"; 42 inch Tires.

TOURING CARS   ROADSTERS   TOURABOUTS   CLOSED CARS

OLDS MOTOR WORKS   LANSING, MICHIGAN

Licensed Under Selden Patent

BRANCH HOUSES at Boston, Philadelphia, Louisville, Detroit, Chicago, St. Louis, and Kansas City.
DISTRIBUTORS IN NEW YORK   REPRESENTATIVES IN EVERY STATE AND IN CANADA

Oldsmobile, 1911

Garford MOTOR CARS

HERE is the Garford "Six"—the most advanced six cylinder car on the market. The wonderful performance of this motor during a series of unusually rigid tests, covering a period of over three years, rightly classes it as the most perfect six cylinder car made. Every six cylinder obstacle has been overcome. It has successfully weathered the storm.

¶ Under any condition the fuel distribution is perfect. At all times you get the full benefit of all of the cylinders—not occasionally. It has a self contained oiling system, guaranteeing perfect lubrication. Oil consumption is remarkably low. On one 15,000 mile test it averaged eleven miles per gallon of gasoline. In this car the six cylinder bugbear—carburetion—has been completely eliminated. It is as mechanically perfect as the best of the engineering world can make it.

¶ The wheel base of one hundred and thirty-five inches permits an unusually comfortable and luxurious seven-passenger body. The body itself is elegantly proportioned. The whole finish is magnificent. The car shown here is the six cylinder seven-passenger touring car priced at $4500.

¶ A polished chassis of this most advanced "Six" will be shown at both the New York and Chicago Automobile Shows. If you attend be sure and look it over.

¶ We have a book about this "Six" which we know will interest you. We would like to send you a copy. Please ask for Book B.

The Willys-Garford Sales Company, Toledo, Ohio

If interested in trucks ask for a truck book.

Hotel Plaza, New York City

Garford "Six," 1911

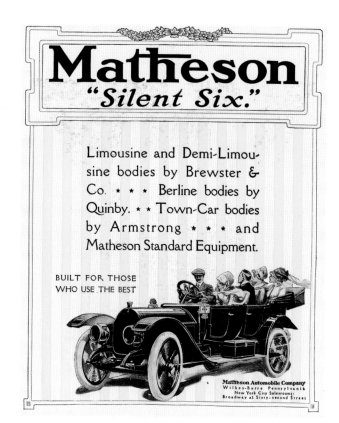

Matheson "Silent Six."

Limousine and Demi-Limousine bodies by Brewster & Co. ✱ ✱ ✱ Berline bodies by Quinby. ✱ ✱ Town-Car bodies by Armstrong ✱ ✱ ✱ and Matheson Standard Equipment.

BUILT FOR THOSE
WHO USE THE BEST

Matheson Automobile Company
Wilkes-Barre Pennsylvania
New York City Salesrooms
Broadway at Sixty-second Street

Matheson "Silent Six," 1911

Maxwell

$1150 EQUIPPED

LIFE contains no greater pleasure than a spin over smooth roads of city or country in a Maxwell Mercury.

A stylish, swift, mile-a-minute roadster, thirty horsepower, test-proven, with a wealth of refinements which makes it easily the best-appointed car of its type.

Other models—Maxwell Special, $1280; Mascotte Touring Car, $980; Mascotte Roadster, $950; Messenger Runabout, $600. There are 47,000 Maxwell cars now in use.

Free Monthly Inspection Service of all our cars for twelve months

Maxwell-Briscoe Motor Company, 17 West 61st Street, at Broadway, New York
Division of UNITED STATES MOTOR COMPANY

Maxwell Team of Three Cars Wins Glidden Trophy

Maxwell Mercury, 1911

Pierce-Arrow, 1911

The Pierce-Arrow at the Aviation Meet

No one thing has done so much to decrease the number of imported cars in this country as the Pierce-Arrow.

THE PIERCE-ARROW MOTOR CAR COMPANY, BUFFALO, N. Y.

Licensed under Selden Patent

IN ANSWERING THIS ADVERTISEMENT PLEASE MENTION COLLIER'S

Pierce-Arrow, 1911

▸ *Pierce-Arrow, 1911*

The Pierce-Arrow

Edward Borein

THE PIERCE-ARROW AT NÜRNBERG

Pierce-Arrow, 1911

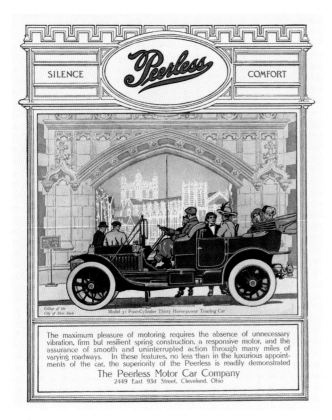

Peerless, 1911

Garford, 1912

Stearns 15-30 H. P. Limousine, 1911

Oldsmobile, 1911

To the man of affairs, whose time is measured in big money value, a motor car of the character, dignity and power of the LOZIER is indispensable. It has become an essential part of his business life and the social life of his family.

6 CYL. 51 HP $5000 - 4 CYL. 46 HP $4,700   Catalog and name of nearest dealer on request   LOZIER MACK AVENUE DETROIT

Lozier, 1912

The Pierce-Arrow

Pierce-Arrow, 1912

Baker Electrics, 1912

Oldsmobile Limited, 1912

Pope-Hartford, 1912

R-C-H "Twenty-Five," 1912

TWENTY-ONE years of consistent progress have resulted in the distinctive individuality for which Stevens-Duryea motor cars are famed—individuality of mechanical design, individuality of finish, and individuality of service.

Our "Individuality" booklet will interest you. Send for it.

STEVENS-DURYEA COMPANY, Chicopee Falls, Massachusetts

Pioneer Builders of American Sixes

Stevens-Duryea, 1912

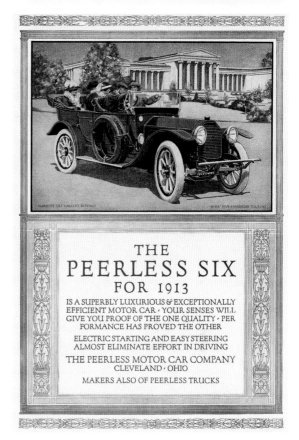

THE PEERLESS SIX
FOR 1913

IS A SUPERBLY LUXURIOUS & EXCEPTIONALLY EFFICIENT MOTOR CAR · YOUR SENSES WILL GIVE YOU PROOF OF THE ONE QUALITY · PERFORMANCE HAS PROVED THE OTHER

ELECTRIC STARTING AND EASY STEERING ALMOST ELIMINATE EFFORT IN DRIVING

THE PEERLESS MOTOR CAR COMPANY
CLEVELAND · OHIO

MAKERS ALSO OF PEERLESS TRUCKS

Peerless Six, 1913

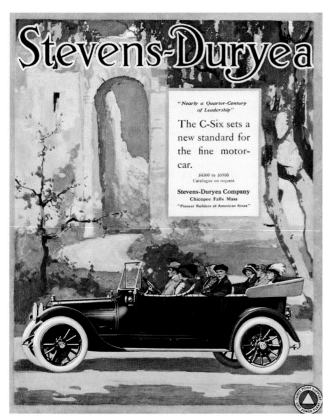

"Nearly a Quarter-Century of Leadership"

The C-Six sets a new standard for the fine motorcar.

$4500 to $5050
Catalogue on request

Stevens-Duryea Company
Chicopee Falls Mass
"Pioneer Builders of American Sixes"

Stevens-Duryea C-Six, 1913

Lozier, 1913

LOZIER
The choice of
'Men Who Know'
Six-Cylinders $5,000 LOZIER 2406 Mack Ave. Detroit

Not only has the Pierce-Arrow turned the tide of imported cars so that there are today far less in proportion than some years ago—not only that, but the Pierce-Arrow in American hands has invaded Europe, giving greater satisfaction to its owners than a native car on its native heath.

The Pierce-Arrow Motor Car Company, Buffalo, New York

Lozier, 1912 ◀   Pierce-Arrow, 1913

Warner Auto-Meter, 1914

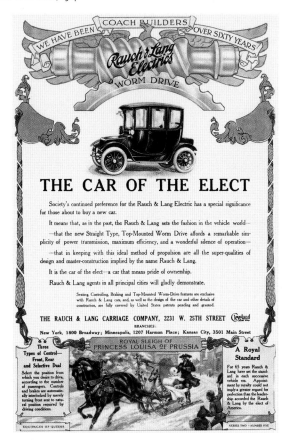

Rauch & Lang Electrics, 1914

Moon Light Six, 1919

Stoddard-Dayton Saybrook

None can go further, none faster—none ride with greater ease and comfort—and none have ever given better service. No finer car for two people was ever designed than this Compartment Roadster. Pull forward the back of the seats and there are your two suit cases, and their contents unsoiled by water or dust. Extra room in body means more than comfort. This style of body is mounted on three chasses; the "Silent Knight," $4900; the "Saybrook," $2700 and the "Savoy," $1350.

Write for Complete Catalog.

DAYTON MOTOR CAR CO.
Division of UNITED STATES MOTOR COMPANY
17 West 61st Street   New York

Stoddard-Dayton Saybrook, 1912

Overland, 1913

Peerless Trucks, 1913

Oakland, 1913

Packard "38" Limousines, 1914

Pleasure

—and your Rauch & Lang or Baker Electric is a car of Pleasure.

You find pleasure in the utility by which you so easily reach the out-o'-way places or make a social call.

Pleasure in the ease of control—in the roomy interior, in the genuine coach work, and in the knowledge that your car *is* a Rauch & Lang or Baker Electric.

THE BAKER R & L COMPANY
Cleveland, Ohio

Rauch & Lang Electrics
"The Social Necessity"

Baker Electrics

Baker And Rauch & Lang Electrics, 1915

New Departure Ball Bearings, 1918

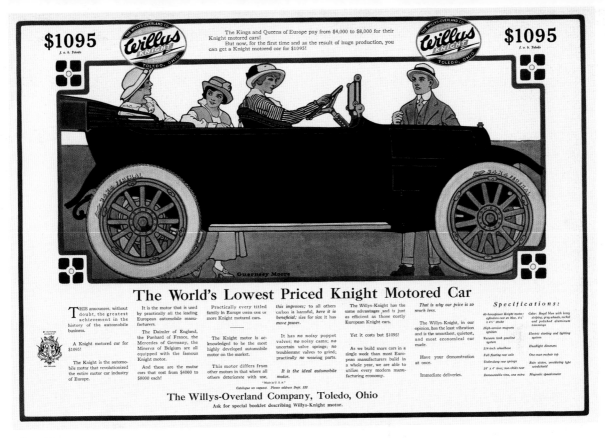

Willys-Knight, 1915

Milburn Light Electric, 1916

Phianna Town Car, 1916

Simplex

Comfort

To know that your Rauch & Lang or Baker Electric is recognized everywhere as Society's Chosen Car means comfort of mind.

To have ample seating room in which you find restful repose means comfort of body. This roominess is richly amplified by genuine coach work, the outcome of over sixty years' leadership in the building of Fashion's equipages.

This, combined with a wonderful operating simplicity, means *comfort* in its fullest sense.

Baker Electrics
QUALITY SERVICE

Rauch & Lang Electrics
"The Social Necessity"

THE BAKER R & L COMPANY, Cleveland, Ohio

Simplex, 1916 ◄ *Baker And Rauch & Lang Electrics, 1916*

Confidence

Wonderful driving simplicity of the Baker and Rauch & Lang Electric inspires utmost confidence on the part of the occupants at all times.

The mother finds comfort in knowing that the safety and pleasure of her little ones are enhanced because of this driving simplicity—this independence from mechanical obtrusion and confusion.

And in full keeping with this is the rich coach work—*genuine* coach work—the best that can come of over sixty years' leadership in fashionable coach building.

Confidence all 'round—in the knowledge that your Baker and Rauch & Lang represents the best, and that it insures the utmost in safety.

Baker Electrics

The Baker R. & L. Company
Cleveland, Ohio

Rauch & Lang Electrics
"The Social Necessity"

Baker And Rauch & Lang Electrics, 1916

THE FRANKLIN CAR

TO have defined motoring fineness as motoring efficiency, has been the unique service of the Franklin Car.

This is the simple explanation of the fact that for seventeen years, in economy, comfort, easy handling and long life, the Franklin has given substance and reality to the somewhat shadowy phrase, motoring satisfaction.

20 miles to the gallon of gasoline
—instead of 10

10,000 miles to the set of tires
—instead of 5,000

FRANKLIN AUTOMOBILE COMPANY
SYRACUSE, N. Y.

Franklin, 1919

▶ *Willys-Knight Limousines, 1916*

Overland, 1916

Chalmers, 1916

Overland, 1916

Overland, 1916

▶ *Overland, 1916*

O. K.'d by the Nation

Exacting, appreciative, practical, hard-headed America—has, as one unit, O. K.'d the small, light, economical $615 Overland.

They like its style; its good-looking lines; that smart, individual air of exclusiveness.

They like its power and pep. It shoots up a hill like a streak of greased lightning. It gives, but seldom gets, the dust.

Put five in (there's lots of room), give her a little gas and away she flies—free from vibration, rattle, stress or strain.

What do you suppose appeals to the more elderly people? Just the solid comfort. This car, unlike most of the smaller and popular priced makes, has none of that stiffness or rigidness about it. Deep, soft, divan upholstery and shock-absorbing cantilever springs take all the stiffness out and put all the comfort in.

Large tires (4-inch) also add materially to the riding qualities of the car. Also, and just as important, they help keep upkeep at a minimum.

Another thing to remember. This car comes complete. No expensive starter or speedometer or anything extra to buy.

It's the little conveniences that seem to have the broadest appeal. The electric control buttons on the steering column, convenient foot pedals and shifting levers bring everything within everyone's reach—even the price.

It is but $615—complete.

The Willys-Overland Company, Toledo, Ohio

"Made in U. S. A."

Buick Sedan, 1916

Overland Country Club, 1917

Cole Aero-Eight, 1916

Buick, 1917

THE CABRIOLET

White
Sixteen valve 4'

A perfect example of custom built quality and an impressive illustration of the distinction to be attained by hand wrought, built in, refinement in every detail of body and chassis.

Upholstery and finish may be selected to suit the owner's individual taste.

The *WHITE COMPANY*, Cleveland

White Cabriolet, 1917

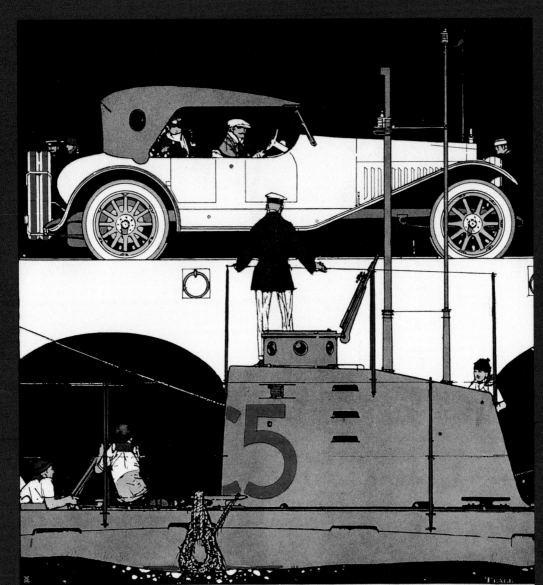

White Sixteen valve 4'

THREE STAGES OF MOTOR DEVELOPMENT

In the first stage, higher power was obtained by building larger cylinders. In the second stage, greater flexibility was secured by adding cylinders. Both involve serious handicaps in a reciprocating engine. In the third stage, upon which gas engine design is now entering, a higher range of inherent capability has been developed—more power from existing plant. Simple and rugged, the sixteen-valve four draws straight from the source of high power and flexible performance: *valve efficiency*.

The White Company, Cleveland

White Runabout, 1917

Milburn Light Electric, 1917

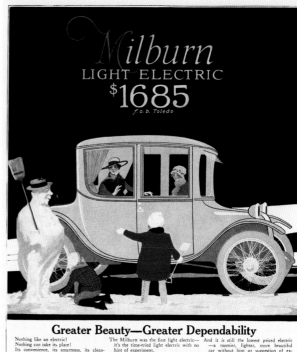

Milburn Light Electric, 1917

Studebaker Big-Six, 1919

Overland Six, 1916

All out of doors coaxes, teases and invites you to get an Overland.

There's one for you. See the Willys-Overland dealer today—let him show you the most comprehensive line of cars ever built by any one producer—make your selection now.

The Willys-Overland Company, Toledo, Ohio
Manufacturers of Willys-Knight and Overland Motor Cars
"Made in U. S. A."

Overland, 1917

She hasn't an Overland — or anything

Probably no one thing makes such a difference in one's whole outlook upon life as the change from lack of an automobile to ownership of an automobile—it changes everything.

The Willys-Overland Company offers the most comprehensive line of automobiles ever built by any one producer; all are beautiful cars, with brand new body designs.

The Willys-Overland Company, Toledo, Ohio
Manufacturers of Willys-Knight and Overland Motor Cars

She has an Overland — an' everything

Every car in the line shares proportionately in the economies of our huge production—every one of these models is, we believe, priced lower than any other car of similar value.

See the Willys-Overland Dealer now, let him help you to select the car best suited to your needs and your purse, and begin now to lead a better, bigger, happier, healthier life.

The Willys-Overland Company, Toledo, Ohio
Manufacturers of Willys-Knight and Overland Motor Cars

Overland, 1917

Do your bit—but keep fit—
The car of the hour

The times demand alertness—energy—efficiency.

The call for extra effort has been heard and answered by men, women and even children.

Do "your bit"—but keep fit.

If you work harder—play harder too.

Have an automobile.

It will enable the whole family to do more each day with less fatigue.

With it you can speed up your work—gain time for play—

and reach your playground quickly—without fatigue.

Have efficient equipment for efficient living—get an Overland Model Eighty-Five Four.

This is the famous 35 horse-power Overland.

Among cars of such comfortable size it has been the leading favorite for years.

And it is the car of the hour.

The new body this season makes it far more beautiful than ever before and with its

Five passenger capacity

new cantilever rear springs is far easier riding.

And we have made it a bigger, roomier car.

No one now has money to waste.

With tremendous resources, unequalled facilities and larger output than any other producer of an economical four cylinder car of such comfortable size—

We effect greater economies and therefore give more for the money in this car than

35 horsepower motor

can be had in any other similar car.

No one now has energy to waste.

This Overland is small enough to be economical to operate yet it is big enough not to cramp you and so easy riding that it will not tire you.

It represents the maximum of economy possible without sacrifice of comfort—true economy—true efficiency.

In this 35 horsepower Overland there is not one hint of experiment—not one hint of

Cantilever rear springs

extravagance—not one hint of false economy.

It is the car of the hour.

Run over the specifications of this car—compare it with others and you will find more car in size, in comfort, in power, in convenience, in beauty, than $895 will buy in any other car.

Go to the Overland dealer and get your Model Eighty-Five Four today—the car of the hour—efficient equipment for efficient living.

Auto-Lite starting and lighting

Willys-Overland Inc., Toledo, Ohio
Willys-Knight and Overland Motor Cars

Overland, 1917

Marmon 34, 1917

Marmon 34, 1918

Overland

The New Four-Door Sedan

Women Especially Appreciate the Easier-Riding and Easier-Driving of Overland 4 With Three-Point Cantilever Springs

NO previous motor car experience is an adequate comparison for the riding-smoothness, the road-steadiness and the greater driving-ease of the new Overland 4 Four-Door Sedan.

The new, exclusive Three-Point Cantilever Springs give to this light weight car the comfort formerly confined to the heavy car of long wheelbase. They are so attached as to give the steadiness of long wheelbase together with the lightness and ease of control of 100-inch wheelbase.

They protect the passengers from road-blows and shield the car from shock, thus prolonging the life of the car and saving repair expenses.

Light weight also is a source of great economy in this car. Fuel consumption is lower. Tires last longer.

The Four-Door Sedan has beauty, smartness, and ample room. It is elegantly furnished and complete in its accommodations. Its equipment is high grade—complete from Auto-Lite Starting and Lighting to Demountable Rims.

See the Overland dealer now. Ask for booklet describing this new car, Overland 4 Four-Door Sedan, $1375; Touring, $845; Roadster, $845; Coupé, $1325. Prices f. o. b. Toledo.

WILLYS-OVERLAND INC., TOLEDO, OHIO
Sedans, Coupés, Touring Cars and Roadsters
Willys-Overland, Limited, Toronto, Canada

Overland 4, 1919

PAIGE
The Most Beautiful Car in America

The Paige occupies an unchallenged position among the finest motor carriages of this country and Europe. It is an artistic achievement and a mechanical masterpiece.

Paige-Detroit Motor Car Co.
Detroit

Paige, 1918

MARMON 34

The Convertible Sedan is one of the most popular of the newer body styles—it can be used as a closed car or easily changed to an open car with only windshield, top and rear portion in place. All seats are enclosed, entrance is by rear doors, the front seats are separate and adjustable. Smart, low lines distinguish this luxuriously appointed car, eleven hundred pounds lighter.

NORDYKE & MARMON COMPANY
Indianapolis, Ind.

Marmon 34, 1918

The New Studebaker BIG SIX

Studebaker Quality, dominant for sixty-six years, is reflected in this car

Beautiful in design
Thoroughly modern
Mechanically right

STUDEBAKER
Detroit, Mich.
South Bend, Ind.   Walkerville, Ont.
Address all correspondence to South Bend

Studebaker Big-Six, 1918

PIERCE-ARROW

Milburn
LIGHT ELECTRIC
$1685
f. o. b. Toledo

"Never a Bit of Trouble"

An automobile which users and dealers say "never gives a bit of trouble"—

An automobile which users and dealers pronounce "the most remarkable motor car ever placed on the market"—

Such is this season's Milburn Light Electric.

Its freedom from mechanical troubles is due to its balanced efficiency.

Its freedom from tire troubles is due to its light weight.

Its remarkable success is due to these things

—to its exquisite appearance and to the low price made possible by our large production,—doubled this year compared with last.

The lowered prices of other electrics give tribute to the Milburn—but Milburn efficiency is greater than ever, Milburn beauty even more exquisite—Milburn value still unapproached and supreme.

See the nearest dealer or if he is not known to you write for our catalogue and nearest dealer's name and address.

Established 1848   **THE MILBURN WAGON COMPANY**   **Toledo, Ohio**
Automobile Division

The Milburn Charger solves the home charging problem—inexpensively—efficiently

A Wonderful Family Gift—Overland 4
With Three-Point Suspension Springs

As a family gift, this new Overland 4, the Four-Door Sedan will contribute smoothness of riding, usefulness and enjoyment every day in the year.

Three-Point Suspension Springs give a *new kind* of riding comfort—a comfort that was unknown until introduced by Overland 4.

Spring attachment at the ends of a 130-inch Springbase give this easy-to-drive, 100-inch wheelbase car the riding-ease and the road-steadiness of a large, heavy car of long wheelbase.

The wheels go up and down, following the irregularities of the road, but car and passengers sail along smoothly.

Car and passengers are free from the ordinary jolts, vibrations and side swaying.

The lightweight of the Overland 4 makes for exceptional economy. Its life is prolonged because the springs *protect* the car from the racking damage of road blows.

This Four-Door Sedan is a quality car throughout, of graceful design, and smart appearance and conveniences.

In equipment is complete, from Auto-Lite Starting and Lighting to U. S. L. Batteries.

Have the Overland Dealer show you this car. Overland 4, Four-Door Sedan, $1375; Coupé, $1325; Touring, $845; Roadster, $845. Prices f. o. b. Toledo.

WILLYS-OVERLAND INC., TOLEDO, OHIO
Sedans, Coupés, Touring Cars and Roadsters
Willys-Overland, Limited, Toronto, Canada

Overland 4, 1919

Overland
The Thrift Car
Top-Notch Value—
Rock-Bottom Cost

See how satisfactorily this car meets all five of the requirements for complete satisfaction.

Its *appearance* commands admiration and its performance is equal to all demands.

The 32-horsepower motor is notoriously stingy with fuel, and liberal with power.

This car is simple to handle, has narrow turning radius, convenient control, Electric Auto-Lite Starting and Lighting and easy operating clutch that women drivers so appreciate.

It is exceedingly *comfortable*, with wide seats, deep upholstery, spacious interior, rear cantilever springs and large tires, non-skid rear.

Wherever you drive, expert Overland service facilities are available. Priced at its remarkably low figure, this Model 90 is truly a bargain.

All of these essentials for complete satisfaction cannot be bought for less.

For point-of-Overland superiority:
Appearance, Performance, Comfort, Service and Price

Willys-Overland Inc., Toledo, Ohio
Willys-Knight and Overland Motor Cars and Light Commercial Cars
Canadian Factory, West Toronto, Canada

Light Four Model 90
Touring Car

"Show me where the highest mileage is but no brakes and nicety. I'll show you the widest number of motor cars in service."
—John N. Willys

Overland, 1918

Here is permanence — in the distinctive lines and the stalwart chassis of this Anniversary Apperson 8—the 8 with 80 less parts.

APPERSON BROTHERS AUTOMOBILE COMPANY KOKOMO, INDIANA

APPERSON 8

Apperson 8, 1918

The New

Studebaker

LIGHT-SIX

FOUR-PASSENGER CLUB ROADSTER

Beautiful in Design
Thoroughly Modern
Mechanically Right

A light-weight, speedy and
powerful close-coupled 4-pas-
senger roadster. Provided with
four doors that open into driver's
compartment and tonneau, elim-
inating the inconvenience of
crowding through front entrance.
A very comfortable and convenient car.

STUDEBAKER

Detroit, Mich.   South Bend, Ind.
Walkerville, Ont.

Studebaker Light-Six, 1918

THE FRANKLIN BROUGHAM

WITH all the charm and intimacy of the individual enclosed car—this Brougham of advanced design still has ample room for four passengers.

And its real fineness is demonstrated in remarkable riding-comfort, ease of handling, and the consistent economy of—

20 miles to the gallon of gasoline
10,000 miles to the set of tires
50% slower yearly depreciation

FRANKLIN AUTOMOBILE COMPANY, SYRACUSE, N. Y.

Franklin Brougham, 1919

The Tudor Sedan

Not even a chilly all-day rain need upset the plans of the woman who has a Ford closed car at her disposal. Knowing it to be reliable and comfortable in all weathers, she goes out whenever inclination suggests or duty dictates.

The car is so easy to drive that it constantly suggests thoughtful services to her friends. She can call for them without effort and share pleasantly their companionship.

All remark upon the graceful outward appearance of her car, its convenient and attractive interior, and its cosy comfort. And she prides herself upon having obtained so desirable a car for so low a price.

TUDOR SEDAN, $590   FORDOR SEDAN, $685   COUPE, $525   (All prices f. o. b. Detroit)

Ford
CLOSED CARS

Ford Closed Cars, 1919

National

TWELVE CYLINDER CARS

Aircraft Type MOTOR

THIS National springs from a race of lean, powerful cars that for eighteen years have served their owners well. Under its bonnet a steady flow of even power that will carry you where you will, smoothly and as swiftly as you dare to ride.

NATIONAL MOTOR CAR & VEHICLE CORPORATION, INDIANAPOLIS
Nineteenth Successful Year

Six and Twelve Cylinder Models

Seven-passenger Touring Car Four-passenger Roadster
Four-passenger Phaeton Seven-passenger Convertible Sedan

National, 1919

Pantasote Top Material, 1919

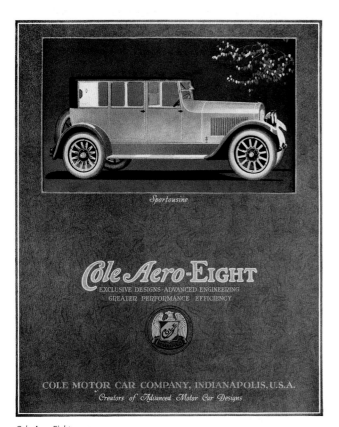

Cole Aero-Eight, 1919

Overland Model 90, 1919

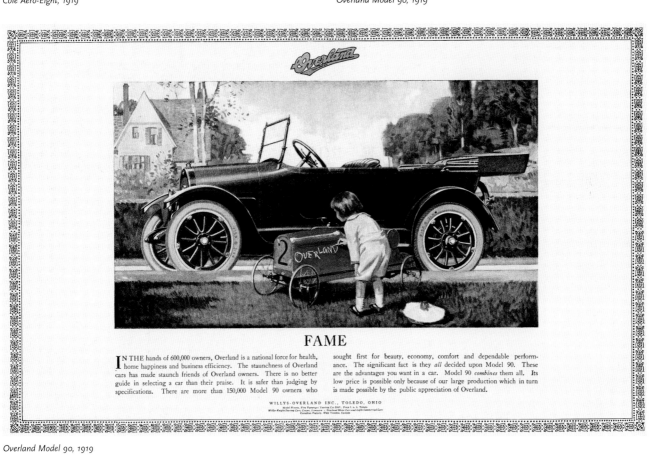

Overland Model 90, 1919

Rauch & Lang Electrics

WHATEVER your ideas today, you are certain to come to the conclusion, sooner or later, that an enclosed automobile, like the Rauch & Lang Electric, combines all the desirable features and eliminates all the well-known annoyances and much of the expense incident to gasoline cars.

Today's Rauch & Lang Electric has more mileage, more speed, maximum economy. An illustrated catalog sent upon request.

The Baker R & L Company, Cleveland

Builders of Custom Coach Bodies of Quality

Baker And Rauch & Lang Electrics, 1919

–beauty enhanced by **Duplex** *engineering*

SAXON MOTOR CAR CORPORATION
DETROIT, MICHIGAN

IT is less difficult to describe Saxon's Duplex power, comfort and economy than its two fold beauty. Truly this must be *seen* — daring, low-hung grace, clear-etched lines, alert design and harmony of color—further enhanced by the *permanence* of Saxon's charm. Duplex engineering eliminates the usual sheet metal parts which develop annoying squeaks and disfiguring dents. Saxon's gleaming silver fittings and luxurious appointments complete this new ideal of motor car attractiveness.

Saxon, ca. 1915

Irresistible Advantages

The Fours
Seven Passenger Touring
$1395

Four Passenger Coupe, $1650
Seven Passenger Touring-Sedan, $1890
Seven Passenger Limousine, $1990

The Eight
Seven Passenger Touring, $2190

*All prices f. o. b. Toledo
Subject to change without notice*

For sheer beauty the new Willys-Knight Four is captivating.

But even the charm of its beauty quickly yields to the sorcery of its completely satisfying comfort.

The most forty-eight inch cantilever rear springs, seat cushions with every spiral separately encased so that it is air cushioned and checked against rebound, together with long 121 inch wheelbase, make it luxuriously comfortable even over rough roads.

Yet both its beauty and its comfort yield to the wizardry of its sleeve-valve motor.

We think you will consider this four-cylinder motor *even when new*, the equal in power, smoothness and flexibility of almost any six you ever drove.

And it actually and very noticeably *improves* with use because it is constantly *revitalized* by carbon, the very deadly element that devitalizes every other kind of motor.

This means more constant use without repair or adjustment, constant, instead of intermittent, efficiency and much longer life.

Let the Willys-Overland dealer tell you more of the advantages of the Willys-Knight motor.

The Willys-Overland Company, Toledo, Ohio
Manufacturers of Willys-Knight and Overland Motor Cars

Willys-Knight, ca. 1918

CHALMERS
WITH HOT SPOT AND RAMS-HORN

The temptation to over-elaboration has been avoided studiously in the interior and exterior decorative treatment of the Chalmers Limousine Landaulet, resulting in an automobile of dignified beauty, reflecting in every possible way the atmosphere of the homes of people of good taste.

CHALMERS MOTOR CAR COMPANY, DETROIT, MICHIGAN
CHALMERS MOTOR COMPANY OF CANADA, LTD., WINDSOR, ONTARIO

Chalmers, ca. 1916

Brougham
$1585
f.o.b. Toledo

Milburn
LIGHT ELECTRIC

Roadster
$1285
f.o.b. Toledo

THE Milburn is by far the lightest electric and by far the easiest to start and stop, to steer and control in every way.

The most timid drive it without the slightest nervousness.

It is positively the safest car in the world for a woman to drive.

See the Milburn—ride in it—drive it.

Then realize that although its beauty is unsurpassed, its comfort unequalled, its safety unapproached—yet it costs from $500 to $1500 less than other electrics and is the least expensive to operate.

See the Milburn dealer—write for our catalogue.

Address Department 201

THE MILBURN WAGON COMPANY

Established 1848

The Milburn Electric Charger solves the home-charging problem—effectively—inexpensively—if your public garage is inconveniently located or lacking in electric facilities.

TOLEDO, OHIO

Milburn Light Electric, ca. 1916

Milburn
LIGHT ELECTRIC
$1685
f.o.b. Toledo

The Greatest Success of Them All

Two years ago the Milburn Light Electric made its bow. And almost instantly it was touched by the fairy wand that brings success.

It grew and grew in popularity until today it is preeminent among electrics—and remember, the electric is more popular than ever before.

The car has always possessed undeniable beauty, finish, charm. This season these features are even more pronounced.

And there are other substantial reasons for Milburn success.

It is the lightest electric built, and by far the easiest to control.

It is speedy, too, with unusually long mileage per charge.

The operating cost is less than any other car—gasoline or electric.

And last, but not least, there is the Milburn price—a price made possible only by our large production and advanced manufacturing facilities.

The nearest Milburn dealer will gladly demonstrate the car for you.

Or, if he is unknown to you, write to us. We will send you his name and address, as well as the new Milburn catalogue.

Established 1848 **THE MILBURN WAGON COMPANY** *Toledo, Ohio*
Automobile Division
The Milburn Charger solves the home charging problem—inexpensively—efficiently

Milburn Light Electric, ca. 1917

CHALMERS

Chalmers, ca. 1917

▶ *Pierce-Arrow, ca. 1916*

The Pierce Arrow

And the winner is...

Money Talks

The Lozier, a luxury car that would quickly disappear from the marketplace, pitched its advertising to a time-tested customer: the male car buyer. The man of the household had been responsible for purchasing the family vehicle since the horse-and-buggy days, but this approach would soon evaporate with the emerging influence of liberated females. By the end of World War I, women's purchasing power would be embraced by automobile advertising as eagerly as men's.

Der schöne Schein des Geldes

Die Werbung für den Lozier, einer Luxuslimousine, die schnell wieder vom Markt verschwand, sprach mit seiner Anzeige ausschließlich verlässliche Kunden an: den männlichen Autokäufer. Zu Zeiten der Pferdekutsche war der Herr des Hauses noch für die Beschaffung des Familienvehikels zuständig gewesen, doch diese Rollenverteilung sollte sich mit dem verstärkten Einfluss emanzipierter Frauen bald in blauen Dunst auflösen. Ab dem Ende des Ersten Weltkriegs wurde die weibliche Käuferschicht von der Automobilwerbung genauso eindringlich angesprochen wie die männliche.

Une histoire d'argent

La publicité pour la Lozier, voiture de luxe qui disparaîtra rapidement du marché, s'adressait au consommateur traditionnel : le mâle acheteur de voitures. L'homme de la maison était responsable de l'achat du véhicule familial depuis le temps des voitures à cheval, mais cette approche devait bientôt disparaître sous l'influence de la libération de la femme. A la fin de la Première Guerre mondiale, la publicité visera aussi bien le pouvoir d'achat des femmes que celui des hommes.

Una cuestión de dinero

El Lozier, un automóvil de lujo que no tardaría en desaparecer del mercado, lanzó este anuncio dirigido a un cliente con tradición a sus espaldas: el comprador de coches. El hombre de la casa había sido el responsable de adquirir el vehículo familiar desde los días de las tartanas, pero este papel empezaría a evaporarse con la influencia creciente de las mujeres liberadas. Hacia finales de la Primera Guerra Mundial, el poder adquisitivo de las mujeres entraría en el punto de mira de la publicidad de automóviles con tanta fuerza como el de los hombres.

金は効果を発揮する

すぐに市場から消えた高級車 Lozier は、男性の車購入者をターゲットとして猛烈に売り込まれた。世帯主である男性は馬車の時代から家族の乗り物を買う責任を負っていたが、このアプローチは解放された女性の勢力が現れてくるとすぐに消え失せた。第一次世界大戦の終結までに、女性の購入力は対男性への広告と同じように熱心な自動車の広告に取り囲まれていった。

LOZIER

"The Choice of Men Who Know"

ON touring highways, at the seashore, on the boulevard, in the mountains, at the country club,—wherever you meet people of wealth and refinement, there, in increasing numbers, you find the Lozier.

Big Six. Touring Cars $5,000, Limousines and Landaulets $6,500.

"LIGHT SIX" $3,250 to $4,450.

LOZIER MOTOR COMPANY

2403 Mack Avenue   Detroit, Michigan

Factory Branches in New York, Chicago, Boston
Philadelphia and San Francisco

Lozier, 1913

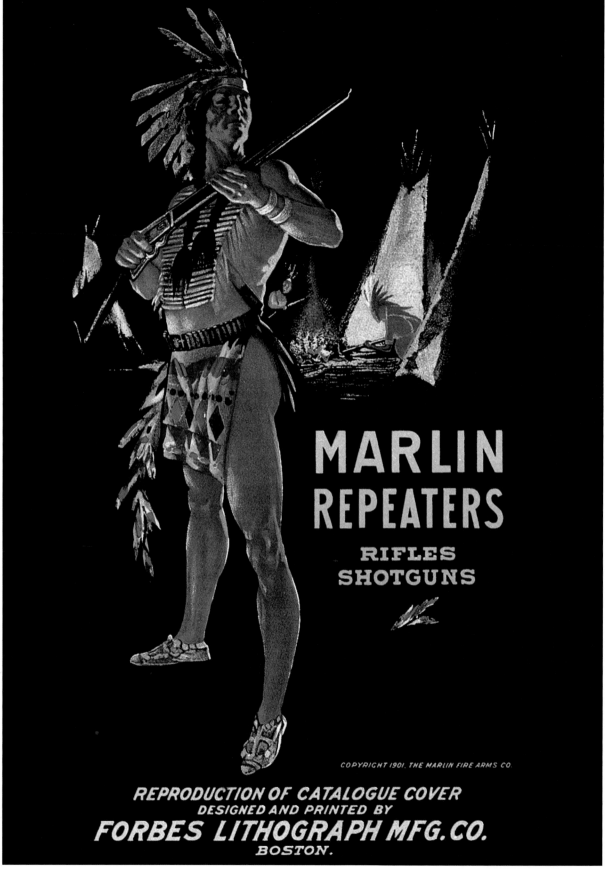

MARLIN
REPEATERS

RIFLES
SHOTGUNS

COPYRIGHT 1901, THE MARLIN FIRE ARMS CO.

REPRODUCTION OF CATALOGUE COVER
DESIGNED AND PRINTED BY
FORBES LITHOGRAPH MFG. CO.
BOSTON.

Randolph & Co., 1915 ◀   *Forbes Lithograph, 1902*

SEND $1.00 FOR A YEARS SUBSCRIPTION FOR

COMMERCIAL ORIGINALITY

FOR THE MAN AT THE HEART OF EVERY BUSINESS

A BUSINESS MAN'S ILLUSTRATED MAGAZINE
CONTAINING PRACTICAL EXAMPLES OF THE BEST AND
LATEST BUSINESS BRINGING ILLUSTRATIONS FOR
CATALOGUES ADVERTISEMENTS ETC.= PUBLISHED MONTHLY
BY THE BINNER ENGRAVING CO. CHICAGO

Binner ENGRAVING CO. 21-25 PLYMOUTH Ct Chicago

W. A. HINNERS
Treas. & Gen. Mgr.

H. C. LAMMERS
V. Pres. & Art. Mgr.

J. L. SHILLING
Secy. & Gen. Supt.

DISTINCTIVE EFFECTIVE DESIGNS PERFECT PRINTING PLATES

O. E. BINNER, Pres. & Res. Mgr. New York Branch

Commercial Originality Magazine, 1902

Butler Paper, 1902

Forbes Lithograph, 1902

THE QUEEN CITY
PRINTING INK CO.

1925 South St., CINCINNATI, O.
345 Dearborn St., CHICAGO.
147 Pearl St., BOSTON.
734 Sansom St., PHILADELPHIA
Saturday Night Bldg., TORONTO.

H·D·
BOOK
INK·

H. D. BLACK, 40.   RED, 2120.   LAVENDER, 2121.

Peninsular Paper, 1903 ◄ *Queen City Inks, 1903*

American Bridge Company, 1903

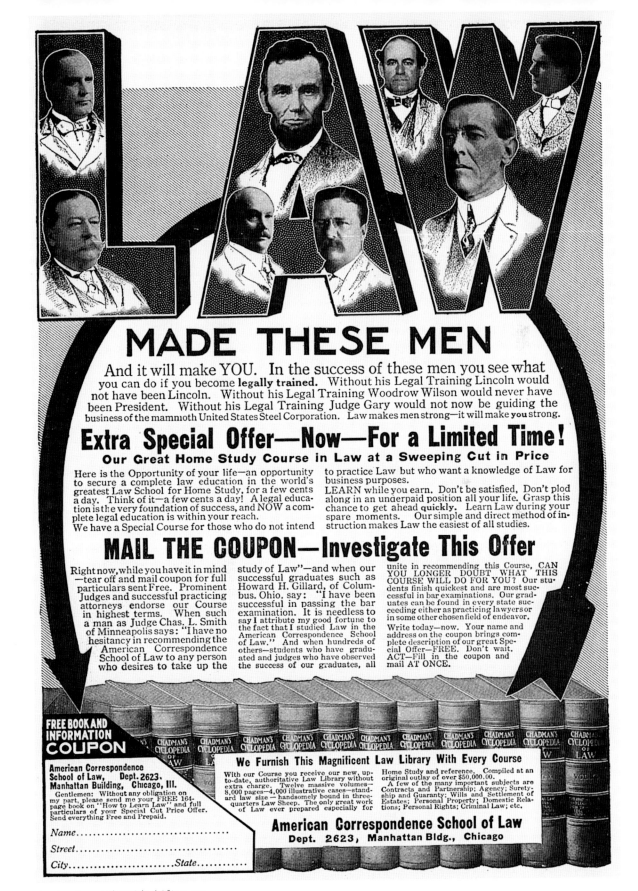

LAW

MADE THESE MEN

And it will make YOU. In the success of these men you see what you can do if you become **legally trained**. Without his Legal Training Lincoln would not have been Lincoln. Without his Legal Training Woodrow Wilson would never have been President. Without his Legal Training Judge Gary would not now be guiding the business of the mammoth United States Steel Corporation. Law makes men strong—it will make **you** strong.

Extra Special Offer—Now—For a Limited Time!
Our Great Home Study Course in Law at a Sweeping Cut in Price

Here is the Opportunity of your life—an opportunity to secure a complete law education in the world's greatest Law School for Home Study, for a few cents a day. Think of it—a few cents a day! A legal education is the very foundation of success, and NOW a complete legal education is within your reach.

We have a Special Course for those who do not intend to practice Law but who want a knowledge of Law for business purposes.

LEARN while you earn. Don't be satisfied, Don't plod along in an underpaid position all your life. Grasp this chance to get ahead **quickly**. Learn Law during your spare moments. Our simple and direct method of instruction makes Law the easiest of all studies.

MAIL THE COUPON—Investigate This Offer

Right now, while you have it in mind—tear off and mail coupon for full particulars sent Free. Prominent Judges and successful practicing attorneys endorse our Course in highest terms. When such a man as Judge Chas. L. Smith of Minneapolis says: "I have no hesitancy in recommending the American Correspondence School of Law to any person who desires to take up the study of Law"—and when our successful graduates such as Howard H. Gillard, of Columbus. Ohio, say: "I have been successful in passing the bar examination. It is needless to say I attribute my good fortune to the fact that I studied Law in the American Correspondence School of Law." And when hundreds of others—students who have graduated and judges who have observed the success of our graduates, all unite in recommending this Course, CAN YOU LONGER DOUBT WHAT THIS COURSE WILL DO FOR YOU? Our students finish quickest and are most successful in bar examinations. Our graduates can be found in every state succeeding either as practicing lawyers or in some other chosen field of endeavor.

Write today—now. Your name and address on the coupon brings complete description of our great Special Offer—FREE. Don't wait. ACT—Fill in the coupon and mail AT ONCE.

American Correspondence School Of Law, 1915

Miles Brothers Moving Pictures, 1906

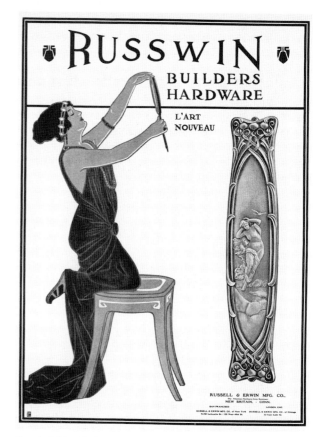

Russwin Builders Hardware, 1914

Equitable Life Assurance Society, 1904

Equitable Life Assurance Society, 1903

Get Rich Growing Ginseng

If you will send us two 2-cent stamps to help pay postage, we will immediately mail you our 55-page book telling all about the enormous, easily-earned profits in this wonderful plant, "Ginseng," its nature, habits, uses, and instances showing the profits growers of it make; we will also send a copy of the current issue of our magazine, "The Ginseng Garden."

Ginseng must be planted in the fall. It requires little ground—a square rod will grow hundreds of plants. Anybody can cultivate it; hardy anywhere in the United States and Canada. Can be grown either in city garden or on farm. Ginseng root brings from $6 to $10 per pound in the American market. Seeds and young plants bring splendid profits from American growers.

We sell stratified seeds and cultivated plants. Our copyrighted directions, fully covering every point of cultivation, sent free with each order. We guarantee safe delivery and prepay express.

The entire Chinese nation, with its population of 400,000,000, uses Ginseng for its medicinal properties.

U. S. Consul Johnson, writing from Amoy, China, says: "It is used as an invigorating tea by all the wealthy Chinese and as a medicine by the native physicians. It enters largely into the list of presents sent by the wealthy to friends and the articles exchanged between high officials. It is bought by the middle classes throughout the entire empire and even the poor peasants give up their hard earned silver for this national panacea. I do not exaggerate when I state it is possible to market annually in China $20,000,000 worth of these roots." For ten years the annual exportation from the United States has been limited to from $600,000 to $1,000,000 worth.

For 175 years wild Ginseng has been dug by "Sang Diggers" in certain mountainous districts of the United States. By them it was sold at good prices to exporters who in turn sent it to China.

Within the last few years, just when the wild supply was almost exhausted and China was demanding more than ever, it was discovered that Ginseng was hardy and could be cultivated with success in practically every part of the United States and Canada. At present prices an acre of four year old plants is worth $40,000, which statement is proved in details given in our printed matter that we will send you.

You can start a Ginseng bed for from $5 up and can realize on your investment annually, beginning with the first year, if you sell the seeds and young plants to other growers. If you enlarge your own garden with them you will harvest fully developed roots at the end of four years that weigh from two ounces to eight ounces each and are worth $6 to $10 per pound. The entire cost of growing them is about 25 cents per pound.

Ginseng is a very certain crop, and no other business pays such enormous returns on money and time invested. It is an absolute staple, like cotton, wheat, and iron, and, like them, is regularly quoted in the world's markets. It is not perishable and may be held in store for an indefinite time. The land needed for its cultivation is so very little that even a restricted city lot will hold a bed yielding hundreds of dollars annually.

All plants and seeds purchased of us will be delivered to any address free of charge. Every order is personally inspected by our botanist. Our copyrighted directions, fully covering every point, are sent free with each order.

Autumn is the time to set out plants and sow the seed, and as our stock for sale is limited and the demand strong it is advisable to place orders at once.

We reserve the right to decline all orders after the stock for sale has been engaged.

Write to-day for our 55-page book telling all about this wonderful Ginseng, and copy of current issue of our magazine, "The Ginseng Garden." Enclose 4c. to help pay postage.

Chinese=American
Department F,

For financial references communicate with First National Bank, Scranton, Pa.

Ginseng Company,
Scranton, Pa.

Chinese-American Ginseng, 1903

We Shall Not Sleep

"In Flanders fields
the poppies blow
Between the Crosses,
row on row,
That mark our place;
and in the sky
The larks still bravely
singing fly,
Scarce heard amidst
the guns below.

We are the dead.
Short days ago we lived,
felt dawn,
saw sunset glow,
Loved and were loved,
and now we lie
In Flanders fields.

Take up our quarrel
with the foe,
To you from falling hands
we throw the Torch-
be yours to hold it high;
If ye break faith
with us who die,
We shall not sleep,
though poppies grow
In Flanders fields."

Courtesy of G.P.Putnam's Sons

In behalf of the brave men who have enlisted in the fight of right against might we reprint the above lines by Col. McCrae.

As an inspiration to war giving and war sacrifice, it strikes a major note. There is no war appeal to which it is not applicable.

This beautiful lyric of the war was written by Lieutenant Colonel Dr. John McCrae of Montreal, Canada, while the second battle of Ypres was in progress.

The author's body now lies buried in Flanders fields.

Is it conceivable that we shall "break faith" with those "who die" for us?

Bauer & Black First Aid Products, 1918

PROBABLY no other area in the world is subjected to foot traffic more severe and concentrated than the great entrance space of the New York Hippodrome. Over the elegant, agreeable, richly-colored, silent surface of

PENNSYLVANIA INTERLOCKING RUBBER TILING

with which the floor is paved, the crowds pour in and out. Here, and in many of the magnificent theatres of the country, where marble or any other material would quickly be reduced to an undesirable state, years of service can only enhance the appearance of this most durable floor covering in existence.

Upon receipt of sketch or description of size, shape and character of any space, full information of its equipment with Pennsylvania Rubber Tiling will be furnished, with estimate of cost.

The Tiling-Book-de-Luxe, containing color plates of designs, with interesting data, will be mailed upon request.

PENNSYLVANIA RUBBER COMPANY

Jeannette, Pa.

New York, ... 1741 Broadway
Chicago, . . 1241 Michigan Avenue
Philadelphia, . 615 North Broad Street
Atlanta, Ga., . 102 North Pryor Street
Boston, . . . 20 Park Square
Buffalo, . . 717 Main Street
Detroit, . 237 Jefferson Avenue
Cleveland
2134-2136 East Ninth Street
San Francisco
512-514 Mission Street

Pennsylvania Rubber Tiling, 1907

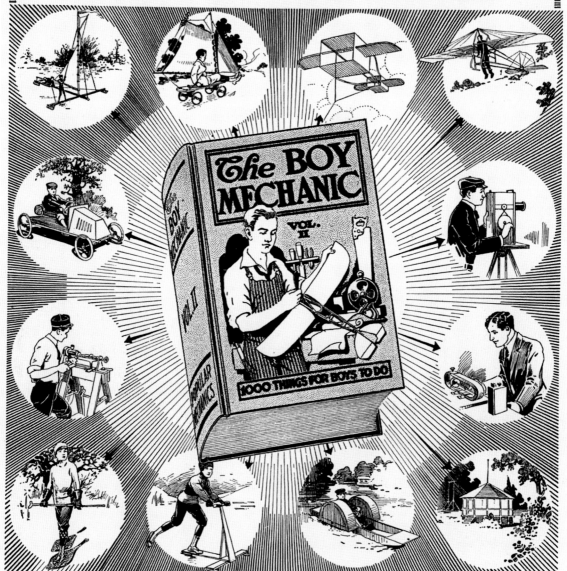

BOYS! BUILD THINGS!

THIS BIG NEW BOOK

Vol. II — THE BOY MECHANIC — Vol. II

Tells All About 1000 Interesting Things To Make and Do

A SEQUEL TO, BUT CONTAINING NOTHING FOUND IN VOLUME I

480 PAGES (6¾x9¾ in.) — **995 ILLS.** — **CLOTH** — **PRICE $1.50**

HOW TO MAKE

Bobsleds — Snowshoes — Ice Boats — Ice Gliders — Boats — Camps — Fishing Tackle — Houses of Poles — Kites — Aerial Gliders — Motion-Picture Camera — Spot-Light Lantern — Mile-O-View Camera — Photographic Appliances — Indoor Games — Tricks — Cyclemobile — Pushmobile — Flymobile — Roller Coaster — Ferris Wheel — Sunlight Flasher — Reed Furniture — Electrical Devices — Mechanical Contrivances — Art-Craft Work and hundreds of equally interesting things.

SENT POSTPAID UPON RECEIPT OF PRICE BY PUBLISHERS

POPULAR MECHANICS BOOK DEPT., 78 EAST MADISON ST., **CHICAGO**

The Boy Mechanic, 1916

Arctic City, 1919

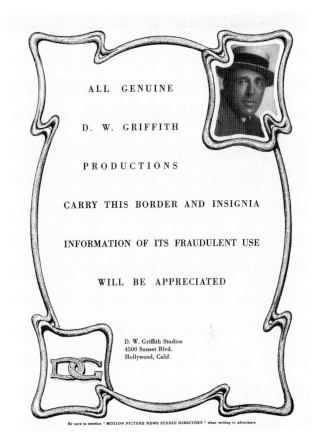

D. W. Griffith Studios, 1919

Selznick Pictures, 1919

Pathé Cinematograph, 1906

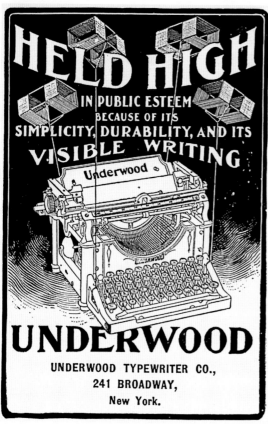

Underwood Typewriters, 1904

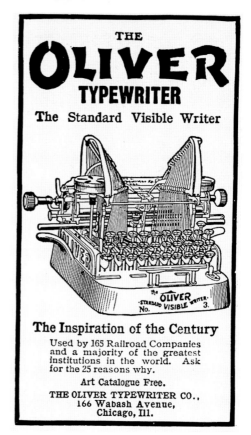

Oliver Typewriters, 1903

GROCERS' FURNISHINGS

Grocers' Tea Canisters

The Queen Tea and Coffee Canisters and Queen Spice Cabinet

Are our newest and latest productions. Nothing handsomer made. Mirror fronts, a dozen different sizes, well made and prices low. Our latest catalogue shows all the attractions in Grocers' Caddies, Floor Cans for Coffee, and a full variety of hand-made Tea and Coffee Scoops, in brass and tin.

THE NEW YORK
Roll-Door Refrigerator

The latest and most perfect. It has every improvement. The Roll Door makes a very attractive appearance. Each door separated with nickel-plated bands. Marble slab across the front. Made of kiln-dried ash, and lined with spruce. Ice chamber lined with galvanized iron. Perfect ventilation. Positively the BEST REFRIGERATOR made.

SEND TO US FOR CATALOGUE

Importers of Chinese Scenery Paper for Tea Stores. General Agents for Coles' Coffee Mills, Fairbank's Scales and Troemner's Fine Balances, and the Star Mills. Send for our Illustrated Price-List. We carry everything in the line of Fittings for Grocers and Tea Dealers.

MORGAN & CORNELL

FACTORY AND SALESROOM,   **213 and 215 DUANE STREET, NEW YORK.**

IN WRITING TO ADVERTISERS KINDLY MENTION "GROCERY WORLD."

Morgan & Cornell Grocers' Furnishings, 1901

Cottrell Printing Press, 1903

The whole world of figures in only 10 keys —one for each numeral. Column selection is eliminated— machine puts each figure into proper column automatically.

Speeding up the handling of figure work for Simmons

The millions of figure items handled by the Simmons Hardware Company of St. Louis are a reflection of the size of its business. Thousands of sales are made daily, thousands of items must be listed and billed, thousands of credits must be checked. Five of the thirteen Daltons used in Bookkeeping, Statistical, Sales and Factory departments are illustrated above.

The use of Daltons by different departments of a business emphasizes its broader application to figure work. Where great amounts of straight adding and listing are necessary, Dalton operators work by *touch method* entirely, handling the figure items without ever looking at the keys, increasing by 40% the volume of daily work.

R. M. Tenant, Chief Accountant for the Franklin Automobile Company, says:

"The Dalton with its simple 10-key keyboard, can be operated by touch method, enabling operator to keep her eyes right on her work — no time lost turning from work to machine and then back to hunt for the next figure. By using the Dalton we save 25% to 30% of time formerly required by other machines."

In Cost, Purchasing, Statistical, Sales, Billing or any department where a *multiplying* machine is necessary the Dalton handles this type of figure work with an ease and speed that can only be appreciated by a demonstration under time-tests. Such a demonstration will convince any business man that a faster multiplying machine does not exist.

The great simplicity of the Dalton keyboard appeals to both operator and executive. Here is the whole world of figures in only 10 keys. No training required — no confusion in column selection — each figure is placed in its proper column by the machine automatically.

Wherever talk turns to figuring machines today, you hear the Dalton

spoken of as "that wonderfully simple machine which anyone can use immediately." The words "Dalton Adding and Calculating Machine" mean a machine which will handle all branches of your figure work.

Have a Demonstration

The service of the Dalton is that of a simpler, faster figuring machine of broader application to figure work for retailer, wholesaler, manufacturer. There are thousands of Dalton users in every State, hundreds in every city. The Dalton Sales Agent in the hundred and more leading cities will gladly bring a Dalton to your office for demonstration —look for "Dalton" in your phone book.

Descriptive catalog by mail upon request.

THE DALTON ADDING MACHINE CO.
136 Beech Street (Norwood) Cincinnati, O.

Representative for Canada—
The United Typewriter Co., Toronto, and its branches

Dalton ADDING AND CALCULATING MACHINE

Dalton Adding Machines, 1918

ELECTRICITY
The 20TH Century Servant

ELECTRICITY is the cleanest, quickest, most willing and most easily controlled household servant. It gets busy instantly where the housewife directs—and never tires. And it charges very little for the perfect service which it renders.

The best-known service of electricity in the home is through the telephone—that marvelous instrument of human sensitiveness—which would be impossible were electricity unknown. The telephone is at the forefront of electrical development.

It is a significant fact that the 8,000,000 telephones used on the world's greatest telephone system—the Bell System—are made by the Western Electric Company. These are in daily use throughout America, and are everywhere recognized as perfect instruments.

This excellence of electric construction is reflected in every device bearing the Western Electric name. The Western Electric vacuum cleaner, the Western Electric washing machine, inter-phones, heaters, fans, toasters, coffee percolators, lamps, etc., etc., all are sponsored by the manufacturer who builds the Bell Telephones.

For thirty-five years this company has been identified in a notable way with the development in electrical progress. It is organized on a nationwide basis to maintain an easily available service for users of Western Electric apparatus.

Write our nearest house for literature descriptive of electrical household conveniences. Ask for booklet No. 169-C.

WESTERN ELECTRIC COMPANY
Manufacturers of the 8,000,000 "Bell" Telephones

New York	Atlanta	Chicago	St. Louis	Kansas City	Denver	San Francisco
Buffalo	Richmond	Milwaukee	Indianapolis	Oklahoma City	Omaha	Oakland
Philadelphia	Savannah	Pittsburgh	Minneapolis	Dallas	Salt Lake City	Seattle
Boston	Cincinnati	Cleveland	St. Paul	Houston	Los Angeles	Portland
New Orleans						Detroit

EQUIPMENT FOR EVERY ELECTRICAL NEED

Western Electric

Western Electric, 1914

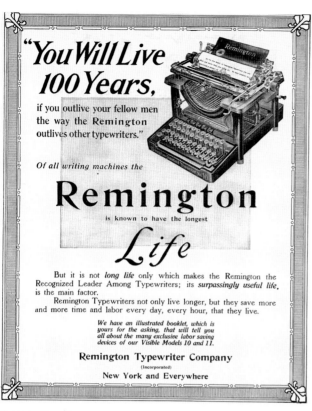

Remington Typewriters, 1913

Remington Typewriters, ca. 1916

Addressograph Duplicating Machine, 1917

Multigraph Duplicating Machine, 1916

▸ *Insurance Agency Listings, 1902*

⚘ "I Forgot"

How much is expressed in these two words—"**I forgot!**"
Thousands of human lives and millions of dollars worth
of property have been sacrificed to a faulty memory!

The **Pelman System of Memory Training**

scientifically trains the Natural Memory. Requires only a few minutes time each day, and is so simple a child can understand it. It is entirely original and of such absorbing interest that the pupil finds the half hour daily study a real pleasure. Our pupils range in age from 15 to 85 years. It is hard to conceive of any man or woman in any profession, business, trade or calling who could not receive permanent benefit of almost inestimable value from a course of training under **The Pelman System.** It will enable any person to remember figures, dates, names, appointments, addresses, speeches, business details, to learn languages, **to avoid mistakes.**

A Test	W. T. Stead	FREE	D. F. Urbahns	D. H. Patterson
One should be able to think of a subject for a half hour or an hour at a time, yet we venture that not one person in a thousand can think of one subject for a single minute by the watch without the mind wandering off to other subjects. Try it yourself. This mind wandering can be cured as surely as sunrise and taxes by THE PELMAN SYSTEM. Taught in six languages: English, German, French, Italian, Dutch, Russian.	Editor of the London Review of Reviews, addressed the following letter under date of March 29, 1902: "The improvement that can be effected in the memory by taking pains is so immense and so little realized that I consider Mr. Pelman one of the benefactors of the human race." I am yours truly, W. T. STEAD.	Mr. Pelman has published two books. "Memory Training; Its Laws and Their Application to Practical Life" and 'The Natural Way to Learn a Language' We will send both books ABSOLUTELY FREE, by mail, postpaid. Write at once. A thing done NOW will not require remembering. You will find these books interesting whether you wish to take instructions or not.	of Fort Wayne, Ind., himself an instructor in memory training, has the following to say in a letter dated July 3, 1903. "I am familiar with every known system of memory training, and will say The Pelman System is superior to any I have ever come in contact with. Not another school, to my knowledge, which teaches by correspondence, can secure the good results which you do." Sincerely-yours, D. F. URBAHNS.	Manager of the Patterson Mineral Spring, Saratoga Springs, N. Y. writes us as follows: "I am simply amazed at the ease with which I absorbed the principles of the system, and at the immediate improvement in my memory. I devoted only about a half hour each evening to the lessons and I have had no trouble in mastering the course in the four weeks. I shall be pleased to answer all inquiries in regard to your system.

Don't forget that Mr. Pelman's books are SENT FREE.

THE PELMAN SCHOOL OF MEMORY TRAINING,

1649 Masonic Temple, CHICAGO.

LONDON, 4 Bloomsbury St. W. C.; PARIS, Ave de Neuilly 109; MUNICH, Mozartstr, 9; MELBOURNE, G. P. O. Box 402; DURBAN, Natal, Lynn Bldg.

Pelman School Of Memory Training, 1903

Quicksands of Business

How to Avoid Them

They swallow thousands of young people who have no special training for important positions. The **I. C. S.** holds out the opportunity that saves you. Thousands have been benefited in salary and position by our method of special training *by mail*. We help you to select an occupation *and succeed in it*. We prepare you to advance in your present work, or we aid you in changing to more profitable work for which we qualify you.

There is no such thing as failure if you will follow our direction.

The cost is small.

Courses, $10 up.

No books to buy.

Terms are easy. Requirements simple.

If you want to do better send for our 48-page book, "1001 Stories of Success," mailed **free** to all who cut out, fill in and mail **This Coupon** 👉

International Correspondence Schools, 1903

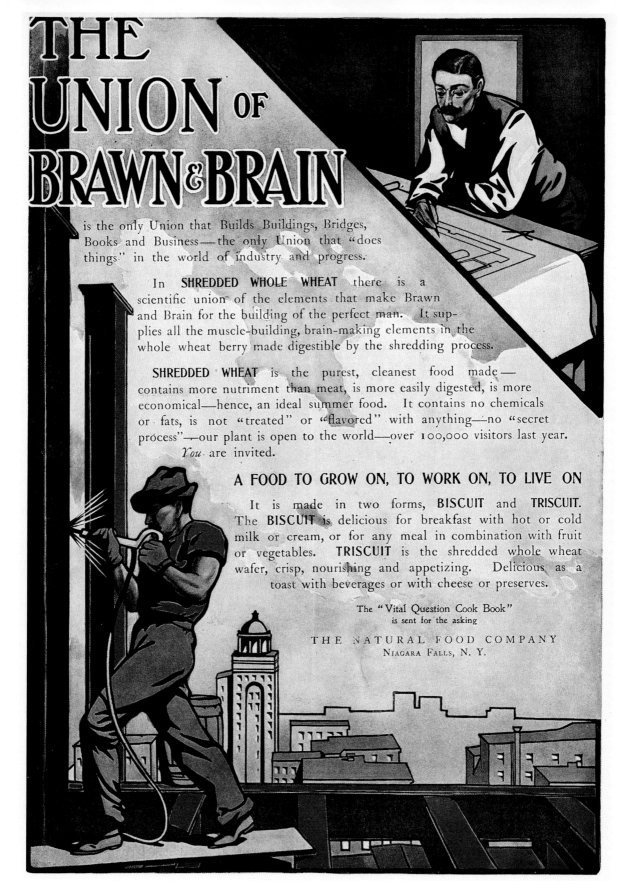

THE UNION OF BRAWN & BRAIN

is the only Union that Builds Buildings, Bridges, Books and Business——the only Union that "does things" in the world of industry and progress.

In **SHREDDED WHOLE WHEAT** there is a scientific union of the elements that make Brawn and Brain for the building of the perfect man. It supplies all the muscle-building, brain-making elements in the whole wheat berry made digestible by the shredding process.

SHREDDED WHEAT is the purest, cleanest food made—— contains more nutriment than meat, is more easily digested, is more economical—hence, an ideal summer food. It contains no chemicals or fats, is not "treated" or "flavored" with anything—no "secret process"—our plant is open to the world—over 100,000 visitors last year. *You* are invited.

A FOOD TO GROW ON, TO WORK ON, TO LIVE ON

It is made in two forms, **BISCUIT** and **TRISCUIT**. The **BISCUIT** is delicious for breakfast with hot or cold milk or cream, or for any meal in combination with fruit or vegetables. **TRISCUIT** is the shredded whole wheat wafer, crisp, nourishing and appetizing. Delicious as a toast with beverages or with cheese or preserves.

The "Vital Question Cook Book"
is sent for the asking

THE NATURAL FOOD COMPANY
NIAGARA FALLS, N. Y.

Natural Food Products, 1906

Citizens National Bank

MARKETS

GEOGRAPHICAL LOCATION makes Los Angeles the logical and practical distributing center for an enormous market. The great Orient, and all the countries bordering on the Pacific, pay millions of dollars annually to United States manufacturers for their exportations. Los Angeles is the natural and economical point from which these manufactured article can be supplied. This market is growing rapidly, and offers a most important field to the American manufacturer.

LOS ANGELES

Citizens National Bank, 1916

And the winner is...

Designing Women

Though women in the first few decades of the century were still expected to partake in traditional female roles, professional opportunities slowly emerged with the advent of World War I, including the burgeoning field of illustration. While this represented an unprecedented advancement for the "fairer sex," it would take the next world war for women to begin to fill historically male jobs. Until then, the gentler field of artistic pursuits would have to suffice.

Frauengestaltung

Auch wenn in den ersten Jahrzehnten des neuen Jahrhunderts erwartet wurde, dass Frauen ihre traditionell weibliche Rolle erfüllten, boten sich ihnen durch den heraufziehenden Ersten Weltkrieg allmählich auch berufliche Möglichkeiten, so zum Beispiel im gerade entstehenden Bereich der Illustration. Dies stellte zwar einen ungeahnten Fortschritt für das „schwache Geschlecht" dar, aber es sollte noch bis zum nächsten Weltkrieg dauern, bis Frauen endlich auch klassische Männerberufe ergriffen. Bis dahin mussten sie sich mit der damenhaften Betätigung im künstlerischen Bereich begnügen.

Les femmes au travail

Si, dans les premières décennies du siècle, les femmes étaient toujours supposées se cantonner dans des rôles traditionnellement féminins, les possibilités d'exercer un métier se multiplièrent avec la Première Guerre mondiale, notamment dans un nouveau domaine : l'illustration. Bien que cela ait représenté un progrès sans précédent pour le sexe dit « faible », il faudra attendre une autre guerre mondiale pour que les femmes occupent des postes historiquement réservés aux hommes. En attendant, elles devaient se contenter d'activités plus « féminines » dans le domaine artistique.

Diseñando a la mujer

Aunque en las primeras décadas del siglo las mujeres seguían desempeñando los papeles femeninos tradicionales, con el advenimiento de la Primera Guerra Mundial empezaron a surgir nuevas oportunidades profesionales para ellas, incluso en el floreciente ámbito de la ilustración. Si bien aquello representó un avance sin precedentes para el «sexo débil», habría que aguardar hasta el estallido de la siguiente guerra mundial para que las mujeres empezaran a ocupar puestos de trabajo históricamente reservados a los hombres. Hasta entonces deberían conformarse con alcanzar pequeños logros artísticos.

デザインする女性達

この世紀の始めの数十年間にはまだ女性達は伝統的な女性の役割を果たすよう期待されていたが、第一次世界大戦の勃発に伴い、急速に発展したイラストレーションの分野を含む専門的な職業に従事する機会がだんだんと現れてきた。こうした "女性" の先例の無い前進もある中で、女性達が歴史的には男性のものであった仕事にまで従事し始めるのは次の世界大戦までかかった。それまでは、芸術のよりおとなしい分野に就くことで満足しなくてはならなかった。

BIG INCOMES for WOMEN!

ARE you an ambitious girl or young woman—eager to make your work count for the very most in these strenuous times? *If you like to draw,* become a Commercial Illustrator. Women with properly trained and developed ability

Earn $25, $50, $75 a Week and *More*

Enter this interesting, well-paid profession, where a woman is not handicapped, but *earns as much as a man with equal ability;* where thousands of advertisers, periodicals, publishers and others buy millions of dollars' worth of designs and illustrations every year. After the War the demand for *well-trained* artists will be intensified. *Be ready!*

Women are naturally fitted for the work. Neysa McMein, Rose O'Neill, Jessie Willcox Smith and numerous others earn incomes that would look good to many a successful business man. You, too, should succeed, *with the proper training. The Federal Course is a proven result-getter*—fascinating, easy to learn and apply.

Develop Your Ability Through Federal Training

Our Advisory Council gives you the benefit of the successful experience of nationally known artists—such men as *Charles E. Chambers,* Magazine and Story Illustrator; *Franklin Booth,* "Painter with the Pen"; *Harold Gross,* Designer for the Gorham Co.; *D. J. Lavin,* Mgr. Chicago Tribune Art Dept.; *Edw. V. Brewer,* of "Cream of Wheat" fame; and others. *Each has contributed an exclusive original lesson to the Federal Course.*

Send To-day for "Your Future"

Be sure to get this 56-page book, beautifully illustrated in colors, and showing remarkable work by Federal Students. It fully describes the Federal Method of home-study, and tells of successes achieved by women, which will open your eyes to opportunities in this field. It will gladly be mailed to you—just send 6 cents in stamps for postage.

FEDERAL SCHOOL OF COMMERCIAL DESIGNING
4703 Warner Building   Minneapolis, Minn.

Those desiring well-trained commercial artists should write us, stating character of work

Federal School Of Commercial Designing, 1918

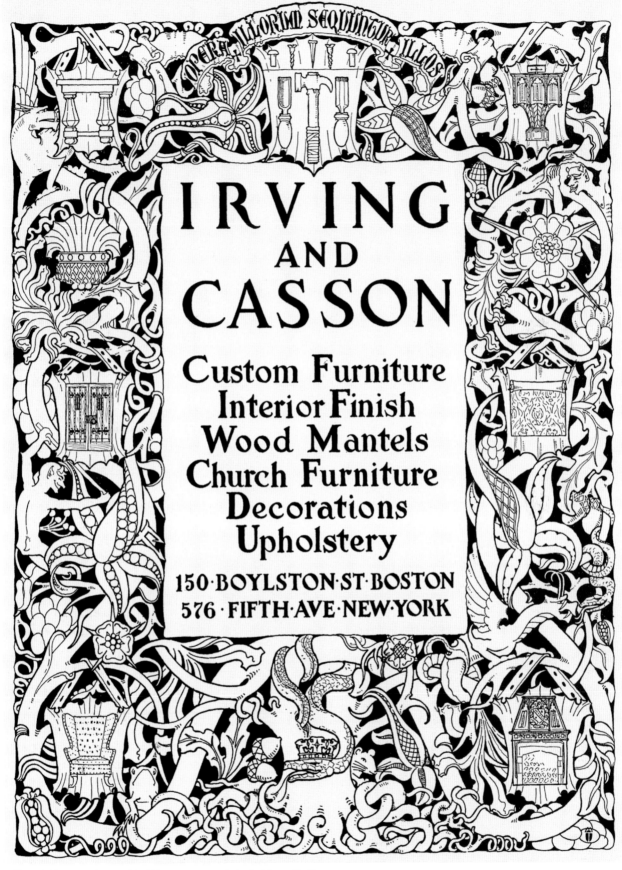

IRVING
AND
CASSON

**Custom Furniture
Interior Finish
Wood Mantels
Church Furniture
Decorations
Upholstery**

**150·BOYLSTON·ST·BOSTON
576·FIFTH·AVE·NEW·YORK**

Old Dutch Cleanser, 1918 ◀◀ *Handel Lamps, 1919* ◀ *Irving And Casson Furniture, 1914*

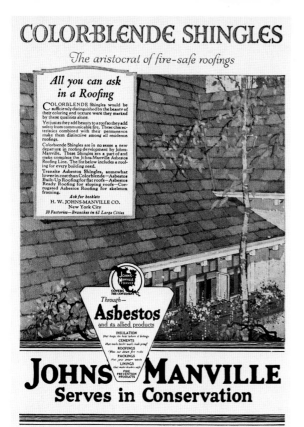

Johns-Manville Shingles, 1919

Bozart Rugs, 1918

Congoleum Rugs, 1919

Blabon Linoleums, 1919

The Whittall rug shown here is an Anglo Persian.   Photograph from Paine's Old English Room, Boston

Whittall Rugs, ca. 1913

▸ *Aladdin Homes, 1917*

ALADDIN

"THE SUNSHINE"

Aladdin Homes, 1919

Gordon-Van Tine Homes, 1918

Vudor Shades, 1919

Restgood Mattresses, 1918

Comfort Swing Chair, 1900

There's a Sherwin-Williams Product for every Surface in your Home

Madam, the Sherwin-Williams Company has been studying the home painting problem for 50 years. Out of this study has come a line of finishes that will beautify and protect every surface in and around your home for the longest possible time and in the best possible way. You do not need to remember the names of these finishes. Just remember the name "Sherwin-Williams" and the surface you wish to protect and beautify. There is a Sherwin-Williams dealer in your town.

Write for Free Book, "The A B C of Home Painting"
Written by a practical painter but without a technical word in it Tells exactly how to paint every surface in and around your home

A Portfolio of Decorative Suggestions
showing artistic color treatment for rooms and exteriors, and giving complete specifications. Our Decorative Department will prepare special suggestions without charge.

BRIGHTEN-UP AMERICA
WITH
SHERWIN WILLIAMS
PAINTS & VARNISHES

Address all inquiries to 617 Canal Road, N. W., Cleveland, Ohio
Showrooms—New York, 116 West 32d Street; Chicago, People's Gas Building; San Francisco, 523 Market Street.
Sales Offices and Warehouses in principal cities. Best dealers everywhere

Sherwin-Williams Paints, 1917

Alabastine Paints, 1917

Scranton Lace, 1917

Chase Mohair Velvets, 1917

Edison Mazda Lamp Works, 1918

Scranton Lace, 1919

▸ *Scranton Lace, 1919*

Nashua Woolnap Blankets, 1919

Nashua Woolnap Blankets, 1919

Nashua Woolnap Blankets, 1919

Nashua Woolnap Blankets, 1919

Nashua Woolnap Blankets, 1918

Nashua Woolnap Blankets, 1918

Nashua Woolnap Blankets, 1919

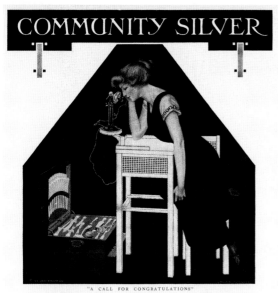

"A CALL FOR CONGRATULATIONS"

OMMUNITY SILVER responds to the Call of Practical Utility as well as to that of Beauty. It is built by overlaying pure silver upon a "backbone" of stiffer metal. This silver is then so especially thickened at the wearing points, and toughened to resist wear, that in a long lifetime you will never see or touch anything but pure silver.

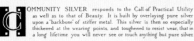

PLATE DE LUXE.   AT YOUR SERVICE FOR 50 YEARS.   SIX TEASPOONS, $2.15 (Engraving extra).   In Canada, $2.75.

Community Silver, 1913

Community Plate Silverware, 1917

Community Plate Silverware, 1917

Community Plate Silverware, 1918

R. Wallace & Sons Silverware, 1916

COFFEE APPROACHES PERFECTION WHEN MADE IN THE SILEX

This is the all-glass coffee-making device that originated on the Continent. Used by the Hotel Vanderbilt and other leading hotels and restaurants

Sold at $4.00 to $9.50 with alcohol lamp—$15.00 to $41.00 with electric heater—by Department Stores, Central Station Stores, Jewelers, Hardware, Drug, Grocery and China and Glass Stores. Three finishes—nickel, copper and sterling. If you do not know a Silex dealer—write us.

THE SILEX COMPANY, 45 High Street, Boston, U.S.A.

Silex Coffee Filters, 1917

Silex Coffee Filters, 1918

The beauty and charm of the right china

The beauty and charm of your dining room can be completely marred by the "wrong" china! It goes without saying that the china must harmonize.

The simple good taste that banished the plush album and wax flowers from the living room has influenced the dining room even more. The brittle, transient, egg-shell china has given place to the permanent "smartness" and luxurious grace of Syracuse China.

Syracuse China is too carefully made to nick or crack easily. It stands the wear and tear of constant handling and you never grow tired of it.

Start with as little as you like. You can always match this made in America china! Syracuse China offers a wealth of lovely designs from which to choose, and all are sensibly priced. The china illustrated is our "Roslyn" pattern, one of the many you will love.

ONONDAGA POTTERY COMPANY, SYRACUSE, N. Y.

SYRACUSE CHINA

Syracuse China, 1919

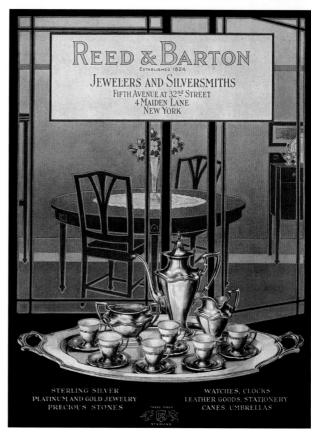

Reed & Barton Jewelers And Silversmiths, 1919

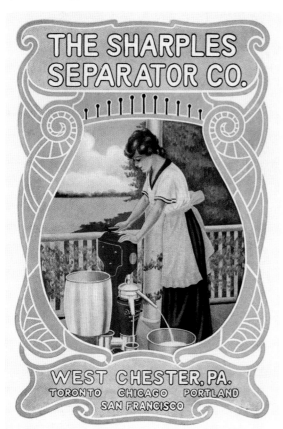

Sharples Separator, 1917

WDC TRIANGLE
THE GENUINE BAKELITE

W D C Triangle Pipes are as good as they are beautiful. They combine the W D C standard of goodness in the bowl, and the lasting beauty of a Triangle Bakelite bit.

There is no substance known to science more suitable for pipe stems, cigar and cigarette holders than Triangle Bakelite. It possesses all the advantages of natural amber but none of the failings.

It has the beautiful coloring of amber—brilliant, rich and translucent—but excels in that it is tougher and more durable than

amber. It has neither taste nor odor and is non-inflammable.

The bowls of the W D C Triangle Pipes are genuine French briar, specially Demuth seasoned and guaranteed against cracking or burning through.

Men who want something distinctive in a pipe will find a variety of select shapes in WDC Triangle Pipes, at the better grade shops, at $1.00 and up. Also a wide selection of cigar holders at 50c and up, and cigarette holders at 35c and up, in many beautiful shapes.

WM. DEMUTH & CO., NEW YORK
WORLD'S LARGEST MAKERS OF FINE PIPES

W. D. C. Triangle Pipes, 1919

American Radiators, 1911

American Radiators, 1916

American Radiators, 1914

American Radiators, 1917

General Electric, 1919

Hotpoint Vacuum Cleaner, 1916

Hotpoint Iron, 1919

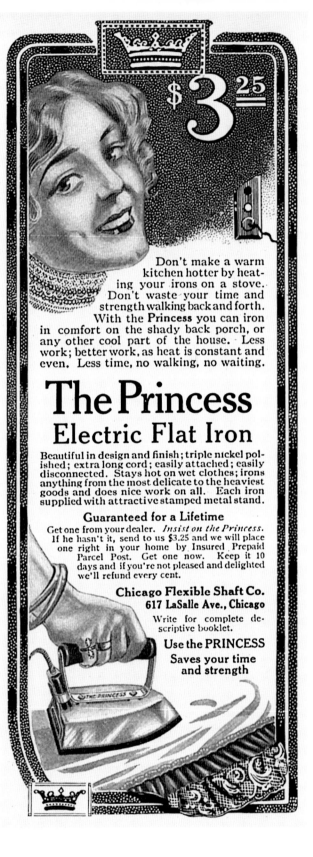

Princess Electric Iron, 1913

New Perfection Stoves, 1919

New Perfection Stove, 1909

Conservo, 1918

Red Cross Stoves & Ranges, 1900

Hartman Furniture, 1919

"We lift the handkerchief, turn the faucet— and presto! the hot water flows"

THIS was formerly possible only in a rich man's house. It is now possible in the home of **every man of average means.**

Hot water instantaneously— fresh hot water as good to drink as it is to bathe in—piping hot— instantly at all hours—in unlimited quantity— **and not a fire in the house.**

Where does it come from?

No coal fires. Nothing to turn on and nothing to turn off **but the faucet.** No light to strike. Nothing to watch.

It is mystifying to the person who is not positively up to date—up to the very minute—in the swift progress of modern household conveniences.

Yet, simple as the twist of the wrist!

It is done by the unobtrusive, unobserved Ruud Automatic Gas Water Heater, tucked away in a corner of the cellar—no dirt, no noise, no odor—requiring absolutely no attention either from yourself or your servant.

The moment **before** you turn on the faucet the water is cold.

The moment you turn on any hot water faucet in the house the water pressure in the pipe is relieved. That automatically opens a valve which turns on and lights the gas in the Ruud heater in the cellar.

In a jiffy the steaming hot water is flowing. The action is positive—unfailing.

It heats the water instantly and keeps heating it as long **and only as long** as the faucet is open, whether you fill a shaving mug or a bath tub.

You turn off the faucet. The water pressure in the pipe is restored. This automatically closes the valve, down in the cellar, which shuts off the gas.

Not a moment's waste. Hot water the moment you want it—never a moment in any season that you can't get it.

That is the simple story of Ruud hot water luxury. Easily connected in any home. The man who builds or improves to-day **without** putting this heater in is overlooking one of the conveniences most treasured in the larger cities and their comfortable suburbs.

The leading gas companies carry the Ruud heater. Write for illustrated booklet giving full description.

Fresh Hot Water vs. Stagnant Hot Water

Water that is heated and kept hot all day or all night undergoes deterioration.

It stagnates—grows stale—much faster than cold water. Unless it is kept at the boiling point it becomes one of the best culture mediums for germs and bacteria.

Animalculæ thrive in warm, or tepid, or hot water, until it reaches the boiling point—which only by accident it does in the ordinary water-tank or hot water reservoir.

It is like a pond in the summer time.

This is what makes the ordinary kitchen water-tank or hot water reservoir undesirable from the viewpoint of sanitation and healthfulness.

It is one of the most unsanitary things about a household.

The water-tank is never quite emptied and the remaining old water communicates its impurities to the new water flowing in—and all of the contents are polluted again.

The feature alone should make a man who likes domestic sanitation and cleanliness investigate this system of instantaneous water heating that is being used in the best homes of America and Europe—from the cottage and the country chateau to the great estate houses.

RUUD MANUFACTURING COMPANY, Dept. A, Pittsburgh, Pa.

Ruud Water Heaters, 1914

BEST INVESTMENT ON EARTH!!

SIMPLE   STRONG

SINGER SEWING MACHINES

THE SINGER MANFG. CO. TRADE MARK

SILENT   SPEEDY

They earn more money, in proportion to cost, than any other product of human ingenuity.

The SINGER MANUFACTURING CO.

Singer Sewing Machines, 1900

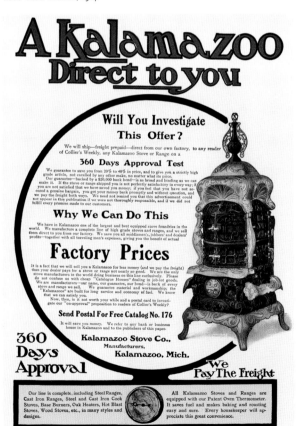

A Kalamazoo Direct to you

Will You Investigate This Offer?

We will ship—freight prepaid—direct from our own factory, to any reader of Collier's Weekly, any Kalamazoo Stove or Range on a

360 Days Approval Test

We guarantee to save you from 20% to 40% in price, and to give you a strictly high grade article, not excelled by any other make, no matter what its price.

Our guarantee—backed by a $20,000 bank bond—is as broad and binding as we can make it. If the stove or range shipped you is not perfectly satisfactory in every way; if you are not satisfied that we have saved you money; if you feel that you have not secured a genuine bargain, you get your money back promptly and without question, and we pay the freight both ways. We need not remind you that this advertisement could not appear in this publication if we were not thoroughly responsible, and if we did not fulfill every promise made to our customers.

Why We Can Do This

We have in Kalamazoo one of the largest and best equipped stove foundries in the world. We manufacture a complete line of high grade stoves and ranges, and we sell them direct to you from our factory. We save you all middlemen's, jobbers' and dealers' profits—together with all traveling men's expenses, giving you the benefit of actual

Factory Prices

It is a fact that we will sell you a Kalamazoo for less money (and we pay the freight) than your dealer pays for a stove or range not nearly so good. We are the only stove manufacturers in the world doing business on this line exclusively. Please do not confuse us with cheap "Catalogue Houses" dealing in job-lot goods. We are manufacturers—our name, our guarantee, our brand—is back of every stove and range we sell. We guarantee material and workmanship; the "Kalamazoos" are built for long service and economy of fuel. We know that we can satisfy you.

Now, then, is it not worth your while and a postal card to investigate our "on-approval" proposition to readers of Collier's Weekly?

Send Postal For Free Catalog No. 176

It will save you money. We refer to any bank or business house in Kalamazoo and to the publishers of this paper.

Kalamazoo Stove Co., Manufacturers, Kalamazoo, Mich.

360 Days Approval

We Pay The Freight

Our line is complete, including Steel Ranges, Cast Iron Ranges, Steel and Cast Iron Stoves, Base Burners, Oak Heaters, Hot Blast Stoves, Wood Stoves, etc., in many styles and designs.

All Kalamazoo Stoves and Ranges are equipped with our Patent Oven Thermometer. It saves fuel and makes baking and roasting easy and sure. Every housekeeper will appreciate this great convenience.

Kalamazoo Stoves, 1904

"Is dish-washing hard? —not in our house!"

WHEN closed, you use the Western Electric Dish-washing Machine as a kitchen table. Into it, when open, you put your finest china, glassware and silver— all safely arranged in wire racks.

Put in hot water with soap or cleansing powder, turn on the electricity, and in a few minutes the dishes will be thoroughly clean. Repeat the operation with scalding hot water and the dishes will quickly dry themselves.

This practical dish-washer will last many years—every day proving that electricity makes easy even the hardest and most disagreeable of household tasks. Five cents worth of electricity will wash the average family's dishes for a week. It is wonderful—that's why you will want to see it demonstrated.

The world's largest distributor of electrical household helps guarantees this practical labor saver. Be sure to see it demonstrated.

Western Electric Dish-Washing Machine

Write for Booklet No. 33CA and we will tell you where you can see this dish-washer demonstrated.

WESTERN ELECTRIC COMPANY, Inc.
New York   Chicago
Kansas City   San Francisco
Other Distributing Houses in Principal Cities

WESTERN ELECTRIC CO., Inc.
Gentlemen: Please send me Booklet No. 33 CA, describing the new Western Electric Dish-washing Machine.

NAME

ADDRESS

Western Electric Dish-Washing Machines, 1919

257

No More Clothes Lines

The Perfection Clothes Drier is held to wall by one bracket, secured by one screw. Has 35 feet of hanging space. Dries clothes in less than half the usual time—you lower the arm, put on the clothes, draw them to the ceiling, out of the way and where all the heat of the room is, by just pulling a cord—always ready; never in the way; a blessing to housekeepers. Sent to any address by express on receipt of $2.50.

Just loose the cord, lower arms to level of your hands, hang on the clothes, pull the cord and they go to the ceiling, out of your way. A postal will bring full information.

Home Elevating Clothes Drier Co.

2029 FIRST AVENUE,   SEATTLE, WASH.

Perfection Clothes Driers, 1906

Eden Clothes Washers, 1919

for Christmas!

BlueBird Superiorities:
Handsome white enamel, cabinet; table top; all mechanism protected.
Heavy copper, extra large tub, can't discolor clothes. Inside perfectly smooth, nothing to tear or wear things.
Washes by rock-a-bye action, quickest, most thorough way.
Built for a life-time of service; extra strong, rigid frame, simple, dependable mechanism.
Large power-driven wringer, swings to any position, adjusts for light or heavy things.
Highest grade guaranteed motor—powerful, dependable.

What a perfectly glorious gift. BlueBird! —solving *forever* the greatest problem, the greatest burden of homework.

An hour or so of a morning and the week's washing vanishes. On the line by nine, without rubbing or puddling— without work, without cost, without wear on the clothes. Every garment *clean*, yet delicately handled. Such is the BlueBird way.

Isn't it *amazing* to realize that now "the washing" is only a source of gladness—a delightful means of unlimited cleanliness.

See BlueBird soon. Arrange with the dealer for a free demonstration. Ask him about the monthly payment plan. Write us for the beautiful BlueBird Book. BlueBird Appliance Company, 2237 Washington Ave., St. Louis, U. S. A.

BlueBird
ELECTRIC CLOTHES WASHER

Blue Bird Electric Clothes Washer, 1919

Save your energy for pleasanter things than washing clothes

YOU can by using P. AND G.—The White Naphtha Soap. *It* will supply the energy which *you* now supply. Its rich, thick suds will loosen the dirt as your hard rubbing now loosens it. Its white, copious lather will keep your clothes so sweet and clean you need not bother with continual boiling.

P. AND G.—The White Naphtha Soap does not merely *help* you wash; it, by itself, actually *washes*. Its work continues where ordinary soaps leave off; it does *your* part too.

P. AND G.—The White Naphtha Soap really washes clothes while they soak. You have for your other work the time you now spend with washboard and boiler. After the clothes are on the line, the best part of the day is before you to sew, read, shop, visit or romp with the children.

A soap that saves so much work in washing naturally is as great an improvement for all kinds of cleaning. Use it every day for everything and you will have more time and energy for the things you like to do.

P. AND G.—The White Naphtha Soap in the Blue Wrapper

A big, long-lasting cake for 5 cents. Complete directions inside the wrapper.

P. And G. Laundry Soap, 1916

Lifebuoy Soap, 1902

Williams' Jersey Cream Soap, 1906

Swift's Pride Soap, 1908

Peet's Crystal White Laundry Soap, 1916

It's Easy to Prolong the Life of the Daintiest Things You Wear

As you see dainty negligees and soft undergarments in the shop windows, do you worry about frequent laundering or, do you, like millions who know, think of *"The Perfect Family Soap"*—

Peet's Crystal White

Insures longer life for the softest and most delicate fabrics, a timely desire of these days of sensible thrift. Unsurpassed for fine laundry work because it is mild; will not roughen or shred. A better soap for every household cleansing task.

PEET BROS. MFG. CO.
KANSAS CITY :: SAN FRANCISCO

Peet's Crystal White Laundry Soap, 1918

Five Reasons Why P. and G.—The White Naphtha Soap makes housecleaning easier

1. It works fast. Being white and of high grade materials it lathers fast and absorbs dirt quickly.

2. It saves energy. The naphtha and other efficient cleansers in it make hard effort unnecessary.

3. It works in cold or lukewarm water. It dissolves dirt so thoroughly that it does not need heat to help it.

4. It works in hard water as in soft. It lathers so freely that it softens hard water and makes suds without delay.

5. It is not harmful. There is nothing in it to injure the hands or the things it cleans.

Use P. and G.—The White Naphtha Soap this year and your housecleaning will be done almost before you know it. This soap combines all the superior features of white soap and naphtha soap. It is the white laundry soap with naphtha in it. A big, solid, long-lasting cake for 5 cents.

P. And G. Laundry Soap, 1917

Kirk's Flake Soap, 1919

Lux Laundry Soap, 1918

Lux Laundry Soap, 1919

Lux Laundry Soap, 1919

Sapolio Soap, ca. 1906   ▸ *Colgate's Soaps And Perfumes, 1916*

COLG

Fine Soaps and

SPLENDOR

COLGATE'S
BABY TALC

MIRAGE CREAM

COLGATE'S MIRAGE CREAM

CHARMIS COLD CREAM

CHARMIS COLD CREAM

SHAVING STICK

COLGATE'S SHAVING STICK

NATURAL ROSE

NATURAL ROSE

NATURAL ROSE

For Her	Florient Perfume	Monad Violet Soap	*For Him*	Shaving Stick or Cream	Mirage Cream
	Charmis Cold Cream	Mirage Cream		Coleo Soap	A box (6 tubes) of
	Cashmere Bouquet Soap	Éclat Face Powder		Lilac Imperial Toilet Water	Ribbon Dental Cream

ATE'S

fumes for Xmas

Colgate's Cashmere Bouquet
Colgate's Cashmere Bouquet
Colgate's Cashmere Bouquet

Cashmere Bouquet Toilet Soap

COLGATE'S
RIBBON DENTAL CREAM

CASHMERE BOUQUET
TOILET WATER

COLGATE'S
SHAVING CREAM

A large tube of Ribbon Dental Cream Week-End Package | Young People's Perfumes Miniature Size Extracts Baby Talc | *Colgate Gifts for Everybody* | Make useful gifts, not gimcracks. The name "Colgate" on Fine Soaps and Perfumes corresponds to "Sterling" on silver

Colgate Violet Bath Water, ca. 1905

WHEREVER you find refined people, you will find DR. LYON'S. It has been identified for over fifty years with those who exercise more than ordinary care in clothes, surroundings and personal appearance.

Fashionable people know the advantages of fine teeth and select their dentifrice to that end.

Dr.Lyon's

The Dentifrice that made fine teeth Fashionable

Powder   Cream

This is the dentifrice of fashionable people. Dentists have used it widely in their practice, praised and recommended it to their patients. It is the most used, the most trusted and the most delightful,—as well as the safest and surest —because it does all that a good dentifrice should do or should pretend to do—*Cleans the teeth*.

One should not trust a drugged dentifrice to overcome unusual or abnormal tooth trouble.

To Cure—get a good dentist; *to Clean*—get DR. LYON'S.

Sample of either Powder or Cream sent on receipt of 6c.

I. W. LYON & SONS, Inc., 520 West 27th Street, New York.

Dr. Lyon's Dentifrice, 1918

THE DELICIOUS

"A miss is
as good as her smile"

COLGATE'S RIBBON DENTAL CREAM

CANNOT ROLL OFF THE BRUSH

COMES OUT A RIBBON LIES FLAT ON THE BRUSH

DELICIOUS ANTISEPTIC ECONOMICAL

COLGATE & CO.   EST. 1806   NEW YORK, U.S.A.

Colgate's Ribbon Dental Cream, 1913

Hinds Cream, 1915

Colgate's Talc, 1901

Colgate's Toiletries, 1906

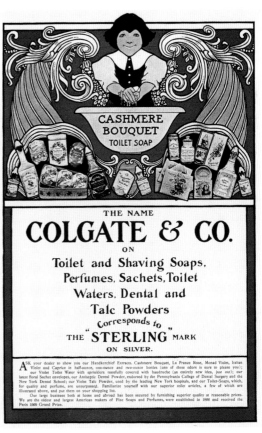

Colgate's Toiletries, 1901

Pro-phy-lac-tic Toothbrushes, 1912

COLGATE'S
CHRISTMAS SUGGESTIONS

Cut Out This Christmas List
to help you with your shopping:

For Him:
Rapid Shave Powder
Shaving Stick
Perfected Shaving Cream
Talc Powder (the "finish" of a perfect shave), either scented or unscented
Lilac Imperial Toilet Water
Ribbon Dental Cream
Pine Tar Soap—for shampoo
Big Bath Soap

For Her:
A Colgate Gift-Box (3 styles: La France Rose, Éclat, Monad Violet)
Florient—Flowers of the Orient—a new Colgate perfume, daintily packaged
Colgate Toilet Waters—of many different perfumes —you may select her favorite
Colgate's Cold Cream—in Jars for the dresser, Tubes for travel
Charmis Face Powder—an exquisitely fine Poudre de Riz
Talc Powder—6 perfumes and Unscented
Sachet Powder
Ribbon Dental Cream
Eclat Soap
Cashmere Bouquet Soap
Natural Violet Soap

And for the Children:
Young Peoples' Perfumes
Miniature Perfumes
Remember to get for their stockings big tubes of Ribbon Dental Cream
Write to Colgate & Co. for a free copy of the merry "Jungle Pow Wow" book for the top of the stocking

COLGATE & CO.
Dept. L, 199 Fulton St., N.Y.

COME IN Full line of Holiday Gifts

A COLGATE CHRISTMAS IS A MERRY ONE

A Delightful Toilet Water
"He" will like this
An Exquisite Perfume
Colgate's Gift Box
Cleanliness Comfort Charm
For the Children
A Dainty Gift

Colgate's Toiletries, 1913

Pro-phy-lac-tic Toothbrushes, 1907

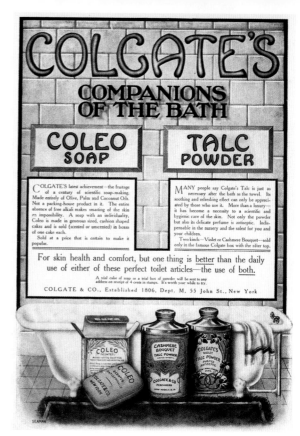

Colgate's Toiletries, 1907

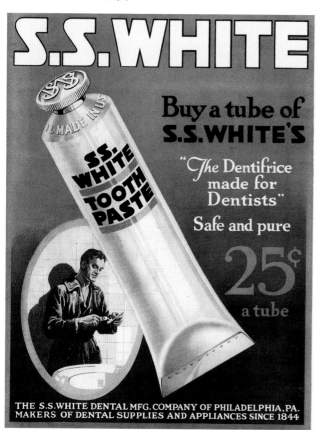

S. S. White Toothpaste, 1919

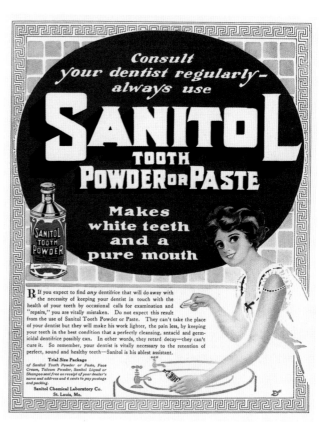

Sanitol Dentifrice, 1912

Colgate's Talc, 1918

Colgate's Ribbon Dental Cream, 1918

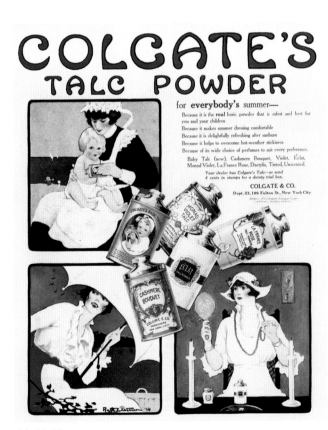

Colgate's Talc, 1914

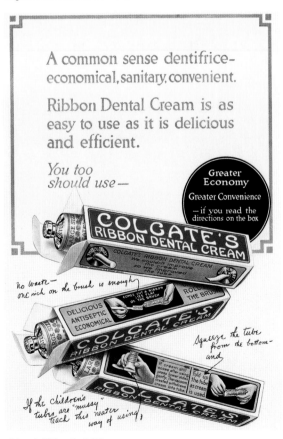

Colgate's Ribbon Dental Cream, 1914

"Another gown ruined by perspiration!"

Don't let perspiration ruin your very nicest clothes when a little precaution would save them.

Two or three applications a week of this exquisite, unscented toilet water make perfect daintiness sure.

Odorono prevents perspiration an-noyance, both odor and moisture, wherever it is applied.

Get a bottle today. All toilet counters 50c and $1.00, trial size 25c. By mail postpaid if your dealer hasn't it. The Odorono Co., 245 Blair Ave., Cincinnati, Ohio.

Your physician will recommend it.

ODO-RO-NO

The toilet water for excessive perspiration

Odo-ro-no Toilet Water, 1917

▸ Pro-phy-lac-tic Toothbrushes, 1916

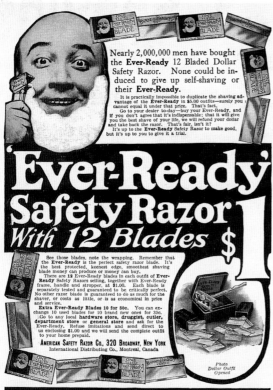
Ever-Ready Safety Razor, 1909

Durham-Duplex Razor, 1910

Durham-Duplex Razor, 1911   ▶ *Williams' Shaving Stick, 1911*

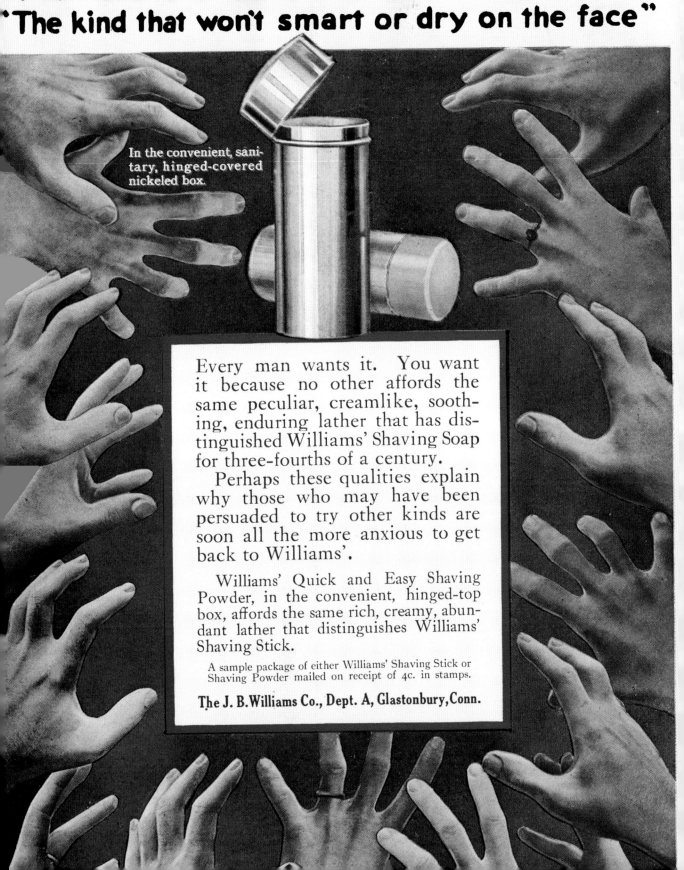

Williams' Shaving Stick

"The kind that won't smart or dry on the face"

In the convenient, sanitary, hinged-covered nickeled box.

Every man wants it. You want it because no other affords the same peculiar, creamlike, soothing, enduring lather that has distinguished Williams' Shaving Soap for three-fourths of a century.

Perhaps these qualities explain why those who may have been persuaded to try other kinds are soon all the more anxious to get back to Williams'.

Williams' Quick and Easy Shaving Powder, in the convenient, hinged-top box, affords the same rich, creamy, abundant lather that distinguishes Williams' Shaving Stick.

A sample package of either Williams' Shaving Stick or Shaving Powder mailed on receipt of 4c. in stamps.

The J. B. Williams Co., Dept. A, Glastonbury, Conn.

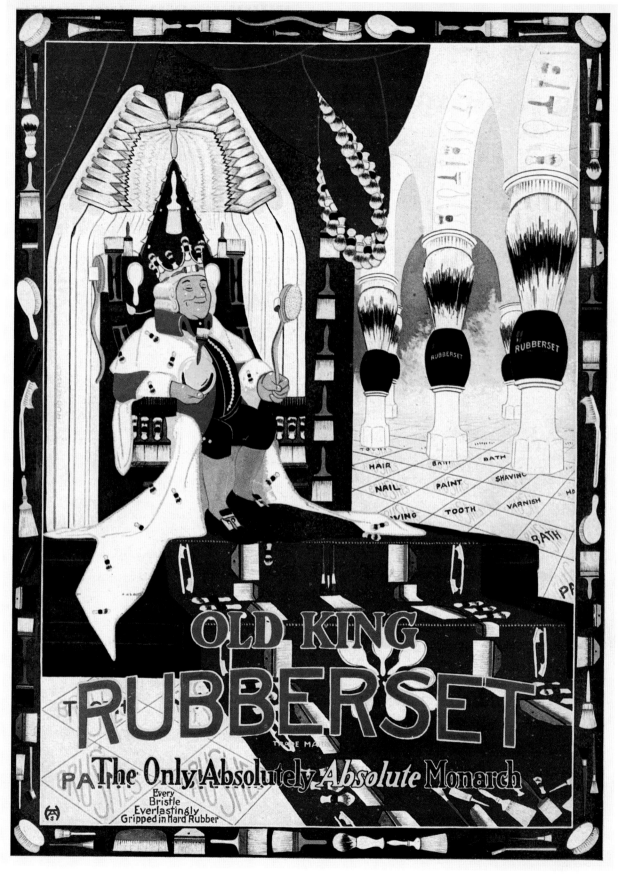

Rubberset Brushes, 1917

Rubberset Shaving Brushes, 1909

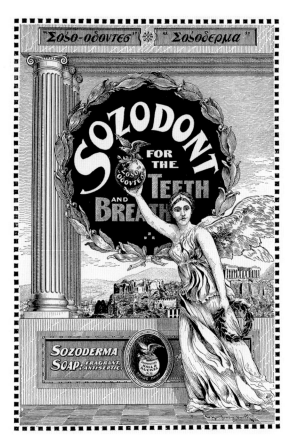

Sozodont And Sozoderma Toiletries, 1900

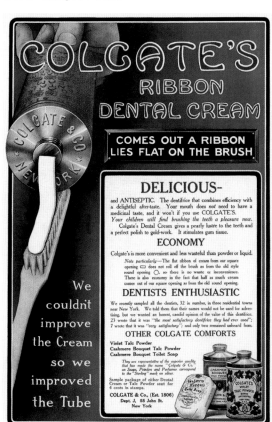

Colgate's Ribbon Dental Cream, 1909

Rubberset Brushes, 1919

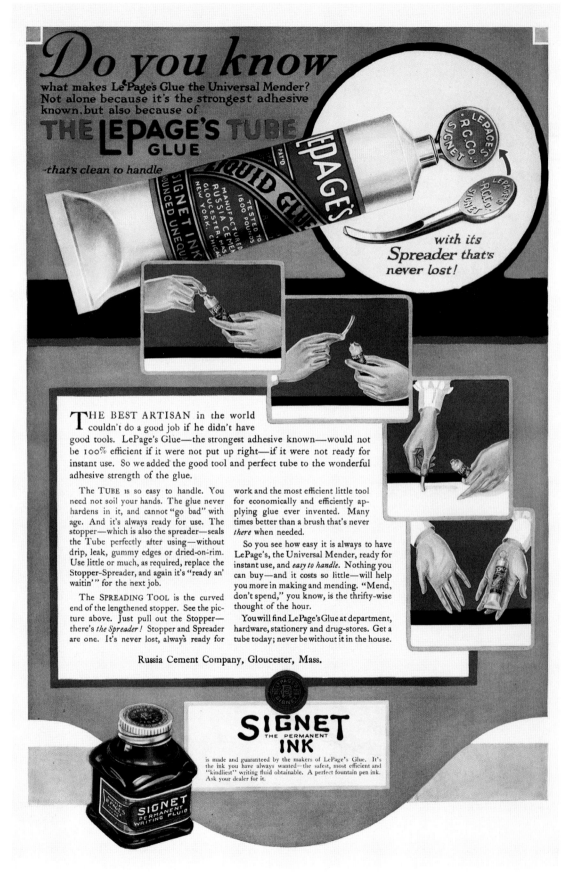

LePage's Tube Glue, 1919

This is the Oldest "Doggone" Advertising Idea In the World

The reason this illustration is used is because it is a real photograph of a real Bull Dog and a real Rubberset Shaving Brush.

It shows that the bristles of a Rubberset Shaving Brush can not even be pulled or twisted out of the setting, while those of an ordinary brush just fall out when the rosin, cement or glue setting is softened by hot water.

The bristles of a

RUBBERSET
TRADE MARK
Shaving Brush

are held in a solid bed of hard, vulcanized rubber — water-proof, soap-proof, alkali-proof, wear-proof. You can boil a Rubberset if you like — it does it good.

Rubberset Brushes are patented and are the only brushes held in hard rubber. Look for the name on every brush.

Every Rubberset Shaving Brush is guaranteed never to lose a bristle from its setting.

At all dealers' and barbers', all styles and sizes, 25, 50, 75 cents to $6.00.

To the average man we commend the $1.00 brush.

If your face is tender.
If your lather dries and tickles.
If your face feels drawn and sore after shaving.
There's a luxurious shave waiting for you when you use

BERSET
TRADE MARK
Shaving Cream Soap

composed of Glycerine and Cocoanut Oil. Prevents dryness — is antiseptic and soothing — contains no free alkali. *Send dealer's name* and 4 cents for 10 cent sample tube.

THE RUBBERSET COMPANY

THE RUBBERSET COMPANY

Sales Dept. No. 9
5204 METROPOLITAN TOWER, NEW YORK CITY

Main Office, Factory and Laboratory:
102 FERRY ST., NEWARK, N.J.

Branch Offices — Boston, Chicago, San Francisco, Montreal

Rubberset Shaving Brushes, 1909

FAULTLESS "Wearever" RUBBER GOODS

"REG. U.S. PAT. OFF"

WEAREVER Nº 40
HOT WATER BOTTLES
SIZES 00, 0, 1, 2, 3 AND 4
PAT. MARCH 20-06

WEAREVER Nº 409
COMBINATION WATER BOTTLE
AND FOUNTAIN SYRINGE
SIZES 2, 3 AND 4
PAT. MAR. 20-06

WEAREVER Nº 24
FOUNTAIN SYRINGE
2 AND 3 QUARTS
OVER CAPACITY

WEAREVER Nº 75
HOT WATER BOTTLE
2 QTS. FULL CAPACITY
PAT.MAR.20-06

WEAREVER Nº 48
FOUNTAIN
SYRINGE
2 QUARTS
FULL CAPACITY

WEAREVER Nº 757
COMBINATION WATER BOTTLE
AND FOUNTAIN SYRINGE
2 QTS. FULL CAPACITY
PAT. MAR. 20-06.

WEAREVER Nº 55
HOT WATER BOTTLE
SIZES 2, 3 AND 4
PAT.MAR. 20-06.

WEAREVER Nº 555
COMBINATION
WATER BOTTLE AND
FOUNTAIN SYRINGE
SIZES 2, 3 AND 4
PAT. MAR. 20-06.

WEAREVER Nº 27
FOUNTAIN
SYRINGE
SIZES 2 AND 3

"WEAREVER" HOT WATER BOTTLES have a PATENTED Oval Neck that makes them stronger where the strain comes, prevents leaking in the neck and protects your hands while filling. The rubber is specifically treated to give long wear. These Bottles have no seams to leak; no bindings to come loose; have a maximum heating surface and are comfortable in use.

"WEAREVER" FOUNTAIN SYRINGES are companion pieces to the Water Bottles. They match exactly in style, color, finish and quality, and have improvements and refinements that will appeal to you.

"WEAREVER" COMBINATION HOT WATER BOTTLES and FOUNTAIN SYRINGES combine all the advantages of "Wearever" Hot Water Bottles and "Wearever" Fountain Syringes. Many prefer a Combination, because it is a convenient two-use outfit.

These are some of many Faultless "WEAREVER" Rubber Goods for Household, Toilet and Sick-Room use. Go to the Faultless dealer for your rubber goods and you will be sure of satisfaction.

If you can not locate the Faultless dealer in your locality, write and tell us what articles you wish to purchase and we will see that you are promptly supplied.

THE FAULTLESS RUBBER COMPANY

Makers of a Complete, High Grade Line of Rubber Goods for the Household, Toilet and Sick-Room.

ASHLAND, OHIO. U.S.A.

Faultless "Wearever" Rubber Goods, 1914

Evans Vacuum Caps, 1905

Faultless "Weurever" Rubber Goods, 1917

red raven is a sparkling aperient or laxative water

red raven not only acts on the liver, but, on account of the <u>natural</u> carbonic acid gas it contains, settles the stomach

red raven is

ideal for any person who has eaten or drank too much; or whose liver is sluggish, or whose stomach is upset from any cause

red raven, by promoting activity of the liver, and by settling the stomach, removes all feeling of nausea, indigestion or headache

this is a perfectly simple proposition; we are convinced that if you are in need of an aperient or laxative water, you cannot buy anything that is bottled under more sanitary conditions, or which will give you better results than red raven

acts in a perfectly natural manner

everywhere 15c

Red Raven Laxative, 1909

Hunyadi János Laxative, 1906

Johann Hoff's Extract, 1901

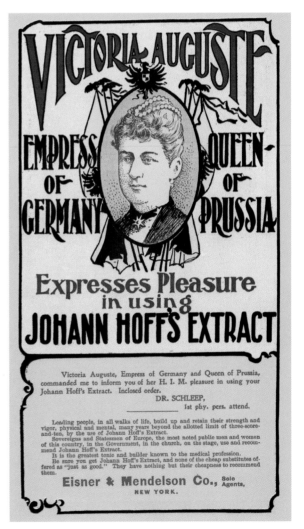

Johann Hoff's Extract, 1902

My Luden Uses

"In wet weather, I take Luden's as a safeguard for nose and throat."

"When traveling, I always take Luden's along to allay thirst, and to relieve coal dust irritation."

"I am fond of motoring, and thanks to Luden's, the wind or dust never bothers my nose or throat."

"When I get overheated or sit in a draught, Luden's quickly relieve any slight cold I contract."

"Luden's help keep my voice in excellent shape. They soothe and clear."

The last thing at night — to relieve throat tickle. The first thing in the morning — to sweeten the breath. Luden's have many uses.

Made by Wm. H. Luden, in Reading, Pa., Since 1881

LUDEN'S MENTHOL COUGH DROPS

The Distinctive Yellow Package.

Give Quick Relief

Luden's Cough Drops, 1918

Bauer & Black First Aid Products, 1919

PISO'S
for Coughs & Colds

Exposure Causes Coughs and Sore Throats

THOSE exposed to winter's storms—perhaps out all day in damp clothing—feet wet and shoulders wringing—are bound to develop sore throat and troublesome coughs.

The important thing is to catch these ills in time. Prompt treatment often keeps real sickness away.

Piso's—always at hand in the medicine cabinet—supplies that ready relief. Good for every member of the family from Baby to Grandmother; it soothes scratchy, tickling throats and allays irritation and inflammation. It relieves hoarseness and troublesome coughs.

Get a bottle of Piso's today—keep it ready in the medicine cabinet for the first symptom of sore throat or cough.

30 CENTS AT YOUR DRUGGIST'S

Contains no opiate   Good for young and old

Piso's Throat and Chest Salve is remarkably beneficial when used in connection with Piso's.

Piso's Throat And Chest Salve, 1919

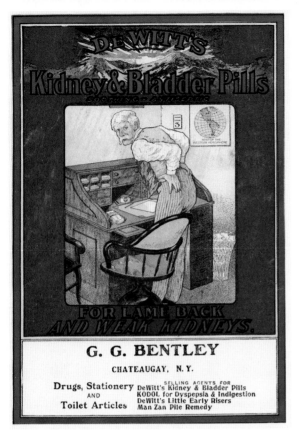

DeWitt's Kidney & Bladder Pills, 1911

California Citrus Cream, 1917

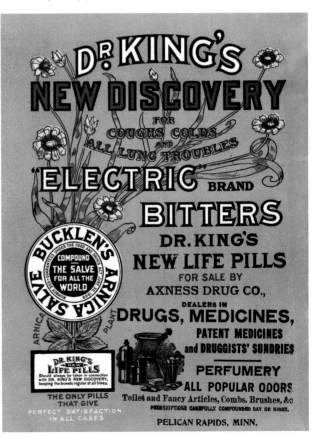

Dr. King's Pharmaceuticals, 1912

The Windows of the Soul

and the most important of your five senses

—YOUR EYES

Your character is read by them, the beauties of the world are seen through them and you would have to depend on others for sustenance if it was not for them.

Furthermore your general health is greatly influenced by the physical condition of this more than often neglected organ, the one that you would miss most if you lost it, that you use most now that you have it.

THE EMBLEM OF
SUPERIOR OPTICAL SERVICE.
LOOK FOR IT WHERE
YOU BUY YOUR GLASSES.

Tired, overstrained eyes cannot inform you of the weakness as would a sprained ankle or an ulcerated tooth—but the condition is fully as wearing on your nerve efficiency and health.

Play fair with your eyesight. Find out if it is a hundred percent efficient. Don't wait until it is gone. You MAY need glasses NOW—and you may NOT, but assure yourself by an examination.

Look for the optometrist who displays this Association Emblem. There are members in every city. If your vision is normal you will be told so very gladly.

Associated Optometrists and Opticians of America

Write for booklet, "The Conservation of Eyesight"
Home Office, Richmond, Va.

Associated Optometrists And Opticians Of America, 1919

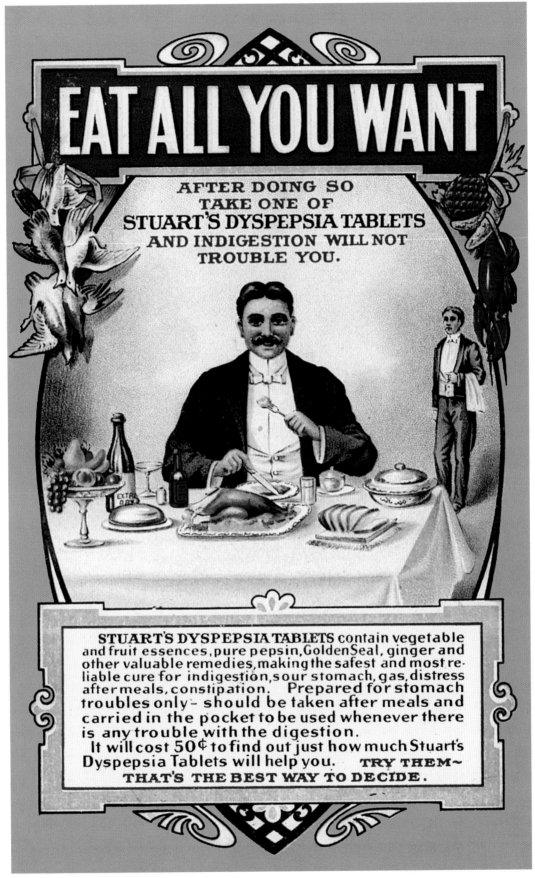

Stuart's Dyspepsia Tablets, ca. 1907

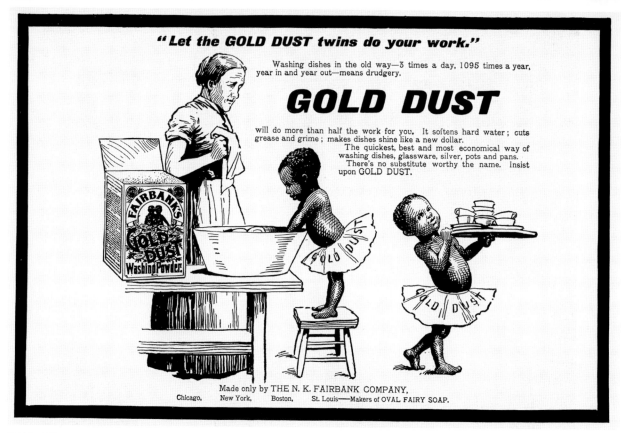

Gold Dust Cleanser, 1902

20 Mule Team Borax Soaps, 1905

Gold Dust cleans the hard-
wood floors;
Also use it on the doors.
— The Gold Dust Twins

Gold Dust changes work to
fun
When your window clean-
ing's done.
— The Gold Dust Twins

GOLD DUST

The Busy Cleaner

for

Spring House-cleaning

Millions of women who are using Gold
Dust daily would not know how to keep
house without it.

A tablespoonful of Gold Dust dissolved
in hot water forms a perfect cleansing
solution on which you can depend absolutely for the following uses:

Scrubbing floors, lino-
leums and cleaning wood-
work, painted walls, etc.

Cleaning bathtubs, wash
basins, tiling, bathroom
faucets and fixtures of
nickel or brass, etc.

Cleaning and sweeten-
ing refrigerators.

Washing windows and
mirrors, glassware, etc.

Washing dishes.

Cleaning pots, pans and
skillets, all kitchen uten-
sils of tin, aluminum or
enamel ware, the kitchen
stove, sink, etc.

You will find directions printed on every package of
Gold Dust. It cleans everything, all around the house.

THE N.K. FAIRBANK COMPANY

Gold Dust makes pans look
so new
That they gleam as mir-
rors do.
— The Gold Dust Twins

Gold Dust meets your fondest wishes
When it's used for washing
dishes.
— The Gold Dust Twins

Five-cent
and
larger
packages
for sale
everywhere

FAIRBANK'S
GOLD DUST
Washing Powder

"Let the
GOLD
DUST
TWINS
do your
work"

Keeping bathrooms clean
and bright,
Gold Dust adds to your delight.
— The Gold Dust Twins

Gold Dust on the kitchen
sink
Cleans it quicker than a
wink.
— The Gold Dust Twins

Gold Dust Cleanser, 1916

Makes
Big Jobs
Look
Small

Old Dutch
Cleanser

Chases
Dirt

MAKES EVERYTHING "SPICK AND SPAN"

Scrubs
Scours
Polishes

Old Dutch Cleanser, 1914

Old Dutch Cleanser, 1918

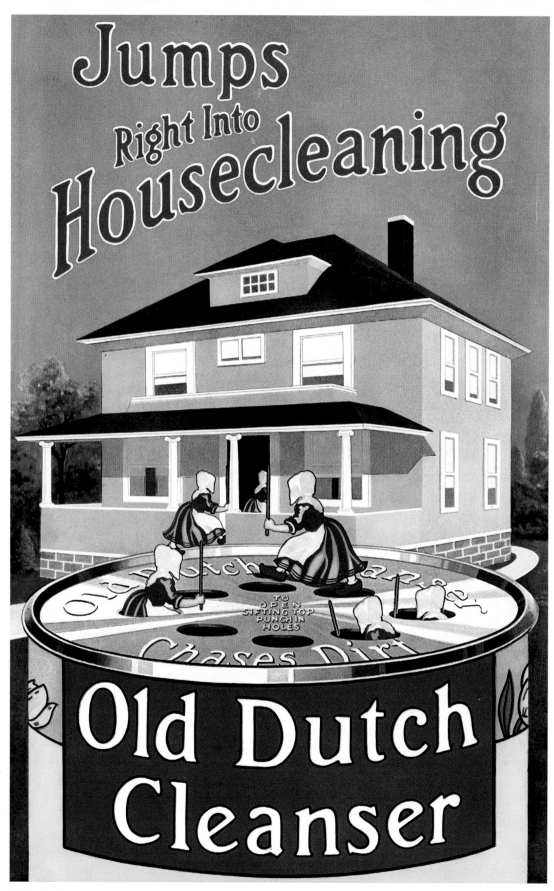

Old Dutch Cleanser, 1915

Old Dutch Cleanser, 1915

Old Dutch Cleanser, 1917

Old Dutch Cleanser, 1909

Old Dutch Cleanser, 1919

Old Dutch Cleanser, 1919

Old Dutch Cleanser, 1917

Bon Ami Cleanser, 1918

Bon Ami

The Missing Panes

After I finish, you will hardly be able to tell whether some of these panes are missing or not!

It's wonderful how invisible you can make good glass with Bon Ami! No smears! No specks!

Use thin, watery lather; it is easier to wipe away after it's dry and it cleans just as well.

"Hasn't scratched yet!"

Made in both Cake and Powder form

Bon Ami Powder

Bon Ami Cleanser, 1918

O-Cedar Furniture Polish, 1918

Bon Ami Cleanser, 1918

O-Cedar Mop Polish, 1915

O-Cedar Furniture Polish, 1916

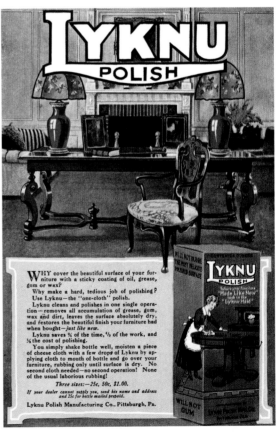

Lyknu Furniture Polish, 1919

2 In 1 Shoe Polishes, 1918

2 In 1 Shoe Polishes, 1918

"AND NIGHT IS FLED
WHOSE PITCHY MANTLE OVER-VEIL'D THE EARTH."
—*Shakespeare*

Edison Mazda Lamp Works, 1919

SAFETY!

A South Bend Watch in the cab of *The Limited* and automatic signals along the right-of-way insure safe travel ¶ South Bend Railroad Watches are specified as "Standard" for service on all the great railroad systems of America. ¶ The same dependable accuracy is available to every man who buys a South Bend Watch. No other watch combines such distinctive beauty with such satisfying accuracy at so reasonable a price. ¶ See your jeweler. Write us for latest catalog.

SOUTH BEND WATCH COMPANY
110 Studebaker Street   South Bend, Indiana
For Years, Makers of Standard Railroad Watches

South Bend
The Watch with the Purple Ribbon

South Bend Watches, 1919

Hamilton Watches, 1913

Hamilton Watches, 1914

South Bend Watches, 1918

Pyrene Fire Extinguisher, 1919

Take a
KODAK
with you

EASTMAN KODAK COMPANY,

ROCHESTER, N. Y., *The Kodak City.*

Kodak Cameras, 1915

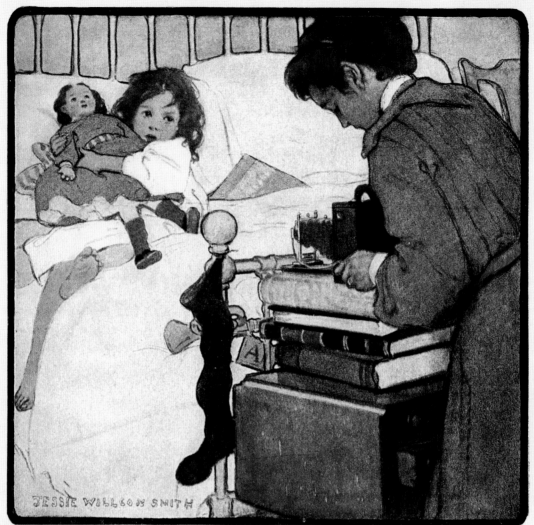

A Christmas Morning

K O D A K

Where there's a child, there should the Kodak be. As a means of keeping green the Christmas memories, or as a gift, it's a holiday delight.

Kodaks from $5.00 to $97.00. Brownie Cameras (They work like Kodaks) $1, $2, $5. Kodak Developing Machines, $2.00 to $10.00.

Catalogue free at the dealers or by mail.

EASTMAN KODAK CO.
Rochester, N. Y.

Kodak Cameras, 1904

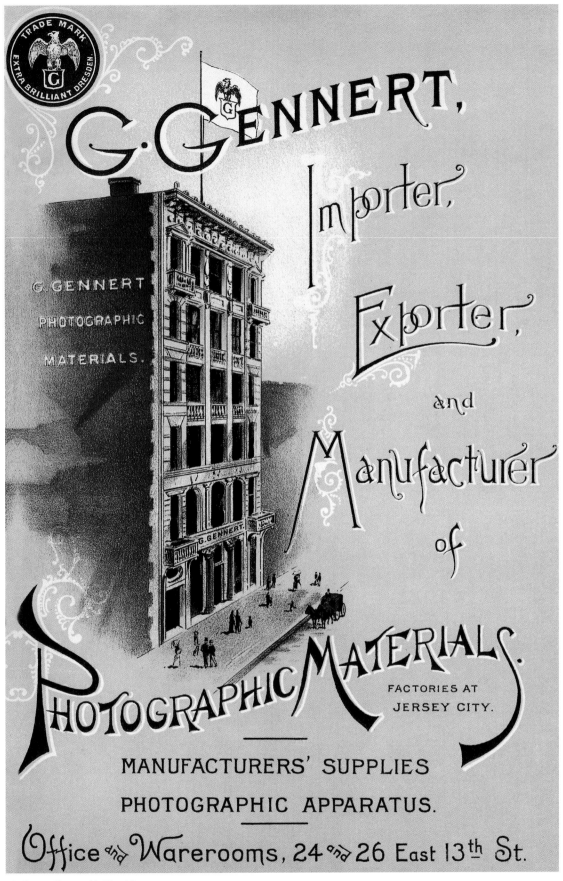

G. Gennert Photographic Materials, 1903

And then again, when snow and ice hold all outdoors—

KODAK

Turn the lens into the home and picture, for the days to come, its hearthstone harmonies. The album of baby and the pictures made by the little folks will be held more precious every year.

And picture making is easy now—the Kodak has made it so. No dark room, few chemicals, no fuss. It's photography with the bother left out.

BROWNIE CAMERAS, they work like Kodaks, $1.00 to $9.00
KODAKS, - - - - - $5.00 to $100.00

EASTMAN KODAK CO.

Catalogue, free at the dealer's or by
Mail. Read it before Christmas.

Rochester, N. Y., *The Kodak City*

Kodak Cameras, 1906

IF IT ISN'T AN EASTMAN, IT ISN'T A KODAK.

LET THE CHILDREN KODAK

There's nothing in which a girl or boy takes greater delight than picture making.

And you will be surprised to find what good pictures even a child of seven or eight can make with a Brownie or a Kodak. Especially interesting is their work when there are two or more children in the family. The pictures they make of each other not only furnish fun for them, but are cherished by father and mother long after the youngsters have outgrown childish ways. Such pictures appeal to *you* because they are natural; they *show the children as they are,* among every day home surroundings.

And photography is educational; it teaches observation; shows the young mind that it's worth while to do things well—and nowadays it's not expensive. The Brownie Cameras at one to twelve dollars, a very, very good one for 2¼ x 3¼ pictures costs only two dollars, and Kodaks from five dollars up, offer a wide variety for all tastes and purses. And in all of them is "Kodak Simplicity."

EASTMAN KODAK COMPANY

Catalogs free at the dealers or by mail

ROCHESTER. N. Y., *The Kodak City.*

Kodak Cameras, 1910

If it isn't an Eastman, it isn't a Kodak

Drawn for Eastman Kodak Co. by Alonzo Kimball

KODAKS

on the tree; then Kodak pictures of the tree; pictures of the baby, of grandmother, of the Christmas house party— all help to keep green the Christmas memories.

Kodaks, $5.00 to $108.00. Brownies, $1.00 to $9.00.

EASTMAN KODAK CO.

Catalogs at the
dealers or by mail

Rochester, N. Y. *The Kodak City*

Kodak Cameras, 1905

All out-doors invites your Kodak

Catalogue free at your dealer's, or by mail.

EASTMAN KODAK COMPANY, ROCHESTER, N. Y., *The Kodak City.*

Kodak Cameras, 1914

▸ *Kodak Cameras, 1916*

Bausch & Lomb Camera Lenses, 1904

Bausch & Lomb Camera Lenses, 1904

Bausch & Lomb Camera Lenses, 1904

Kodak, as you go

Wherever the purr of your motor .lures you, wherever the call of the road leads you, there you will find pictures, untaken pictures that invite your Kodak — intimate pictures of people and places that you and your friends can enjoy again and again as you thumb the leaves of your Kodak album.

And you can take them.

Ask any Kodak dealer.

EASTMAN KODAK COMPANY, ROCHESTER, N. Y., *The Kodak City.*

Kodak Cameras, 1917

Kodak Cameras, 1908

Vanity Fair Magazine, 1914

Vanity Fair Magazine, 1914

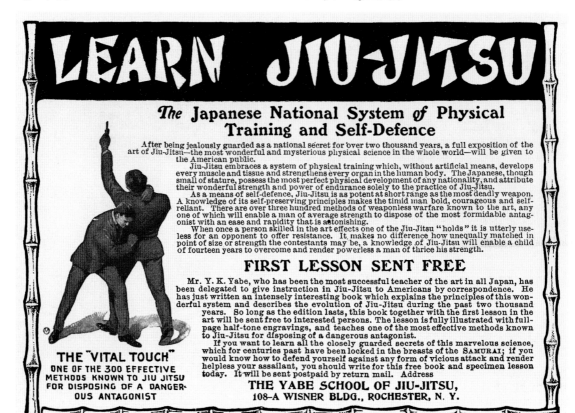

Yabe School Of Jiu-Jitsu, 1905

The American Home Magazine, 1903

Collier's Magazine, 1903

Sunset Magazine, 1905

Fairy Calendar, 1903

Vanity Fair

Vogue Magazine, 1912 ◀ *Vanity Fair Magazine, 1917*

Jos. DeRoy & Sons Diamonds, 1916

Dennison Christmas Goods, 1919

F.W. WOOLWORTH CO.
5 AND 10 CENT STORE

MORE than 800 Woolworth 5 and 10 Cent Stores covering the entire United States sell the famous *Woolco* Cottons. These Cottons have literally leaped into favor for all kinds of crocheting and embroidery work. Sales are enormous — the strongest proof of popularity and *quality*.

Woolco QUALITY CROCHET and EMBROIDERY Cottons

are *smooth-working*, non-shrinkable and hold their color and lustre. They do not *"rough-up" or "kink."* American made and superior, we believe, to any you can buy, domestic or imported.

When you do some especially fine needlework or crocheting, try *Woolco*.

Woolco is sold *exclusively* by F. W. Woolworth Co. Stores — more than 800 of them. You can buy it there — and only there.

If you are not near a Woolworth Store, send your order, at the price quoted, plus postage (at the rate of 3 cents a large ball, 2 cents for 4 balls of tatting cotton, and 2 cents for 3 skeins) to F. W. Woolworth Co., 490 Washington Street, Boston. Circular and color list upon application.

F. W. WOOLWORTH CO.

(Prices quoted are for stores in the United States only)

Woolco Cottons, 1916

F.W. WOOLWORTH CO.
5 and 10 CENT STORES

"BULLSEYE" RINGS
—real 10 K gold-filled—
10c.—*Sold only by*—10c.
WOOLWORTH STORES
all over the United States

"BULLSEYE" RINGS
—new Spring designs—
prettier than ever. See
these new "Bullseye" Rings
in your home Woolworth Store

Beginning March 20th, Watch the Woolworth Windows
10 cents—   for Easter Displays of   —*10 cents*
Famous "Bullseye" Gold-filled Rings

YOU know the "Bullseye" Rings, sold only by the Woolworth Stores. They are the finest *gold-filled rings* ever sold at the remarkably low price of *10 cents*.

Remember, these Rings are *genuine gold-filled* (10 K-$\frac{1}{20}$). They are not merely washed or plated with gold, like so many rings *called* "gold-filled."

They are made by exactly the *same method* as the most *costly gold-filled* ring, pin, bracelet or watch-case—with a *solid surface* of 10 K gold. *Nothing but real gold touches your finger.* Every Ring stamped with the "Bullseye" Trademark *(reg. in U. S. and Canada).*

Now, just before Easter, the Woolworth Stores have an entirely *new and stylish set of designs for Spring*.

Every Woolworth Store in the United States will show these new "Bullseye" Rings in a special window display beginning March 20th.

Be sure to visit the nearest Woolworth Store and see the "Bullseye" Rings for Spring.

No matter what kind of ring you want, you are sure to find one or more to suit your taste in this display. Dainty designs set with fine reproductions of cameos, precious and semi-precious stones, full of brilliant sparkle and color. Solitaires, Pinkies, Marquise settings, and Mannish Signet Rings for Boys.

Notice especially the *delightful Baby Rings.* These are a new "Bullseye" feature and sure to be very popular.

REMEMBER— every "Bullseye" Ring is *real 10 K gold-filled*—You can get any "Bullseye" Ring for only *10 cents*—"Bullseye" Rings are sold by every *Woolworth Store* in the United States —the only place to get Rings of such value and beauty at anything like this price is in one of the Woolworth Stores—Your home *Woolworth Store* will show this Easter display of the Spring designs of "Bullseye" Rings *beginning March 20th.*

In the U. S.
10 cents

In the U. S.
10 cents

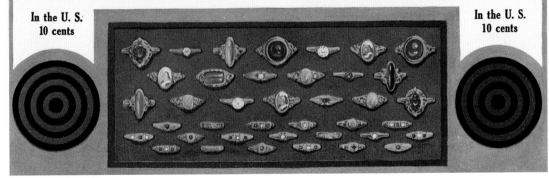

"Bullseye" Rings, 1917

AUTOCRAT

THE STATIONERY OF QUALITY.

EXCLUSIVE STATIONERY

¶ The attractive package in which AUTOCRAT Stationery reaches your hands is but a preliminary verification of that rare, distinctive quality which has made AUTOCRAT Paper the desk companion of clever, discriminating women.

OUR SPECIAL OFFER

¶ To quickly acquaint you with the exceptional qualities of AUTOCRAT Stationery, we will send for ten cents, in stamps or silver, a liberal assortment of these papers in their varying sizes and tints — including our newest Linen Velour — with envelopes to match. Also our interesting booklet "Polite Correspondence," giving the approved forms of extending and accepting social invitations.

The best dealers sell AUTOCRAT Stationery

If you have any difficulty in obtaining it, send us your dealer's name, and we will see that you are supplied.

WHITE & WYCKOFF MFG. CO. - - - - - - - 86 Water Street, Holyoke, Mass.

Autocrat Stationery, 1906

He says
"Be sure and get a **Waterman's Ideal Fountain Pen** before you start It's the one indispensable vacation companion"

The Clip-Cap is a protection against loss. Grips the pocket but is easily detached.

For Sale by Dealers.
L.E. Waterman Co.
173 Broadway, New York
138 Montgomery St., San Francisco.
160 State St., Chicago.
8 School St., Boston.
12 Golden Lane, London.
136 St. James St., Montreal.
6 Rue de Hanovre, Paris.

Waiting for a bite

Waterman Fountain Pens, 1907

Loftis Jewelers, 1915

Deltah Pearls, 1919

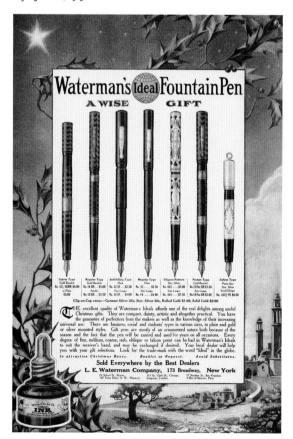

Waterman Fountain Pens, 1910

Colt Fire Arms, 1916

The Greeting Card Association, 1919

Sheaffer Pens, ca. 1919

Society Of American Florists, 1919

Woolco Cottons, 1919

Keep up the Christmas Spirit

with a message of cheerfulness

If ever you should send out generously those friendly cards of Christmas greeting, it is this year.

There is hardly anyone for whom the war has not already caused some hardship. Every friend you have needs a word of courage from you.

Begin *now* to jot down the names so that no one will be overlooked. The boys in the service—their lonely mothers, fathers, wives—the folks back home—your neighbors, relatives, business acquaintances.

Send them all Christmas cards this year. Thus you will help in this fight to bring back *Peace on Earth*, by giving voice to your *Good Will to Men*.

Do it With Holiday Greeting Cards

THE NATIONAL ASSOCIATION OF GREETING CARD MANUFACTURERS, U. S. A.

The stores in your town are ready now with a fine selection of Christmas Cards.

National Association Of Greeting Card Manufacturers, 1918

Santa Claus of to-day

Three types
REGULAR
SAFETY
SELF-FILLING
$2.50 and up
Sold by Best Dealers

Waterman's Ideal Fountain Pen

Brings immediate pleasure and years of appreciation to all ~~

L.E. Waterman Co. 191 Broadway New York
Chicago. Boston. San Francisco. Montreal.

Waterman Fountain Pens, 1919

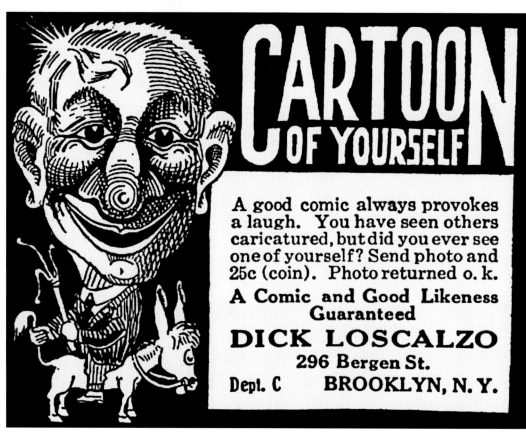

Dick Loscalzo Cartoons, 1916

LOTS OF FUN FOR A DIME

Ventriloquist Double Throat

Fits roof of mouth; always invisible; greatest thing yet. Astonish and mystify your friends. Neigh like a horse; whine like a puppy; sing like a canary, and imitate birds and beasts of the field and forests. **Loads of fun.** Wonderful invention. Thousands sold. Price: only 10 cents; 4 for 25 cents, or 12 for 50 cents.

Double Throat Co., Dept. 89., Frenchtown, N.J.

Ventriloquist Double Throat, 1912

Ives Toys
MAKE HAPPY BOYS

TRANS AND ACCESSORIES

CUT THIS OUT WITH

IVES MANUFACTURING CORP.
225 Holland Ave., Bridgeport, Conn.
GENTLEMEN: I would like to know how to build a model railroad. I enclose 10 cents for which please send me your new, smashing 28-page book (thirteen beautiful pages in full colors) showing Ives Trains and Power Boats—it describes electric and mechanical locomotives; parlor cars, buffet cars, mail cars, freight cars, flat cars, semaphore signals, tunnels, stations, etc.

Name ....
Address ....
City...State.............

THE train illustrated below consists of a Locomotive, Buffet Car, Parlor Car, and Observation Car and 8 pieces of curved and 4 pieces of straight track (2 gauge, 2¼″ from center to center), one terminal section, control switch and connecting wire

Go to your dealer today and ask to see IVES TRAIN No. 701. If he can't supply you, send us $25 00 and we will ship direct to you.

*"Side-track that freight!
Here comes the express!"*

Ives Toys, 1918

Erector Sets, 1915

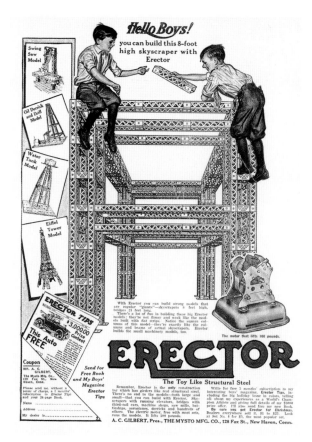

Erector Sets, 1915

Meccano Models, 1915

Never too late to mend
with the Universal Mender

MENDING is saving. To mend is to be thrifty. And thrift, after all, is just plugging up the leaks—it's waste-prevention.

Nothing will help you stop the waste-leaks around the home more efficiently and easily than a Tube of LePage's Glue.

Every day you will find something to mend or make with it. No matter what it is, "it's never too late to mend." Jot down on paper what it would cost to replace the mended articles. At the end of the year add up the total cost. The amount saved will astonish you. *That's money made!*

LePage's Liquid Glue in the Handy Tube is but 15 cents. Only glue that is scientifically prepared will hold "for keeps." Poor glue is worthless. LePage's has been the acknowledged standard for 50 years.

The New Tube with its Spreader is easy to work with and clean to handle. See below how it works. The Spreader fits into the neck of the Tube and acts as Stopper. The Spreader, therefore, can never be lost—glue, tube and spreader, "inseparable," always ready for instant use. No waste—no muss—no fuss! Keep a tube in the house.

LePage's is for sale at department, hardware, stationery and drug stores. Russia Cement Company, Gloucester, Mass.

THE LEPAGE'S TUBE GLUE

with its SPREADER that's never lost

Caption text around image:
For mounting photographs
For mending glasses
For loosened wall paper
Saves the cost
For "skinned" shoes
Keeps rubbers on
Tips for chair legs
Mending toys

LePage's Tube Glue, 1919

LITTLE brother, would you be
Very tall and strong like me?
Then you will, if you are wise,
Take your daily exercise.

Even though you cannot talk,
And have not begun to walk
You are big enough to own
A Kiddie-Kar, and ride alone.

Don't you think that it is pleasant
To have a birthday and a present?
Now that you are one year old
You must be a warrior bold.

I'm sure you will enjoy it more
Than simply creeping on the floor.
There is very little to it,
Let me show you how to do it.

Never fear that you will fall,
See, it does not tip at all.
Sit upon this comfy seat
And push it onward with your feet

Then as soon as you can learn
To travel swiftly and to turn,
You shall come outdoors and see
What fun it is to race with me.

Gaily, gaily we shall ride
On our journeys, side by side.
And come in these frosty nights
With O! such awful appetites!

KIDDIE-KAR is the one universal vehicle for children of all ages, from babyhood up to seven or eight years. Your child should have one on the first birthday, or the first Christmas, after passing one year old. It is a great help in learning to walk. And for the older children, both girls and boys it affords healthful exercise, outdoors and in. It is the only practical indoor vehicle and is used the year round.

It is perfectly safe—close to the ground, and almost impossible to tip over—nothing to pinch fingers—no sharp corners—no paint to come off—no adjustments to get out of order.

You will find Kiddie-Kar wherever juvenile vehicles are sold.

Note the list of sizes and prices at the lower left-hand corner of this page. Don't wait until Christmas. Your dealer may be sold out.

REAL KIDDIE-KARS ARE MADE ONLY BY WHITE

Made in five sizes
No.1—for 1-2 years, $1.25
No.2—for 2-3 years, 2.00
No.3—for 3-4 years, 2.50
No.4—for 4-5 years, 3.00
No.5—for over 5 years, 3.50
Higher west of the Mississippi

KIDDIE-KAR
MADE IN AMERICA FOR AMERICAN GIRLS AND BOYS

Kiddie-Kar, 1919

Buy American-Made Toys

SANTA CLAUS—the good American that he is—this year has turned to Uncle Sam for his toys. In fact the pair of them have been working together for months and months for our American kiddies.

They have planned and arranged and built really wonderful things. They are original—there is a host of new toy ideas.

They are conceived and built by American men and women—they are not the thoughts or work of foreign countries.

American-made toys are best for the children because each toy is perfect. The design is right, the craftsmanship is careful—there are more to pick and choose from. They are educational—they are amusing.

This Christmas make children happier with American-made toys.

This season—this coming New Year—resolve to support American industries—to protect American trade.

Patronize the toy store that shows the circle of Uncle Sam and the laughing, happy children. You will find there the greatest assortment of Christmas and all-year-round toys—the best ones, too.

Patronize the toy store that displays these signs

This space is contributed to the cause of American industries by the Toy Manufacturers of the U.S.A. Flatiron Building, New York

Toy Manufacturers Of The U. S. A., 1919

HERE'S A WONDERFUL VALUE IN A FINE COLLAPSIBLE GO-CART
A YEAR TO PAY

Let HARTMAN Feather Your Nest

$8.35

Very High Grade, Operating With One Motion

WE KNOW THAT NEVER BEFORE HAS SUCH A GREAT BARGAIN BEEN OFFERED AND MOST LIKELY NEVER AGAIN

THE BEST COLLAPSIBLE ONE MOTION GO-CART ON THE MARKET TO BE OFFERED AT OUR SPECIAL PRICE

It Comes to You Complete With Storm Dash and Fine Hood.

The Strongest and Most Durable Go-Cart Made

No. 7G358.

YOU WILL WONDER how it is possible for us to offer so handsome a Go-Cart as this for the small sum of $8.35, while other retail dealers are asking a higher price for Go-Carts not as good as the one illustrated. Knowing you will be amazed at such a wonderful offering we will gladly ship it to you on approval so that you can compare it with any Cart at this price you have seen and thus be convinced that WE OFFER RARE BARGAINS that cannot be duplicated by others.

WHY OUR PRICE IS SO LOW Just before we bought the stock of these Go-Carts from the maker, we figured that by taking so large a quantity, we would get them at factory cost price. We made this offer—it was accepted by the manufacturer and we have included the Carts at factory price with but our one small profit added. That's why our price is so much lower than other dealers would ask you to pay for the equal of the Go-Cart herewith offered.

FOLDS WITH ONE MOTION The simple operation of closing up this collapsible Go-Cart with one motion makes it very desirable. By taking hold of the cross handle with one hand and the front rail of frame with the other, and bringing these two points together, the entire cart collapses and folds together and the wheels fold underneath. It folds with ONE MOTION—almost as simple and as easily as closing an open book. When folded this Go-Cart makes a small package and can be carried about as you would carry a suit case.

View shows as simple and as easily as closing an open book. When folded.

FEATURES of this desirable go-cart are as follows: It has tubular pushers, two position back, nickel plated braces and arm rests, friction hood adjustment, patent unlocking device, luxury springs, large rubber tires, is light in weight, is of generous size, has fancy cross handle and padded seat.

MATERIALS AND DETAILS Only the very best materials obtainable enter into the construction of this collapsible go-cart. It is as strong and rigid when opened as though it were not collapsible. The automatic folding front, or storm dash, and new top give great protection to the child; storm dash, hood and body are of the best selected leatherette, in dark green, brown or black (in ordering state color desired). It has a luxurious spring construction and strong wheel brake, large 10-inch steel wheels equipped with ¾-inch rubber tires and broad nickel plated mud fenders. Size of body, 14x36 inches. At the extremely low price quoted we know the splendid workmanship, high grade materials and beauty of design are beyond the result of competition.

OUR BINDING GUARANTEE We have so much confidence in the merits of this go-cart that we will ship it to you on approval. If you do not feel satisfied that you have received a most exceptional value the go-cart may be returned at our expense. Do not hesitate one minute to send us your order. You run absolutely no risk under this guarantee. Shipping weight, about 50 pounds. No. 7G358. Price only.............$8.35

See Page 1 For Easy Credit Terms

Collapsible Go-Cart, 1914

Dad's "One of the Boys" Again!

YOUNGER than the youngest of them—that's dad when there's a Janesville Ball-Bearing Coaster around.

The "good old days" were nothing like this. No ball-bearing coasters, no auto-type wheels, when dad was a boy.

And speed? Dad's boyhood coaster just snailed along compared with the speed of the ball-bearing Janesville. It's the speed-king of coasters, the winner of every race, the pride of every boy who owns one.

Never before has a coaster wagon been built so well. Spokes are tenoned in rims. Heavy steel tires are set with hydraulic pressure and securely riveted just like big wagon wheels. Has perfect-fitting, nickel-plated dust caps; steel braced bolsters. Body is tough, close-grained white ash. Wheels, body and metal parts are all durably finished. A wagon fit to hold a foremost place in the ranks of America's finest-made products.

No need to wait until tomorrow for the ice-man

When mother wants groceries in a hurry

Easy to haul big loads of kindling or sawed cord wood with this light-running coaster

Janesville BALL BEARING Coaster

It is built to stand the knocks, bumps and strains that a wagon gets in the hands of a vigorous, active outdoor boy. Your boy will get more fun out of this wagon. He will also get lots of exercise and fresh air, something every parent should encourage. And the Janesville will help him make himself useful, too, running errands and doing chores. With it he can easily haul heavy loads—wood, coal, ice, groceries, milk cans, etc. The ball-bearing wheels lighten the load. The "rake" of the tongue makes it easy to steer.

The Janesville Ball-Bearing Coaster is sold at leading hardware, department and furniture stores. If your dealer hasn't it, he can easily get it for you. Don't accept any other. Your boy should have the best—the Janesville, the speediest, most useful coaster made.

Dealers: If your jobber does not handle the Janesville ask us for the name of the jobber in your territory who does.

Janesville Products Co.,
Janesville, Wisconsin

Made in U.S.A.

Skudder Car
no-dead-center Ball-Bearing

HERE'S another Janesville product as remarkable as the Janesville Ball-Bearing Coaster. It's ball-bearing too—a coaster and a power-car in one. Simply shifting the weight from one foot to the other on the tilting board makes it go. And it speeds up to 10 or 12 miles an hour. Three sizes, for boys and girls from 3 to 12.

Other Janesville products are the Jiffy Scoot and Spee Dee Hand Car—all well built, and each a real achievement. See them at your dealer's.

Janesville Coaster, 1919

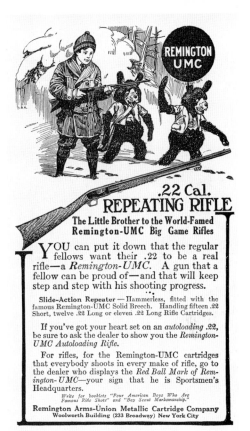

337

Great Bicycle Offer

Send the coupon below today for free catalog of the 1916 Arrow Bicycle. Find out about our special rock-bottom direct offer on the new 1916 Arrow. See below the remarkable improvements and new features in the new 1916 model. Built with all the durability and elegance of highest grade motorcycles. *Guaranteed for 5 years.* The new Arrow offers to bicycle riders the utmost in speed, comfort and easy riding. If you ride an Arrow you will have every reason to be proud of your bicycle—no one in your neighborhood will have one to equal it. You can have the Arrow in a wide variety of new models—the motorcycle type shown above and others. All sizes for men, boys and women. Send the coupon today for free catalog. Get full details of this great offer.

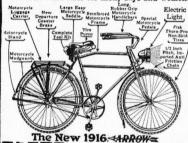

The New 1916 ARROW

Pay As You Ride!

Get our rock-bottom prices. See the great savings you make by dealing direct with the factory. We are now making a special 30-day reduced price offer. We ship the bicycle to you without a penny down. Start riding and enjoying the Arrow right away, and pay the special, rock-bottom, reduced price—**a small amount each month**—while you ride. Now why should you **even consider** paying cash for a bicycle when you can get the wonderful 1916 model Arrow at the lowest, rock-bottom cash price and on small, easy monthly payments while you are riding it? Send coupon for our new catalog.

Free Inspection The ARROW is sent to you without a penny down. If you do not agree when you see it that this new 1916 model Arrow is one of the most wonderful bicycle bargains you ever saw you may send it back at our expense. You alone will be the judge. It will cost you nothing if you decide you do not want the Arrow.

Make Money Riding An Arrow

The coupon brings our liberal rider-agent proposition. The easiest ever! Just ride your Arrow around. People will admire your handsome bicycle and ask about it. Just answer their questions. You can pay for your Arrow and get extra money besides. Just send the coupon for full particulars and New 1916 Catalog, free.

Send Coupon for New Catalog
Showing All Models—It's FREE!

Don't delay. Learn about the sensational 1916 Arrow right away. Take advantage of our special, 30-day, rock-bottom price offer. Get full particulars about the wonderful 1916 improvements. Get the free catalog and details of our easy rider-agent offer by which the Arrow will pay for itself. Also full particulars of our liberal, easy-payment offer and how we can afford to extend to you our sensational rock-bottom prices. See also all the beautiful new Arrow models—the most attractive styles that you ever imagined. No obligations. Send coupon, letter or post card *now*.

Arrow Cycle Co., Dept. 1245, 19th St. & California Ave., Chicago, Ill.

Arrow Bicycle, 1916

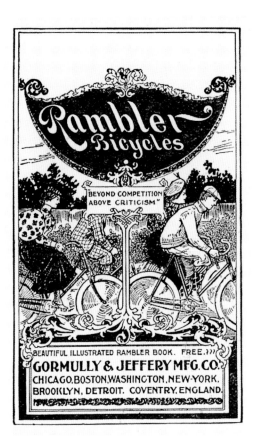

Rambler Bicycles, 1900

Miami Cycle Racycle, 1902

Pope Bicycles, ca. 1907

Pope Bicycles, 1902

Hypnotism

BE A HYPNOTIST AND MAKE FUN and MONEY

It takes but a few hours to learn. The study is both easy and fascinating. Hypnotism is an endless source of fun and wonder. If you know how to hypnotize you can perform the most marvelous feats imaginable. You can do a thousand amazing things that other people cannot do. You can surprise all your friends and make yourself famous. You can place any one you wish under this strange and magic spell. You can compel them to think, act and feel just as you wish. If you want to **make money** you can do it by giving entertainments, curing diseases or teaching the art to others. These are three sure and easy ways to win a fortune. Why be poor? Why work for others, when you can master this money-making profession so easily? Investigate now.

You can learn at home without cost. I will send you my **big free book** for the asking. It tells all about Hypnotism. It is the most elaborate and valuable work of the kind ever published. It contains hundreds of beautiful pictures and explains all the mysteries and secrets of the art. Anybody can learn from it all about the Hypnotic Spell, how it is operated, how it sways the will of its subjects, heals the sick, reforms the degraded, wins undying love, helps to trade or position, amuses an audience for profit, and gains for the operator himself health, wealth and happiness. It also treats fully on Personal Magnetism, Magnetic Healing and kindred subjects, and how to **cure yourself** of any pain, ache or disease. Remember, this book is **absolutely free**. Simply write for it, and it will be sent by next mail, all charges paid. Don't send any money or stamp, but send your name and address to-day.

PROF. L. A. HARRADEN, Dept. 51, Jackson, Michigan.

HYPNOTIZING

AWAKENING

Hypnotism, 1904

A Tour of the World in the BURTON HOLMES TRAVELOGUES

250,000 Miles of Travel

Through 30 Cities and Countries

Cost $250,000 and 20 Years' Work

3,500 Pages of Descriptive Text

4,000 Half-tone Etchings

30 Full-Page Color Plates

(and you can secure all of them for a few cents a day)

PERHAPS YOU ARE NOT ONE of the army of Americans which is now enjoying the interesting sights of the Old World?

Business or some other cause prevented your taking this most fascinating and educating journey—you found yourself compelled to remain at home and forego the trip that possibly you had been planning. Is this so? Then—

Perhaps, too, you are not aware of the fact that all the pleasures, experiences and value of a foreign tour may be had for a tithe the cost of an actual tour, and without stirring from your own threshold? *We are prepared to demonstrate this to you.*

If you will avail yourself of this opportunity to secure the Burton Holmes Travelogues, you will retain more vivid recollections of a trip through the strangest parts of the World, with the famous world-traveller, E. Burton Holmes, as companion and guide, than if you had made the actual tour alone.

In a series of splendid journeys Mr. Holmes unfolds before your eyes the beauties of travel in foreign lands, with such narrative skill, with so many strange experiences, incidents and humorous episodes, and so admirably illustrated by over 4,000 photographs taken on the spot by Mr. Holmes himself as to carry you in spirit over 22,000 miles of travel, through thirty of the most interesting countries and cities of the world.

It would cost you $50,000.00 and many years of your time to take these journeys; but don't take our word for it

—WRITE US TODAY and we will send you a beautifully illustrated booklet containing sample pages and color plates—a full description of the work, and tell you how you may secure the TRAVELOGUES for a few cents a day.

Mail the Coupon Now

McClure's Tourists' Agency
44 E. 23d St.
New York City

Aug. McClure's

McClure's Tourists' Agency
44 East 23d St., New York City

Gentlemen:—I am interested in the **Burton Holmes Travelogues** and will be glad to receive specimen pages in colors and to learn the terms upon which I can secure the ten handsome volumes referred to in the foregoing advertisement.

Name..................................

Address..................................

TEAR OFF, SIGN AND MAIL TODAY

Burton Holmes Travelogues, 1908

Be a Doctor of Mechano-Therapy

Make $3,000 to $5,000 a Year

THIS BOOK IS FREE

Have you ambition?

Do you seek a life position—one in which you can earn both a name and a fortune?

Would you like to be forevermore independent of position-hunting and employers?

Do you wish to advance yourself both financially and socially to an equality with the best professional class of people within the next six months?

Then write at once for the book I hold in my hand, which proves by documentary evidence that the American College of Mechano-Therapy, the largest and best equipped institution of its kind in the world, is turning out daily highly successful graduates—Doctors of Mechano-Therapy (M. T. D.)—men and women who have advanced themselves socially in a few months in a truly marvelous way and who are now able to, and actually are making incomes of from $3,000 to $5,000 a year.

Write at once for this book, which proves, beyond possibility of contradiction, that any man or woman of ordinary common-school education may come to this college in person and learn in class—or be taught with the greatest success at his or her convenience at home by mail—the principles and practice of Mechano-Therapy—an elevating, absorbing and fascinating profession that has the unqualified indorsement and the active support of the medical profession.

WRITE AT ONCE FOR THIS BOOK

Which shows how we guarantee our students success in the study of this absorbing calling, make them the possessors of unusual and exclusive ability, advance them socially and financially, and give them a highly-paid, short-houred and interesting calling, which anyone of average attainments can master in his own home in a few months' spare-time study. This book, which describes the authorized diplomas granted our graduates, the reasonable cost of tuition, the convenient terms of payment, and the actual bona fide realness of the new and unusual opportunity this college course opens up to all enterprising men and women, *is free,* and, if you are ambitious, if you are looking for a life position in which you can make a name and fortune, if you would like forevermore to be independent of position-hunting and employers and wish to advance yourself financially and socially within a few months' time by home study—at small cost and on convenient terms—then write for it at once—write now while the special terms of tuition are in force.

How to become A MECHANO-THERAPIST

Address

THE AMERICAN COLLEGE OF MECHANO-THERAPY

Dept. 650, 120-122 Randolph Street, Chicago, Ill.

American College Of Mechano-Therapy, 1909

▸ *YMCA, 1918*

"Water Flying"—*top-notch sport!*

Speed faster than the fastest motor boat—*on* the water, *over* the water, *cross country*—in the practical Curtiss Hydro-Aeroplane.

"As safe as yachting"

Curtiss Hydro-Aeroplanes

arise and alight on the water and minimize aviation dangers. Add a hundredfold to the joy of flying. Safest air craft ever built. Carries two and either person can drive, with Glenn H. Curtiss' natural dual control. Training stations: New York, Middle West and California. You can learn with little practice and without cost, because tuition applies on purchase. Write today for full information.

Curtiss Aeroplane Co., Hammondsport, N. Y.

Curtiss Hydro-Aeroplanes, 1912

Drive an Aeroplane

¶ The operating of an aeroplane, readily handled by the amateur, is now an assured fact.
¶ In the number of aeroplanes already purchased Europe is far in advance of America. This was likewise true with the introduction of the automobile.
¶ Our Paris correspondent writes us that hundreds of aeroplanes have been sold to private individuals in Europe. One manufacturer, alone, has sold 112—many of the early deliveries at large premiums.
¶ A substantial interest has also begun to arouse Americans. A great wave of enthusiasm has set in, and, although more different makes of heavier-than-air machines are to be had abroad, to America belongs the distinction of producing the lightest, speediest, and most practical aeroplane yet designed.

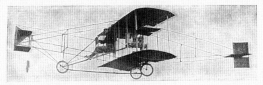

The Herring=Curtiss Aeroplane

amply demonstrated its supremacy at the recent Rheims international meet by winning the coveted International Cup, which brings to America next year the big world's contest.
¶ We invite those interested to favor us with a call. Americans desiring to enter the international contest next year should order machines early to secure prompt delivery, so as to be ready for the different events.
¶ A special inducement will be made to those ordering now for delivery after Jan. 1st, 1910.

Every HERRING-CURTISS AEROPLANE is demonstrated in flight before delivery to the purchaser.

Call or write to **Aeronautical Department,**

Wyckoff, Church & Partridge

1743 Broadway, at 56th St., New York City

Herring-Curtiss Aeroplane, 1909

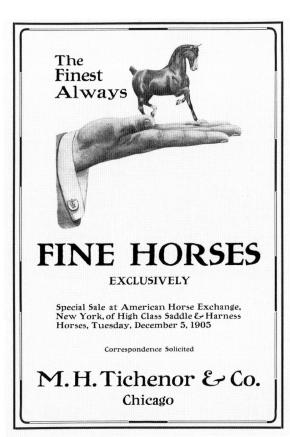

The Finest Always

FINE HORSES

EXCLUSIVELY

Special Sale at American Horse Exchange, New York, of High Class Saddle & Harness Horses, Tuesday, December 5, 1905

Correspondence Solicited

M. H. Tichenor & Co.
Chicago

M. H. Tichenor Fine Horses, 1905

Winchester Rifles, 1909

Winchester Guns And Ammunition, 1910

Marlin Cartridges, 1903

Remington Guns And UMC Shells, 1910

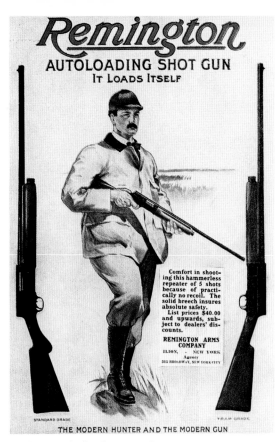

Remington Autoloading Shotguns, 1906

Iver Johnson Shotguns, 1903

And the winner is...

Just What the Doctor Ordered

Patent and quack medicines flourished in this era of invention and discovery. Electricity, the new energy resource, was marketed as healing a variety of ills through many dubious medical products, among them the electric vibrator. Targeted at women, it claimed to cure weak eyes, constipation, and catarrh. Those who read between the lines knew the phallic-shaped attachments could also cure "nervousness" and give "life and vigor, strength, and joy to everyone." Ahhh! The wonders of science.

Der Doktor hat's empfohlen

Patentrezepte und Wunderheilmittel gediehen in dieser Zeit technischer Erfindungen aufs Prächtigste. Die neue Energiequelle Elektrizität wurde in Form von vielerlei dubiosen medizinischen Gerätschaften vermarktet und half angeblich gegen eine Unmenge von Krankheiten. Der elektrische Vibrator war eines dieser Geräte. Der weiblichen Kundschaft wurde die Heilung von schwachen Augen, Verstopfung und Katarrh versprochen. Wer zwischen den Zeilen lesen konnte, erfuhr auch, wie die phallusförmigen Aufsätze „nervöse Überspannung" heilen und „jedermann zu Lebenskraft, Elan und Freude" verhelfen würden. Gepriesen seien die Wunder der Technik!

Sur prescription médicale

L'époque des inventions et des découvertes engendra une prolifération de charlatans et de remèdes miracle. L'électricité, une nouvelle source d'énergie, était réputée soigner toutes sortes de maladies grâce à une variété d'instruments médicaux hasardeux, dont le vibrateur électrique. S'adressant aux femmes, il prétendait guérir la mauvaise vue, la constipation et le rhume. Ceux qui savaient lire entre les lignes apprenaient que les divers accessoires de forme phallique pouvaient aussi remédier à la « nervosité » et apporter « l'entrain et la vigueur, la force et la joie pour tous ». Aaaah ! Les miracles de la science ...

Acatando las órdenes del médico

Los medicamentos con patente y los ungüentos de curanderos florecieron en esta época de inventos y descubrimientos. La electricidad, el nuevo recurso energético, se vendía como medio sanador de todo un abanico de enfermedades por medio de artilugios médicos de beneficios dudosos, entre los que figuraba este vibrador eléctrico. Destinado a las mujeres, se le atribuían propiedades para curar defectos de visión, el estreñimiento y el catarro. Aquellos que eran capaces de leer entre líneas sabían que los accesorios con forma fálica también podían curar el «nerviosismo» y dar «vida, vigor, fuerza y alegría a todo el mundo». ¡Ah, las maravillas de la ciencia ...!

まさにお医者様が指示したこと

この発明と発見の時代、新案特許でインチキな医薬品が世に満ち溢れた。新しいエネルギー資源、電気は、電動バイブレーターを含むたくさんのいかがわしい医療品を通じて色々な病気の治療方法として売り出された。女性をターゲットにして、弱い視力や便秘やカタルまでを治療すると喧伝した。言外の意味を読み取った人々は、男根の形をしたアタッチメントが "神経症" を治し、"活力や元気や強さやそして喜びをも万人に" 与えることに気が付いた。ああ! 科学の驚異。

VIBRATION IS LIFE!

Read What Others Say

Here are a few of the hundreds of unsolicited testimonials from people who have used the White Cross Electric Vibrator and know what it has done. It will do the same for you.

PARALYSIS TREATED BY VIBRATION

Upon the request of my sister, who urged me to use her great Electric Vibrator on my son when I was thoroughly hopeless of his cure from physicians' treatment, I write you this recommendation. My son is 16 years old, and eight months ago became paralyzed from the after-effects of diphtheria. He was so badly afflicted that his arms and limbs were twisted out of shape and was confined, all doubled up, in his bed. Medicine and attention did no good, and I had become discouraged in all ways. After treating first his spine at the base and then his limbs with your vibrator he felt such relief that I kept up the treatment regularly, with the result that we soon had him around in a wheel chair. Next he was going around on crutches, and now, after three months' treatment, he is going around with a cane and will soon be entirely cured.

3122 Indiana Ave., Chicago. MRS. C. KNIGHT.

WHAT A DOCTOR SAYS

I have received your Vibrator, and to say that I am well pleased with it is not enough. I wish I could tell every physician just how bad he needs one in his office. I am sure he would not hesitate to place his order for one at once.

Longmont, Colo. DR. W. H. EASTER.

VIBRATOR BEST FOR RHEUMATISM

My husband uses your vibrator for rheumatism and says he never had anything so good in all his experience. I would not be without it myself, as I find it is good to relieve stomach pains, back ache, and besides I continually use it for face massage. I used to go down town for that, while now I save the money and the time, besides being comfortable in my own home. MRS. S. H. BROWN,

2935 Vernon Ave., Chicago, Ill.

Here is a Picture of the wonderful WHITE CROSS ELECTRIC VIBRATOR,

the only vibrator in the world which combines the three great forces of Vibration, Galvanic and Faradic Electricity. This is the very same machine which has cured thousands of cases which had been given up by the best physicians as incurable. Read the letters above, then send the free coupon at once.

The secret of the ages has been discovered in *Vibration*.

Great scientists tell us that we owe not only our health but even our very life to this wonderful force.

Vibration gives life and vigor, strength and joy to everyone.

Vibration is the most marvelous curative agent known. It is the remedy provided by Nature for all illness and disease. It cures like magic. Simple, sure and inexpensive—it banishes drugs and doctors forever.

The White Cross Electric Vibrator On Free Trial!

This wonderful instrument gives you the three greatest natural curative forces in the world—Vibration, Faradic and Galvanic electricity.

We want to prove to you at our expense what the great White Cross Electric Vibrator will do for you. We want you to actually feel its invigorating, health-giving thrill coursing through your own body. We want you to see for yourself how quickly it removes pains and aches—how marvelously it cures. We take all the risk.

Cures These Diseases

Rheumatism, Headache, Backache, Constipation, Kidney Disease, Lumbago, Catarrh, Scalp Diseases, Skin Diseases, Deafness, Weak Eyes, General Debility, Nervousness.

A Vibrating Chair Free

With the White Cross Vibrator you can make a perfect vibrating chair out of any chair. A chair which will give you the same results as the kind used in the biggest hospitals and sanitariums. You cannot do this with any other vibrator in the world. **Swedish Movement** right in your own home. You can give yourself the very same treatments for which specialists and sanitariums charge from $2.00 to $3.00 each. The nervous, irritable, worn-out man or woman will obtain quicker and more permanent benefit from a few minutes each day in the vibrating chair than from hundreds of dollars worth of medicines.

This Valuable Book, "Health and Beauty," NOW SENT FREE

This wonderful book describes the human body in health and disease so plainly and clearly that anyone can understand. It tells how to get healthy and beautiful and how to keep so. This book tells you what vibration will do for you and how you can get the **White Cross Electric Vibrator** sent right to your home for an actual free trial.

SIGN this COUPON

Get this valuable free book at once. No matter how healthy you may be now, the time will come when you will need this book **badly**. It may save your life or the life of some of your loved ones. Learn all about our offer—the most astounding and generous offer ever made. Don't wait. Don't delay. Sign the coupon **NOW!**

LINDSTROM SMITH CO.,
253 LaSalle Street,
Dept. 2011,
CHICAGO,
ILL.

SIGN THIS COUPON AND MAIL TODAY

LINDSTROM SMITH CO.,
253 La Salle St.,
Dept. 2011,
CHICAGO, ILL.

Without obligations on me please send me free your special reduced price offer, free Book on Health and Beauty, treatment of disease by vibration and electricity, and complete catalog.

Name.....................................

....

Address ....

....

White Cross Electric Vibrator, 1909

VICTOR

Won the First Prize at St. Louis

The *Victor* was awarded the GRAND PRIZE over all other talking machines at the St. Louis Exposition.

This is the first prize and the highest award given.

The *Victor* was also awarded the first prize at Buffalo in 1901.

This proves that the *Victor* is the best talking machine. It is also the greatest musical instrument in the world.

Victor Talking Machine Company Philadelphia

Original makers of the Gram-O-phone

Victor Phonographs, 1905 ◄ *Victor Phonographs, 1904*

Victor Talking-Machine

"His Master's Voice"

The voice of Melba

can now be heard on the *Victor Talking Machine*.

These records of the great soprano were made for her own private use—to send to her relatives in Australia. She has been persuaded to make them public.

The Melba Records have delighted the King and Queen of England. They have been eagerly sought by other famous singers. Melba herself says they are really wonderful. You can hear Melba only on the *Victor*.

Caruso and others

famous in the operatic world have also sung for the *Victor* and you can have grand opera at home whenever you want.

Besides the living voices of the leading artists of both continents, you can hear the music of celebrated bands and orchestras, and the best entertainment of every sort.

The *Victor* is more than a mere talking machine. It is the greatest musical instrument in the world.

Victor Phonographs, 1904

Columbia Grafonola Phonographs, 1913

Victor Phonographs, 1904

Edison Phonographs, 1917

Victor Phonographs, ca. 1912

Victor Victrola Phonographs, 1918

Victor Victrola Phonographs, 1913

Why do these great artists all make records only for the Victor?

Because they realize that the Victor is the only instrument that does full justice to their magnificent voices.

They want every part of every selection to be as sweet and natural when they sing in your home as when they sing on the grand opera stage — and this can be accomplished only on the Victor.

And you can depend upon it, the instrument that perfectly renders the highest achievement of a Caruso or a Melba does equally well with the lighter forms of music.

It is only a matter of the choice of records, and in looking through the catalog of Victor Records you will find there is a variety of entertainment to satisfy every taste.

> Always use Victor Records, played with Victor Needles — there is no other way to get the unequaled Victor tone.

Victor Talking Machine Co., Camden, N. J., U. S. A.

Berliner Gramophone Co., Montreal, Canadian Distributors

And be sure to hear the
Victor-Victrola

Victor Victrola Phonographs, 1911

Edison Phonographs, 1908

Edison Phonographs, 1910

Edison Phonographs, 1906

Edison Phonographs, 1908

EDISON
PHONOGRAPH

SOMETHING to enjoy in the evening, at home, in comfort, without effort. Something that is cleaner, brighter and more fascinating than most entertainment that is planned for and paid for.

GO to a dealer and hear the Edison Phonograph play the new Records, including Amberols. Get a catalogue of Phonographs and Records from him or from us.

NATIONAL PHONOGRAPH COMPANY, 12 Lakeside Avenue, Orange, New Jersey.

Edison Phonographs, ca. 1910

I am your Christmas wish, the realization of your Christmas desire. I am the voice of Slezak, the soul of Sylva, the dramatic art of Sarah Bernhardt—I am the laugh of Lauder, the coon shouts of Stella Mayhew—I am Sousa and his entire band, Herbert and his orchestra—I am the

EDISON PHONOGRAPH

I hold, on a little sapphire button, scarcely bigger than the point of a pin, the ability to produce exactly the kind of music you and each member of your family like best. No one in your family is too young, none will *ever* be too old to enjoy my presence. I am supreme as an entertainer—the greatest *kind* of Christmas gift—a gift for *all* the family.

And I am the greatest Christmas gift *of its kind*. For I have four great advantages: Exactly the right volume of sound for your home; the sapphire reproducing point that never wears out—no needles to be changed after each record; Amberol

(four-and-one-half minute) Records rendering every composition *completely*, without cutting or hurrying; and home recording. This is a great feature: Talk to me, sing to me! I answer you back in your own words, in your own voice. I, the Edison Phonograph, am you *yourself*.

Go to an Edison dealer and hear and see me—be sure to have me in your home on Christmas Day.

There is an Edison Phonograph at a price to suit everybody's means, from $15.00 to $200.00; sold at the same prices everywhere in the United States. Edison Standard Records, 35c; Edison Amberol Records (play twice as long), 50c; Edison Grand Opera Records, 75c to $2.00.

Thomas A. Edison
INCORPORATED
11 Lakeside Ave., Orange, N.J.

Edison Phonographs, 1908

Just two ways of hearing
all the Music
of all the World

Columbia Grand $500
Grafonola

The Columbia Grafonola is the one incomparable instrument of music. This new Columbia "Grand" has made the very words "talking machine" obsolete. Its tone is beyond compare. No winding—it runs by electric motor. It stops automatically at the end of each record. Ask your dealer for the Book of the Columbia "Grand"—or write us.

Columbia Grafonolas now range from $50 to $500. Catalogs on request.

Important Notice

All Columbia Records can be played on Victor talking machines. Likewise all Columbia instruments will play Victor records.

DESTINN   FREMSTAD   BONCI   NORDICA   GARDEN   SLEZAK   ZENATELLO

NIELSEN   PASQUALI   BISPHAM   WHITE   GAY   CAVALIERI   HARROLD

Columbia

Columbia "Grand" Grafonola Phonographs, 1913

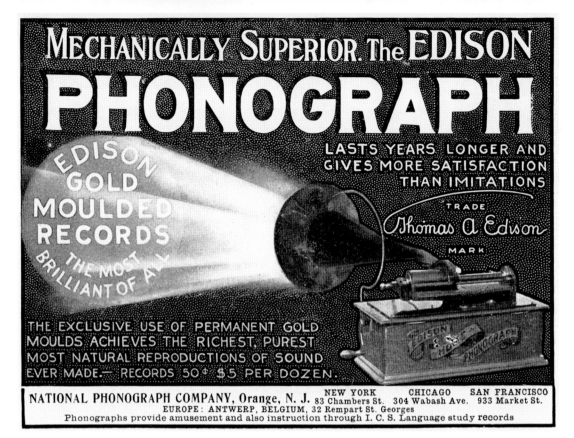

Edison Phonographs, 1904

Duplex Phonographs, 1906

COLES PHILLIPS

CAROLA

THE ALL-SEASON PHONOGRAPH

Cabinet Phonograph
$15

In the Far West - - - $17.50
Dominion of Canada - 25.00
Australia - - - - £6 6s

THE CAROLA in a very short time has won an amazing nation wide popularity. Its convenient light weight and size have helped to do it; its beauty of design and elegance of finish have helped too; its top, dustproof compartment for records and other exclusive features have helped, *but the real reason is its marvelous interpretation of all standard disc records.*

Weighs but 11 pounds.

Cabinet made entirely of acoustic metal, with handsome mahogany finish.

Music does not pass thru metal, but thru violin fibre tone arm.

If you don't know the Carola dealer in town, write us for free demonstration in your home.

Size 11x13x22 inches, 31 inches high in playing position.

One winding of the sturdy motor plays one 12-inch or two 10-inch or three 8-inch records.

DEALERS: We have an exceptional opportunity for you. Good territory still open. Write for details.

THE CAROLA COMPANY, *513 Leader-News Building,* Cleveland, Ohio

Carola Phonographs, 1916

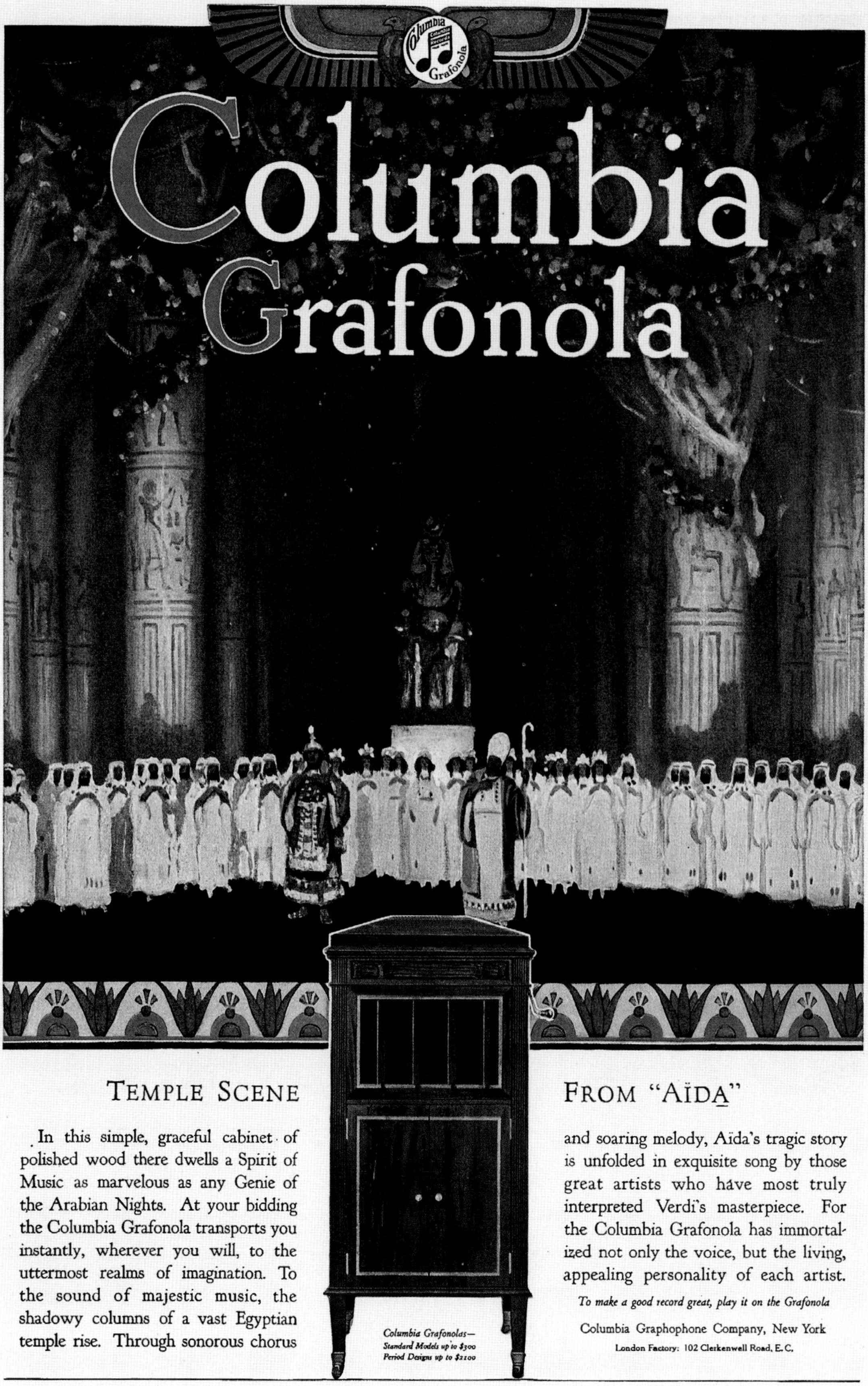

Columbia Grafonola Phonographs, 1919

The Gateway to a Thousand-and-One Entertainments

THE Columbia Grafonola is an instrument of infinite possibilities. It can make an instant reality of a longing to hear the art of great singers; it can improvise at call a concert-platform on which the magicians of music appear; it can summon, one by one, the star entertainers who make the entire country laugh; or bring the brilliance of a full orchestra within the confines of the drawing room.

Its power to thrill, amuse, inspire—its mastery of every sound and emotion—and, above all, its sheer perfection in all the numberless roles it plays, make the Columbia Grafonola the one incomparably versatile and delightful entertainer.

The Columbia Grafonola, playing Columbia Double-Disc Records, is the living, breathing embodiment of art; for the *tone* of Columbia Double-Disc Records is *life itself*—REALITY! "Hearing is believing." Arrange a hearing at your dealer's *today*.

New Columbia Records on sale the 20th of every month

Columbia Grafonola

The instrument illustrated above is the $200 Grafonola—a notable achievement in cabinet instruments
Prices in Canada plus duty

Columbia Grafonola Phonographs, 1916

Columbia Records, 1917

Edison Phonographs, 1908

Columbia Grafonola Phonographs, 1918

Columbia Grafonola Phonographs, 1918

Columbia Grafonola Phonographs, 1919

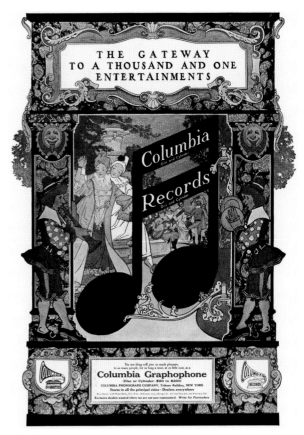

Columbia Records, 1908

Columbia Grafonola Phonographs, 1918

Columbia Grafonola Phonographs, 1919

Columbia Grafonola

Songs Across the Sea

Singing, they march and fight for freedom over there — thousands on thousands of America's best and dearest. And to war-worn Europe the tread of their marching feet and the sturdy lilt of their brave young voices sound the music of liberty.

Day and night the self-same music is echoing over here. In thousands on thousands of loyal American homes, these inspiring, patriotic melodies on the Columbia Grafonola cheer and sustain the patriotic men and women who work and wait and save and serve. This is Columbia's war-time task.

Columbia Grafonolas—Standard Models up to $300.
Period Designs up to $2100.

COLUMBIA GRAPHOPHONE COMPANY, NEW YORK

Columbia Grafonola Phonographs, 1919

Victor

Only on Victor Records or on the grand-opera stage can you hear the wonderfully sweet and powerful voices of Caruso, Melba, Sembrich, Eames, Scotti, Schumann-Heink, and other world's famous operatic stars.

But not even at the opera can you hear in one evening such a celebrated group of artists as you can hear on the Victor anywhere at any time.

Any Victor dealer will gladly play grand-opera or any other Victor Records for you. Call and ask to hear them.

Victor Talking Machine Co., Camden, N. J., U. S. A.

Berliner Gramophone Co., Montreal, Canadian Distributors.

Victor Phonographs, 1908

COLUMBIA

Double-Disc Records

Music on both sides

Fit any Disc Machine and Double its Value

Two records at a single price

[10-inch 65 cents]   **65 cents**   [12-inch $1.00]

Columbia Records, ca. 1913

The Gift for all the Family

With this incomparable instrument of music in your home "all the music of all the world" is yours to command. No other gift can assure so much in genuine delightful pleasure and entertainment, for so long a time, at so little cost, as a Columbia Grafonola.

Columbia

GRAPHOPHONE CO., Box L-270, Woolworth Building, New York

Toronto : 365-367 Soranren Ave.   Prices in Canada plus duty.   Dealers wanted where we are not actively represented.   Write for particulars.

Any one of 8500 Columbia dealers will gladly demonstrate any Grafonola, from the one at $17.50—and it's a real Columbia—to the magnificent model at $500. A small initial payment places any Columbia in your home—and on Christmas morning if you wish.   Balance can be paid, at your convenience, after the holidays.

We illustr ate the new "Leader" Columbia Grafonola, typical of every other Columbia in its wonderful tone-quality.   The "Leader" equipped with the new Individual Record Ejector, an exclusive Columbia feature.   Price, $85; with regular record rack, $75.   Others $17.50 to $500.

Columbia Grafonola Phonographs, 1914

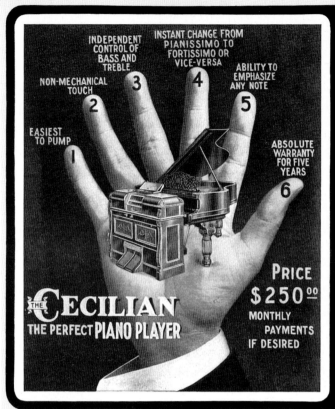

Cecilian Piano Players, 1903

Beethoven Pianos, 1902

▸ *Chickering Pianos, 1919*

Chickering Quarter Grand in Dull Mahogany $1150

Art and science combine with the ideals and traditions of nearly a century to create, year by year, new standards of excellence for the Chickering Piano. Golden beauty of tone, perfect action and finest workmanship are the attributes of the Chickering of today. It represents the highest development of the piano-makers' art.

Made at the Great Chickering Factories. Boston. Massachusetts

The Chickering with the Ampico reproduces in your home the playing of the world's greatest pianists and all the music you love best, ideally interpreted

Gloria's Romance, 1916

Intolerance, 1916

Upstairs And Down, 1919

Fox Entertainments, 1919

Selznick Pictures, 1919

Fox Entertainments, 1919

Paramount-Artcraft Motion Pictures, 1919

Anne Of Green Gables, 1919

Mutt & Jeff, 1919

Chaplin Classics, 1919

When The Desert Smiled, 1919

Broken Blossoms, 1919

The Autoharp, 1903

Fox News, 1919

The American Beauty, 1919

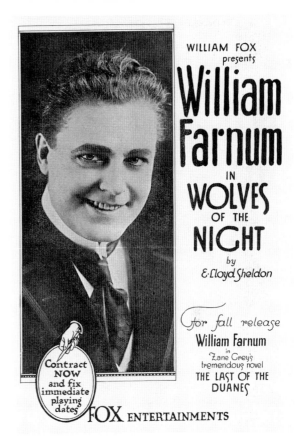

Wolves Of The Night, 1919

Rough Riding Romance, 1919

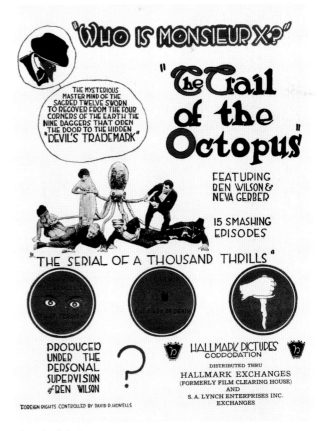

The Trail Of The Octopus, 1919

The Spite Bride, 1919

Kathleen Mavourneen, 1919

Sunshine Comedies, 1919

Laurant, ca. 1907

And the winner is...

Not So Phat

The comic darling of the silent film era, Fatty Arbuckle, was at the height of his popularity when *Back Stage* was released in 1919, co-starring his pal Buster Keaton. Two years later, Arbuckle was accused of raping a starlet at a wild party and tried for her death. The claims turned out to be false, but no public exoneration could reverse the bad publicity. A broken man, Arbuckle died of a heart attack in 1933.

Der kriegt sein Fett weg

Der beliebteste Komiker der Stummfilmzeit, Fatty Arbuckle, stand auf dem Höhepunkt seines Ruhms, als „Back Stage" 1919 – mit seinem Kumpel Buster Keaton als Ko-Star – ins Lichtspieltheater kam. Zwei Jahre später wurde Arbuckle vorgeworfen, bei einer wüsten Party ein Starlet vergewaltigt zu haben, und er stand wegen ihres Todes vor Gericht. Die Vorwürfe erwiesen sich als falsch, doch auch der Freispruch konnte die schlechte Meinung der Öffentlichkeit nicht wieder umkehren. Arbuckle starb als gebrochener Mann 1933 an einem Herzinfarkt.

La fin tragique d'un comique

Le comique le plus populaire du film muet, Fatty Arbuckle, était au sommet de sa gloire lorsque sortit *Back Stage* en 1919, un film dont il partageait la vedette avec son copain Buster Keaton. Deux ans plus tard, Arbuckle fut accusé d'avoir violé une starlette lors d'une folle soirée et jugé pour avoir causé sa mort. Les allégations se révélèrent fausses et toutes les disculpations publiques ne purent rien faire pour enrayer la mauvaise publicité. Arbuckle, brisé, mourut d'une crise cardiaque en 1933.

Falsas acusaciones

En 1919, la estrella cómica de la era del cine mudo, Fatty Arbuckle, se hallaba en la cima de su carrera cuando se estrenó *Keaton entre bastidores*, en la que compartía protagonismo con su amigo Buster Keaton. Dos años más tarde, Arbuckle fue acusado de violar a una *starlet* en una fiesta salvaje e intentar asesinarla. Las acusaciones demostraron ser falsas, pero ninguna exoneración pública podía subsanar la mala publicidad. Hundido, Arbuckle falleció de un ataque al corazón en 1933.

それほど太ってないよぅ～

無声映画時代の人気者ファッティ・アーバックルは、彼の相棒バスター・キートンと共演した「Back Stage」が発表された1919年に人気の絶頂であった。2年後、アーバックルは乱痴気パーティーで新進女優を強姦した容疑で起訴され、殺人の罪で裁判にかけられた。この告発は間違いであったと判明したが、公式な免罪も悪い評判をくつがえすことはなかった。悲嘆の男アーバックルは1933年に心臓麻痺で他界した。

Joseph M. Schenck *presents*

STAGE ENTRANCE

"FATTY ARBUCKLE"

IN PARAMOUNT-ARBUCKLE COMEDIES

"BACK STAGE" is one of the funniest comedies Arbuckle has ever made. This is a strong statement. You don't have to take it on trust. You can see the picture at your exchange.

"Fatty" is stage manager. And he quarrels with the strong man. And the strong man quits. So "Fatty" gives the show himself. It's some show! See the electric shock strong man; the trunk full of weights and its purpose; the Keaton dive into the stage box; the Al. St. John snow storm; Molly Malone as Fatima, Queen of the Harem; "Fatty" as King Murad; Buster as Bull; "Fatty's" glorious dance; Keaton's giant swing from the theatre balcony to the stage; the falling scenery; the gorgeous fights.   See it all!

Then arrange to give all the folks their chance to roar and applaud. Good for a longer run.

FAMOUS PLAYERS-LASKY CORPORATION
ADOLPH ZUKOR *Pres* JESSE L LASKY *Vice Pres* CECIL B DE MILLE *Director General*
ARTCRAFT PICTURES

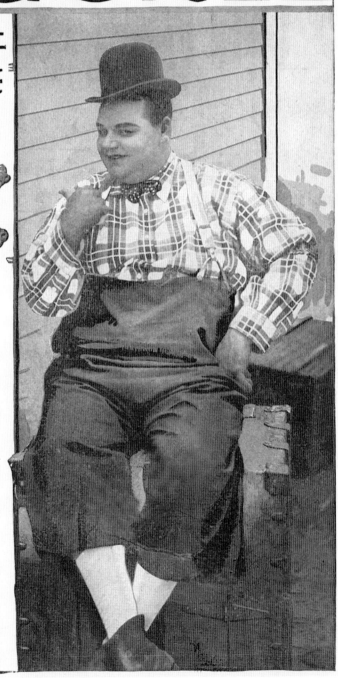

Back Stage, 1919

PROPER SHAMPOOING is what makes beautiful hair. It brings out all the real life, lustre, natural wave and color, and makes it soft, fresh and luxuriant.

Your hair simply needs frequent and regular washing to keep it beautiful, but it cannot stand the harsh effect of ordinary soap. The free alkali, in ordinary soaps, soon dries the scalp, makes the hair brittle and ruins it. This is why discriminating women use

WATKINS
MULSIFIED
COCOANUT OIL
FOR
SHAMPOOING

This clear, pure and entirely greaseless product cannot possibly injure, and does not dry the scalp or make the hair brittle, no matter how often you use it.

Two or three teaspoonfuls will cleanse the hair and scalp thoroughly. Simply moisten the hair with water and rub it in. It makes an abundance of rich, creamy lather, which rinses out easily, removing every particle of dust, dirt, dandruff and excess oil. The hair dries quickly and evenly, and has the appearance of being much thicker and heavier than it is. It leaves the scalp soft and the hair fine and silky, bright, fresh-looking and fluffy, wavy and easy to do up. You can get WATKINS MULSIFIED COCOANUT OIL at any drug store. A 4-ounce bottle should last for months.

Splendid for Children

THE R. L. WATKINS COMPANY, Cleveland, Ohio

GET THE GENUINE
LOOK FOR THIS SIGNATURE
R.L. Watkins
ON EVERY ORIGINAL BOTTLE

MULSIFIED
COCOANUT OIL
SHAMPOO FOR THE HAIR
ALCOHOL 3%

DISTRIBUTED BY
THE R.L. WATKINS COMPANY
CLEVELAND, OHIO, U.S.A.
NET CONTENTS 4 FL. OZ.

Arrow Collars And Cluett Shirts, 1911 ◀ *Watkins Mulsified Cocoanut Oil, 1919*

CRANI TONIC

The Food that Does The Hair Good

"Purity"

Makes
Hair Grow
Stops Hair
Falling Out
Prevents and
Cures Dandruff

The Neglect of Your Hair May Be Its Ruin

If you have neglected your hair and scalp or have any serious hair or scalp trouble, and are alarmed or worried because you have used or done the wrong thing and do not know what to do, read the following offer and start now, to stop your trouble.

350,000 TRIPLE SIZE BOTTLES TO BE DISTRIBUTED

COLLIER'S WEEKLY has over 350,000 paid subscribers, all of whom would find pleasure and benefit in the use of Cranitonic Hair Food, if they but knew how delightfully refreshing its use is to all who suffer from dandruff, itching scalp, falling hair. We have therefore empowered the Chief Chemist attached to our Laboratories to send to every reader of COLLIER'S WEEKLY, as an Introductory Offer, a Large Two Pound Physicians' Size, $3.00 bottle of Cranitonic Hair Food with two cakes of Cranitonic Shampoo Soap (regular price 50cts a cake) and one tube of cream (regular price $1.00) making $5.00 worth of the Greatest Hair and Scalp Food in the World, all for $1.00. Post Office and Express Money Orders, Checks and Drafts are Safer than Currency or Stamps. Any of the above can be sent.

CRANITONIC HAIR AND SCALP FOOD IS ABSOLUTELY PURE AND NON-ALCOHOLIC

Cranitonic Hair and Scalp Food destroys the microbe that causes dandruff and falling hair, and nourishes the hair-root back to health.

Cranitonic Hair and Scalp Food makes hair grow — prevents hair splitting — renders coarse hair soft and silky.

Cranitonic Hair and Scalp Food cleanses the scalp of all irritation and keeps it healthful. The life of the hair is in the scalp.

Cranitonic Hair and Scalp Food restores gray hair to its natural color, not by dyeing, but by gently stimulating the pigment cells that give color to the hair.

CRANITONIC HAIR AND SCALP FOOD is absolutely pure, harmless, contains no grease, no vulgar perfume, sediment, dye matter or dangerous drugs. It is pure, clean, clear as a crystal, delightful to use and certain in its results.

"Two years ago my hair was so badly burned that I was obliged to stay indoors. My doctor prescribed Cranitonic. The result was magical; the burned hair all came out and a healthy new growth took its place. My photo shows its present condition."
(MISS) LILLIAN M. TOTTEN.
No. 72 West 105th St., New York City.
March 10, 1903.

"The diagnosis made by the Chief Physician of your Medical Department was so accurate, his attention so courteous and the results of the Cranitonic Treatment so beneficial that I feel it my duty to write you and send photograph."
(MISS) L. MAE CRANSTON.
No. 248 West 24th St., New York City.
January 15, 1903.

"My success with Cranitonic has been so great that I feel if I could convince the public of the great benefits that can be obtained from its use that all persons with poor hair would at once adopt Cranitonic."
M. CAMILLE MULLER.
No. 862 Lafayette Avenue, Brooklyn, New York.
May 21, 1903.

"My hair was dry and brittle and falling out in an alarming manner. A friend suggested Cranitonic. Its use restored my hair to health. It is soft, strong and easy to arrange. I have recommended Cranitonic to many friends, all of whom praise it."
(MISS) JENNIE CUTHEL.
No. 728 East 139th St., New York City.
March 31, 1903.

For Sale by Dealers in—THREE SIZES—for One, Two and Five Dollars the Bottle. Sent to Any Point on Order. EXPRESS PREPAID

HAIR EDUCATION

All readers of COLLIER'S WEEKLY who are troubled about their hair and who would like a microscopic examination of their hair, and will call or send a few hairs pulled from the head, or a sample from the daily combings, will receive from our Medical Department, by mail, Absolutely Free, a full report and diagnosis.

HAIR-FOOD FREE

To enable the public to observe its Purity, Learn of its Possibilities and what it has done for others, a Trial bottle of Cranitonic Hair-Food and a book entitled Hair Education will be sent, by mail, prepaid, to all who send name and complete address, and Ten Cents in stamps or silver to pay postage.

CRANITONIC HAIR=FOOD CO., 526 WEST BROADWAY, NEW YORK

57 HOLBORN VIADUCT, LONDON, E. C.   (Incorporated May 6, 1899, under the Laws of New York State)   5 RUE DE LA PAIX, PARIS

Crani Tonic Hair-Food, 1903

Le Jade Perfume, 1916

Jonteel Face Cream, 1919

Ed. Pinaud's Hair Tonic, 1903

▶ *Rexall "93" Hair Tonic, 1906*

Rexall
"93" HAIR TONIC
Two Sizes, 50c. and $1.00

Keeps scalp and hair clean - promotes hair health
Your Money Back if it Doesn't

Sold and guaranteed by <u>Only One Druggist</u> in a place.   Look for *The* Rexall Stores

They are in nearly 3000 towns and cities in the United States and Canada

UNITED DRUG COMPANY. 43 TO 93 LEON STREET. BOSTON, MASS.

COLES PHILLIPS

PROPER Shampooing is what makes your hair beautiful. It brings out all the real life, lustre, natural wave and color, and makes it soft, fresh and luxuriant.

Your hair simply needs frequent and regular washing to keep it beautiful, but it cannot stand the harsh effect of ordinary soap. The free alkali, in ordinary soaps, soon dries the scalp, makes the hair brittle, and ruins it. This is why discriminating women use

WATKINS
MULSIFIED
COCOANUT OIL
FOR
SHAMPOOING

This clear, pure, and entirely greaseless product, cannot possibly injure, and does not dry the scalp or make the hair brittle, no matter how often you use it.

Two or three teaspoonfuls will cleanse the hair and scalp thoroughly. Simply moisten the hair with water and rub it in. It makes an abundance of rich, creamy lather, which rinses out easily, removing every particle of dust, dirt, dandruff and excess oil.

The hair dries quickly and evenly, and has the appearance of being much thicker and heavier than it is. It leaves the scalp soft and the hair fine and silky, bright, fresh-looking and fluffy, wavy and easy to do up.

You can get MULSIFIED COCOANUT OIL at any drug store, and a 50-cent bottle should last for months. Splendid for children.

If your druggist does not have it, an original bottle will be mailed direct upon receipt of price

THE R. L. WATKINS CO., Dept. F **CLEVELAND, OHIO**

Watkins Mulsified Cocoanut Oil, 1917

Watkins Mulsified Cocoanut Oil, 1918

Milo Violets, 1918

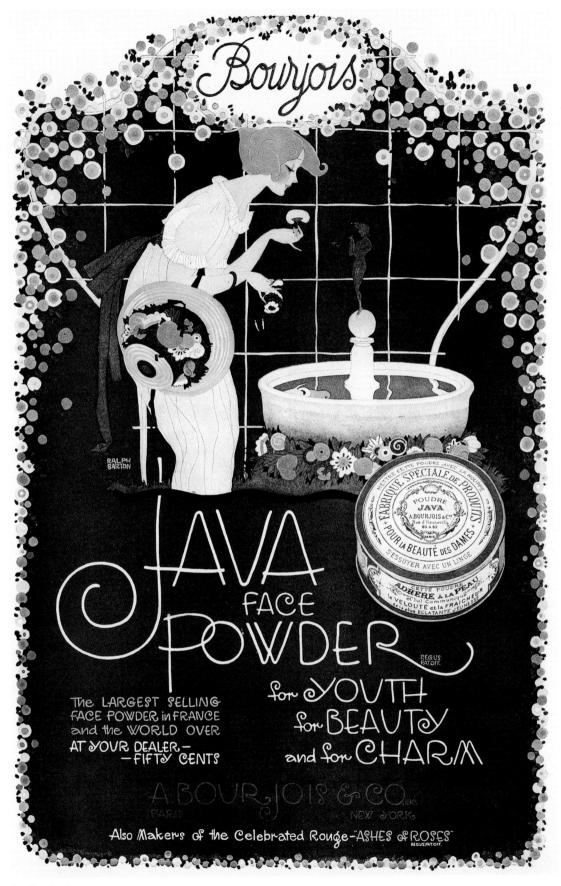

Java Face Powder, 1919

Tetlow's Pussywillow Powder, ca. 1917

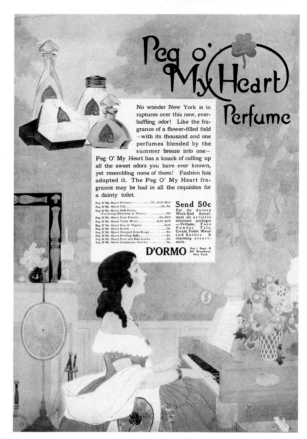

Peg O' My Heart Perfume, ca. 1919

Peg O' My Heart Perfume, 1915

Mavis Toiletries, 1919

Mavis Toiletries, 1919

Mavis Toiletries, 1918

Mavis Face Powder-Talc, 1918

Un Air Embaumé

Un Air Embaumé

— the exclusive perfume with a touch of the Orient — and a clinging atmosphere of distinction all its own.

Extract, Toilet Water, Face Powder, Solid Powder, and Rouge (in handsome metal case) Talcum Toilet Powder, Sachet, Vanity Case

At exclusive stores in America

Rigaud

16 Rue de la Paix, Paris

Rigaud Toiletries, 1918

Rigaud Mary Garden Perfume, 1918

Rigaud Un Air Embaumé Perfume, ca. 1914 ◀ *Fine Art Soap, 1900*

Armour's Sylvan Soup, 1912

© 1918 A. H. S. Co.

L'harmonie de la toilette

There is in the *Spécialités de Djer-Kiss* an appeal that is at once haunting and irresistible.

Pervaded with an individuality of Paris, they breathe a freshness, a charm, an *odeur délicate*, indescribably of France. The great *parfumeur* Kerkoff produces them in Extract, Face Powder, Toilet Water, Talc, Sachet, Végétale, *et* Soap. Let Madame embrace them all. In their entirety she will indeed achieve a veritable harmony of toiletry.

Djer-Kiss
Made in France only

EXTRACT · FACE POWDER
TOILET WATER · SACHET
TALC · SOAP · VÉGÉTALE

R.J. + E.D.FORKUM

Djer-Kiss Toiletries, 1918

Djer-Kiss Toiletries, 1918

FOR the bath, talc powder is almost as essential as soap. The silken touch of Williams' Talc, the delicate flower-fragrance that it imparts, are necessary to the fullest sense of delightful, cleanly comfort. And you can use it freely, for there is a more generous quantity in the Williams' can—qual- ity considered—than you get of any other powder. The hinged-top— opened or closed with a slight push of the thumb—prevents leakage and waste, and makes it very convenient to use.

Shaving soaps, talc powders, toilet soaps, toilet waters, dental cream and powder, cold cream and toilet luxuries.

Williams' Talc Powder

What is your favorite perfume in talc? Williams' has five— Violet, Carnation, English Lilac, Matinée and Rose—also Baby Talc. Send 4c. in stamps for sample of any of these, to
THE J. B. WILLIAMS COMPANY Glastonbury, Conn.

Williams' Talc, 1919

La Toilette Complète

"La France magnifique, ayant rejeté les chaînes de la guerre,
reprend en entier sa faculté de produire tout ce qui est beau."
—Kerkoff, Paris

Translation:—France the magnificent, having thrown off the shackles
of war, resumes to the full her ability to produce that which is beautiful.

EACH day we feel that we may more confidently assure you
that the supply of Djer-Kiss will be no longer uncertain—that
you will be able at all times to procure one and all the *Spé-*
cialités de Djer-Kiss—Extract, Face Powder, Talc, Sachet,
Toilet Water, Végétale, Soap *et*—*Rouge!

Voilà! There is now a new *Spécialité*—*Rouge—in a
dainty box. You will want, without delay, to add this new
Spécialité to your toilet table.

Si chic, si charmant, si français, the *Spécialités de Djer-Kiss!*

(*Rouge ONLY *prepared in America*)

ALFRED H. SMITH COMPANY　ᵧ　*Sole Importers,* NEW YORK

SEND FOR THESE SAMPLES

In return for fifteen cents, Monsieur Kerkoff's importateurs, the Alfred H. Smith
Co., of 40 West 34th Street, New York City, will be happy to send you samples
of Djer-Kiss Extract, Face Powder and Sachet.

Djer-Kiss
Made in France only

SMIRNOFF'S RUSSIAN SHAMPOO
adds a crowning touch to hair beauty. In quality
worthy of Djer-Kiss. Send for sample, 10c

A. H. S. Co.
1919

Djer-Kiss Toiletries, 1919

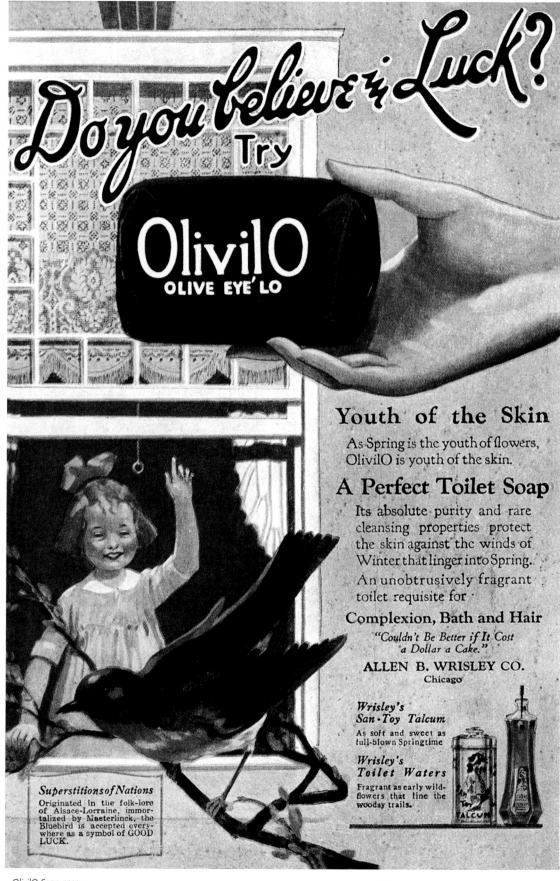

OlivilO Soap, 1919

Djer-Kiss Toiletries, 1918

Djer-Kiss Toiletries, 1918

Djer-Kiss Toiletries, 1917

Palmolive Soap, 1918

OlivilO Soap, 1919

Pompeian Massage Cream, 1914

Mennen's Violet Talcum Powder, 1913

Sempre Giovine Facial Soap, 1916

Pompeian Night Cream, 1917

Mennen's Borated Talcum, 1915

FAIRY SOAP

Do you, too, enjoy the refreshment of the pure, floating, oval cake? How freely it lathers— how agreeably it cleanses! Fairy soap adds real pleasure to toilet and bath.

THE N.K. FAIRBANK COMPANY

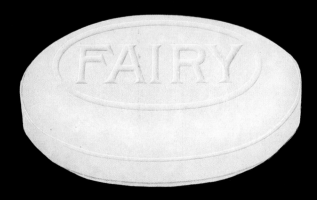

"Have you a little Fairy in your home?"

Fairy Soap, 1918

"The WOOL SOAP has come, Mama—
may we have our bath now?"

"BUBBLES"

PEARS' SOAP

Beautifies the complexion, keeps the hands white and imparts a constant bloom of freshness to the skin.

Pears' Annual for 1905 with 117 illustrations and three large Presentation Plates. The best Annual published — without any doubt. However, judge for yourself. Agents : The International News Company.

Wool Soap, 1914 ◀ *Pears' Soap, 1905*

FAIRY
SOAP

*For Toilet
and Bath*

SOAP

REFRESHING

FAIRY

WHITE, oval, floating—Fairy Soap combines purity and convenience with a fine cleansing quality that is most refreshing.

Its use adds real pleasure to toilet and bath.

THE N.K. **FAIRBANK** COMPANY

"Have you a little Fairy in your home?"

Fairy Soap, 1915

▶ *Mennen's Borated Talcum, 1909*

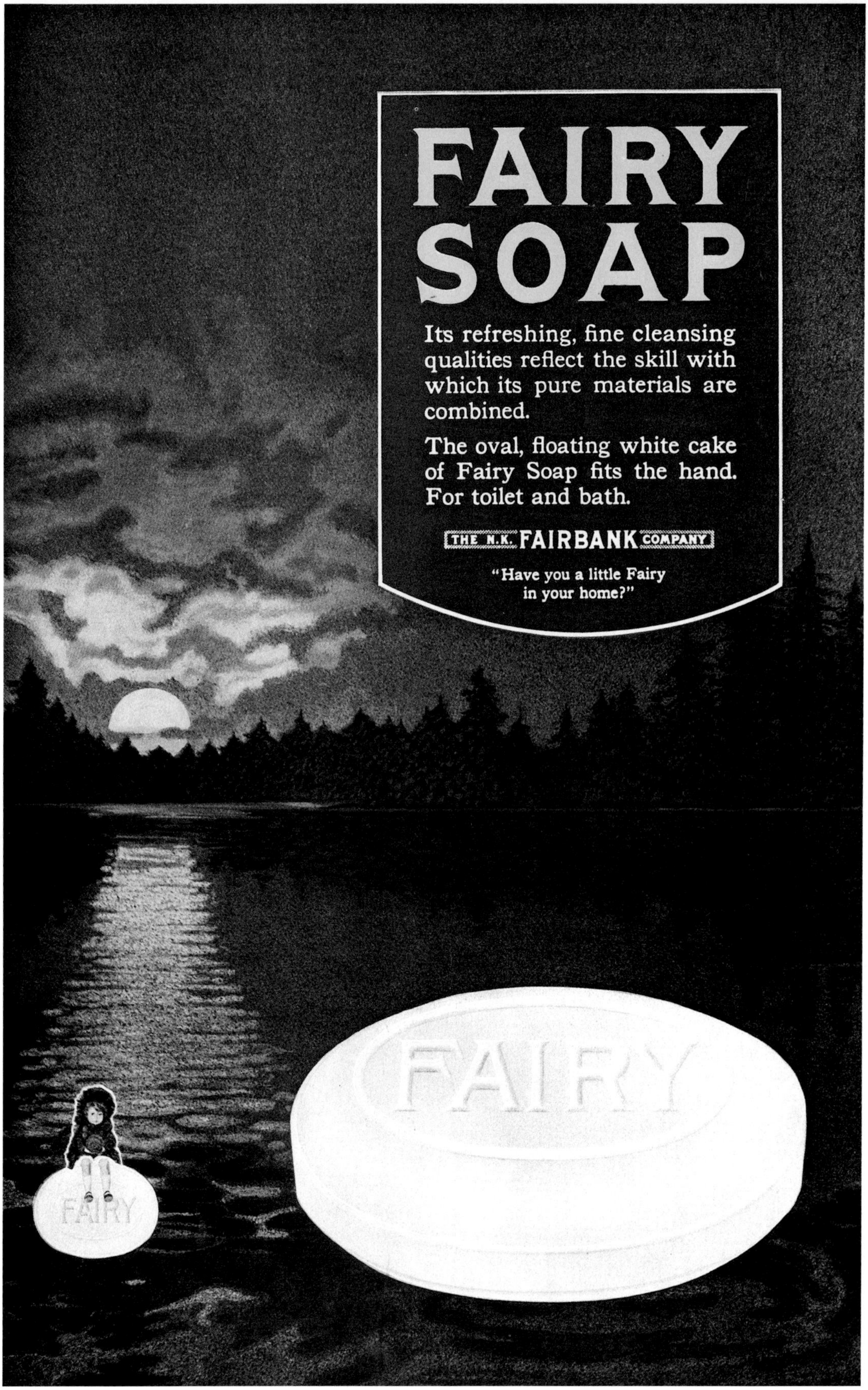

Fairy Soap, 1917

Fairy Soap, 1916

PEARS' SOAP

© WALTER JANVIER, 1918

"THE BEGINNING OF A GOOD COMPLEXION"

A beautiful full-color reproduction of this famous painting, together with a generous sample of Pears' Soap, will be sent anywhere in the United States for 10 cents in stamps.

THE picture is handsomely printed, without any advertising text, on an excellent quality of paper, 14 by 11 inches, suitable for mounting or framing. The sample of soap is illustrated below in actual size. It is big enough to let you make a really pleasant trial of Pears' Soap—so that you can appreciate its generous, free-flowing lather, its rapid, thorough cleansing and its delightful effect on the complexion.

"Good morning, have you used Pears' Soap?"

FULL SIZE CAKES

Unscented
17c a cake, $1.90 per doz.

Scented Glycerine
22c a cake, $2.50 per doz.

WALTER JANVIER, U. S. Agent for A. & F. Pears, Ltd., 419 Canal St., New York City

Dear Sirs: I enclose 10 cents in stamps for which send me color reproduction of painting and sample of soap as above.

Name

Address

Pears' Soap, 1919

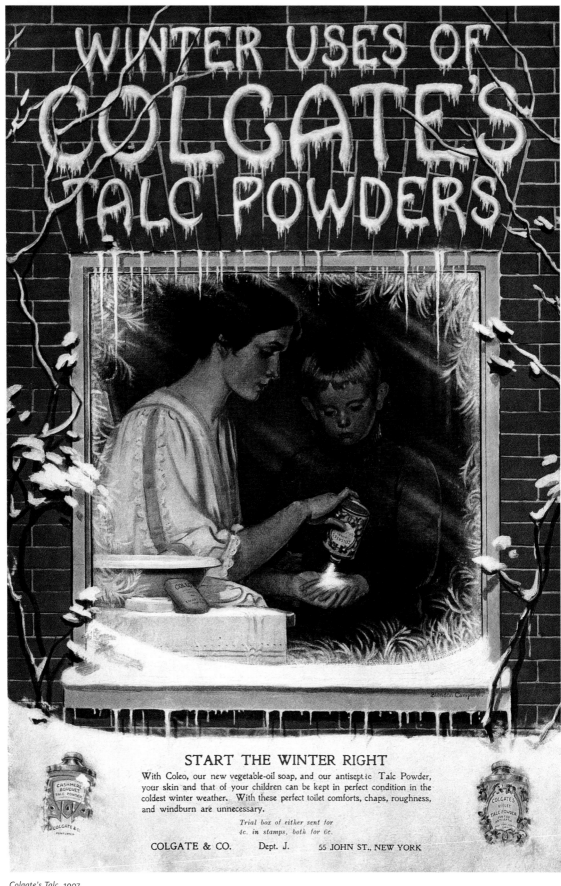

WINTER USES OF COLGATE'S TALC POWDERS

START THE WINTER RIGHT

With Coleo, our new vegetable-oil soap, and our antiseptic Talc Powder, your skin and that of your children can be kept in perfect condition in the coldest winter weather. With these perfect toilet comforts, chaps, roughness, and windburn are unnecessary.

Trial box of either sent for
4c. in stamps, both for 6c.

COLGATE & CO.   Dept. J.   55 JOHN ST., NEW YORK

Colgate's Talc, 1907

That Feeling
of
Delightful Cleanliness

The unquestioned purity, the transparency, the distinctive Rose perfume, fragrant yet elusive, impart a delightful charm to

KIRK'S

JAP ROSE
SOAP

Its instant lather, so smooth, creamy and "bubbly" leaves a satisfying feeling of perfect cleanliness and the *best* test of a toilet soap is how your skin "feels" after you have used it. .

All the resources of the great Kirk Laboratories, the purest oils and the most expensive perfumes have been called upon to make Jap Rose the premier toilet soap of America.

As a "Shampoo" it is a constant delight.

JAMES S. KIRK & COMPANY
Chicago, U. S. A.

TRIAL OFFER
Send 20c for an attractive Week-End Package containing four Jap Rose Miniatures, consisting of one each of Soap, Talcum Powder, Cold Cream and Toilet Water.

So Refreshing— Jap Rose Talcum Powder

Jap Rose Soap, 1918

Jap Rose Soap, 1919

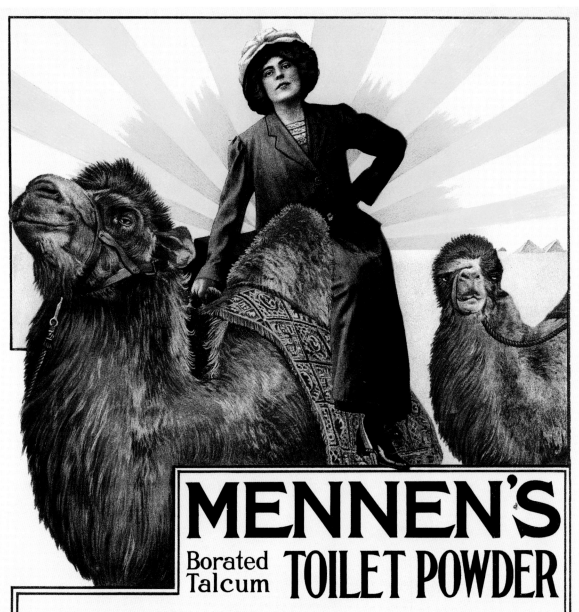

MENNEN'S
Borated Talcum TOILET POWDER

In Every Land

A can of MENNEN'S is an absolute traveling necessity. Due to its **antiseptic** and **antizymotic** properties, it gives instant relief to all **skin irritation** and such bodily discomfitures as travelers are subjected to.

MENNEN'S is the Pioneer Borated Talcum **Toilet Powder**, and is the recognized standard the world over. Use the **original**—avoid **over-medicated** substitutes.

Sample Box 4 Cents, Stamps

GERHARD MENNEN CO.

1 Orange Street   NEWARK, N. J.

Mennen's Borated Talcum, 1911

Garden Court Face Powder, 1919

Williams' Talc, 1919

Mennen's Borated Talcum, 1911

Mennen's Borated Talcum, 1906

MENNEN'S
BORATED TALCUM
TOILET POWDER

"The Sentiment of Sunburn"

soon dies when the summer season ends, and sober contemplation and the mirror reveal the harsh blending of spoiled complexion and the dainty toggeries of fall and winter functions. **Genuine**

MENNEN'S BORATED TALCUM TOILET POWDER

protects and improves the complexion and gives immediate relief from **Prickly Heat, Chafing, Sunburn,** and all skin troubles of summer. After **bathing** and after **shaving** it is refreshing and delightful. Put up in **non-refillable** boxes—the **"box that lox"**—for your protection. If **Mennen's** face is on the cover it's **genuine** and a **guarantee of purity.** Guaranteed under the Food and Drugs Act, June 30, 1906. Serial No. 1542. Sold everywhere, or by mail **25 cents.**

SAMPLE FREE

Gerhard Mennen Co., 1 Orange St., Newark, N. J.

Try Mennen's Violet (Borated) Talcum Toilet Powder. It has the scent of fresh-cut Parma Violets.
Sent free, for 2 cent stamp, to pay postage, one set of **Mennen's** Bridge Whist Tallies enough for six tables.

Mennen's Borated Talcum, 1907

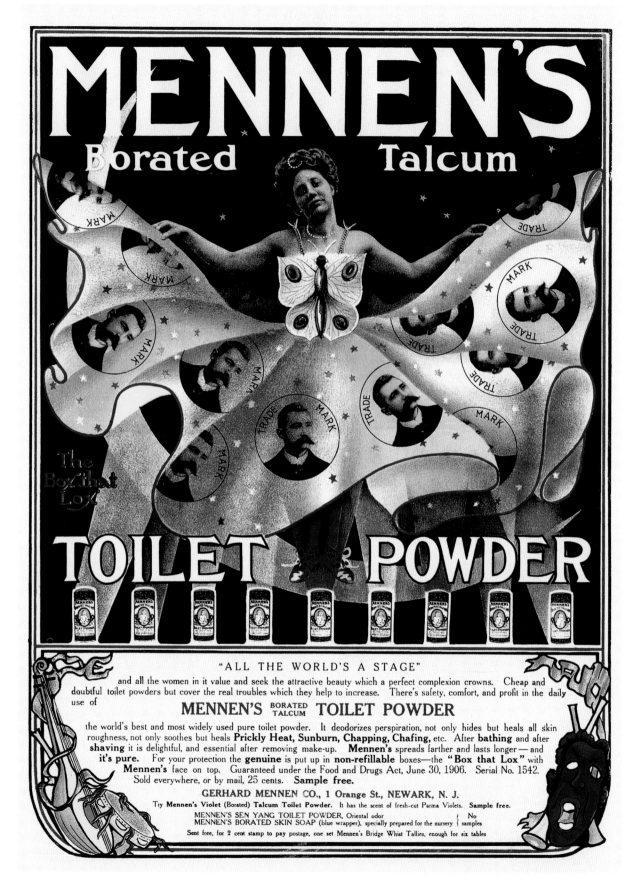

Mennen's Borated Talcum, 1908

"A skin you love to touch"
painted by Neysa McMein
Copyright 1917 by The Andrew Jergens Co.

Given away —

This beautiful picture for framing

Get it today from your druggist or at your toilet counter

THIS picture in exquisite colors and four times as large as shown here! Actual size 15 x 19 in. Reproduced on a fine quality antique paper by a special process which brings out exactly the beautiful colors of the original.

Painted by Neysa McMein, the popular artist, whose lovely women you see every month on the covers of your favorite magazines. This painting is her conception of "A skin you love to touch." Contains no printing or advertising of any kind. Get one while they last.

How to get it

Go to your dealer's today; buy a cake of Woodbury's Facial Soap, and he will give you without additional charge one of these beautiful pictures. Be sure to ask for it before

the supply is gone. Offer is good only until October 5th.

The daily use of Woodbury's Facial Soap will bring to your skin the charm of "A skin you love to touch." There is a Woodbury treatment just suited to the needs of your skin. A booklet giving them all comes with every cake of Woodbury's Facial Soap.

Get a cake and your picture today and begin at once to get the benefit of your Woodbury treatment. A 25c cake is sufficient for a month or 6 weeks. At every drug store and toilet goods counter in the United States and Canada.

If your dealer cannot supply you send us 25c and we will send the picture and the soap direct. Address **The Andrew Jergens Co., 110 Spring Grove Ave., Cincinnati, Ohio.**

If you live in Canada, address The Andrew Jergens Co., Ltd., 110 Sherbrooke St., Perth, Ontario.

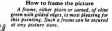

How to frame the picture
A frame, either plain or carved, of olive green with gilded edges, is most pleasing for this painting. Such a frame can be secured at any picture store.

Woodbury's Facial Soap, 1917

A·SKIN·YOU·LOVE·TO·TOUCH

Write today for this picture! See offer below

You, too, can have its charm if you will begin the following treatment tonight:

Just before retiring, lather your wash cloth well with Woodbury's Facial Soap and warm water. Apply it to your face and distribute the lather thoroughly. Now with the tips of your fingers work this cleansing, antiseptic lather into your skin, always with an upward and outward motion. Rinse with warm water, then with cold—the colder the better. Finish by rubbing your face for a few minutes with a *piece of ice*. Use this treatment persistently and in ten days or two weeks your skin should show a marked improvement—a promise of that greater loveliness which the daily use of Woodbury's always brings.

Send now for this beautiful picture

This new painting of "A Skin You Love to Touch," by Mary Greene Blumenschein, has been reproduced in nine colors, 15 x 19 inches, by a new and beautiful process. No printing or advertising appears on it. Just send us your name and address with 10c in stamps or coin, and we will mail you the picture, together with a cake of Woodbury's Facial Soap large enough for a week of the "skin you love to touch" treatment given here. Write today! Address **The Andrew Jergens Co., 430 Spring Grove Ave., Cincinnati, Ohio.**

If you live in Canada, for picture and sample address The Andrew Jergens Co., Ltd. 430 Sherbrooke St., Perth, Ontario, Canada

25c a cake. Get a cake today. For sale by dealers everywhere throughout the U. S. and Canada.

JOHN H. WOODBURY'S FACIAL SOAP For Skin, Scalp and Complexion.

Copyright 1916, The Andrew Jergens Co.

Woodbury's Facial Soap, 1916

▶ *Jap Rose Soap, 1917*

421

Ours
the Greater
Luxury

The luxury loving Greeks equipped the bath with extravagant accessories — but they lacked PALMOLIVE, the *famous modern luxury* for toilet, bath and shampoo. True, Palm and Olive oils were the favorite cleansing agents — but obtainable only in their crude natural state. Their scientific combination in the smooth, creamy PALMOLIVE lather is a triumph only twentieth century users know in

PALMOLIVE SOAP

The wholesome PALMOLIVE cake with its natural attractive color and agreeable faint fragrance is known to millions of users. Its perfect cleansing qualities originated the PALMOLIVE "doctrine of soap and water."

PALMOLIVE SHAMPOO—liquid PALMOLIVE—is equally popular. Its use constitutes a perfect means for thoroughly cleansing the hair—an essential for healthy growth. The Olive and Cocoanut Oils in this shampoo are unequalled ingredients of a perfect hair and scalp application. Our new Palmolive Booklet about the complete Palmolive Line, together with threefold sample package, will be mailed on receipt of 10 cents in stamps.

B. J. JOHNSON SOAP COMPANY, Inc., Milwaukee, Wis.
CANADIAN FACTORY: 155-157 George Street, Toronto, Ont.   (513)

Palmolive Soap, 1917 ◀   *Palmolive Soap, 1916*

425

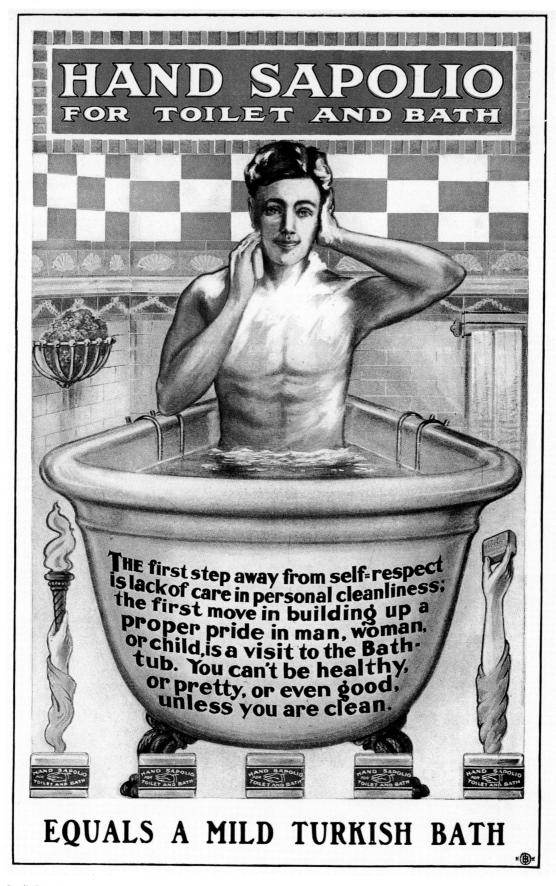

Sapolio Soap, 1900

If You had been a Princess 3000 Years ago

If you had lived when old Egypt was in her glory, Palm and Olive oils would have been your most valued toilet essential.

Now, modern progress gives you these two famous oils scientifically combined in the most popular cleanser this age knows.

The toilet lore of 30 centuries has found its fullest expression in the smooth creamy lather of

PALMOLIVE SOAP

Other Palmolive Products

Palmolive Shampoo
Palmolive Cream
Palmolive Powder
Palmolive Talcum
Palmolive Vanishing
Cream
Palmolive Shaving
Stick

PALMOLIVE

If your dealer cannot supply you with PALMOLIVE preparations write us, enclosing price of article desired. PALMOLIVE Shampoo, Creams and Powder are each fifty cents, Talcum or Shaving Stick, twenty five cents

B. J. JOHNSON SOAP CO., Inc.
MILWAUKEE, WISCONSIN
CANADIAN FACTORY 145-147 George Street Toronto Ontario

Palmolive Soap, 1916

▸ *Palmolive Soap, 1916*

Palmolive Soap, 1913

Palmolive Soap, 1919

Palmolive Soap, 1919

Colgate's Soap, 1919

Palmolive Shampoo, 1918

Kuppenheimer Uniforms, 1918

Kuppenheimer Clothes, 1907

Hart Schaffner & Marx Clothes, 1908

Kuppenheimer Beaufort Suit, 1916

Kuppenheimer Uniforms, 1917   ▸ *Hart Schaffner & Marx Clothes, 1916*

Copyright Hart Schaffner & Marx

Hart Schaffner & Marx

New Varsity Fifty Five
designs for Spring have
the style that young men
want.

Look for this picture in color, in the
window of the store that sells these clothes

PAINTED BY SAMUEL NELSON ABBOTT

Benjamin Clothes, 1909

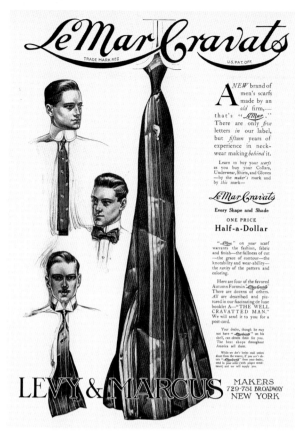

LeMar Cravats, 1909

Signal Shirts, 1915

OshKosh B'Gosh Overalls, 1915

Society Brand Clothes, 1919

Society Brand Clothes, 1919

Kuppenheimer Clothes, 1919

Tom Wye Knit Jackets, 1919

Mallory Hats, 1911

Mallory
CRAVENETTE HATS

Sun Proof

Rain Proof

STYLE and SERVICE

The Mallory Cravenette Hat is like the product of other first class hat makers in that it has unquestioned quality of material, refined shape and exclusive, correct style.

The Mallory Cravenette Hat is different

from all other hats whatsoever, because it has been made rain proof and sun proof by the Priestley Cravenetting process which we control for all hat fabrics.

All the approved shapes and styles in Derbies and Soft hats, $3.00, $3.50 and $4.00.

For sale everywhere by the better class of dealers. In Greater New York and Philadelphia by John Wanamaker.

Send to Dept. C for our Free Booklet of Hat Styles for 1907

E. A. MALLORY & SONS, Inc.
Established 1823
Astor Place and Broadway, New York
FACTORY, DANBURY, CONN.

Mallory Hats, 1907

Arrow Collars And Cluett Shirts, ca. 1916

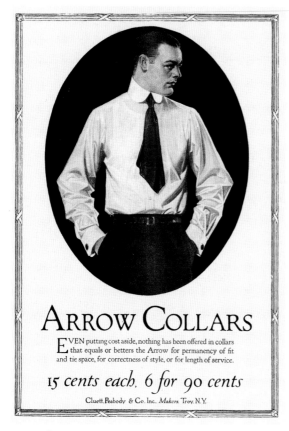

Arrow Collars, 1916

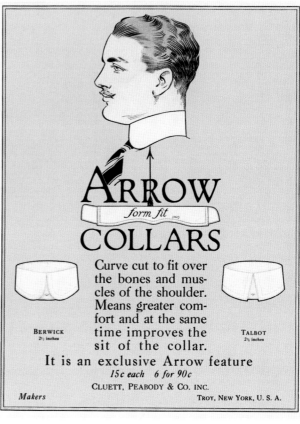

Arrow Collars, 1916

Lion Brand Collars, 1900

Arrow Collars, 1910

Cluett Shirts, 1911

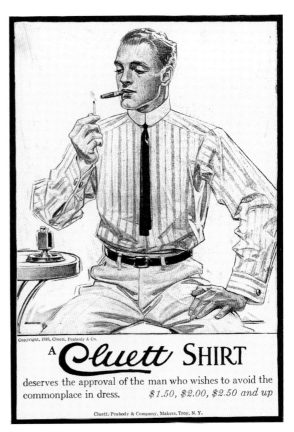

Cluett Shirts, 1910

Boston Garter Cord Type

Boston Garter Pad Type

C. COLES PHILLIPS

At Stores Everywhere
Lisle, 25 cents; Silk, 50 cents

George Frost Company
Makers   Boston

"EVERYMAN"

Boston Garter, 1911

▸ *Kuppenheimer Clothes, 1914*

Wick Hat Bands, 1908

B. V. D. Underwear, 1906

▶ B. V. D. Underwear, 1915

McCallum Hosiery, 1914

Luxite Hosiery, 1919

Beacon Falls Rubber Shoes, 1918

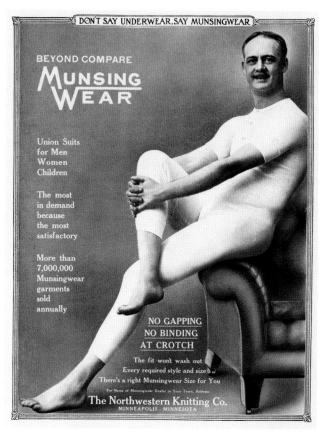

Munsingwear Underwear, 1913

Cooper's Underwear, ca. 1914

Everwear Hosiery, 1911

Boston Store Underwear, 1916

THE SEASON'S MOST ATTRACTIVE FOOTWEAR

6K105. Women's Ocean Pearl Gray Kid, high cut lace shoe. 2½ to 7. D and E. Pair............ **$3.79**

6K107. Women's Golden Brown Kid High Cut Lace Shoe. 2½ to 7. D and E. Pair............ **$3.79**

6K103. Women's All White Kid High Cut Lace Shoe. Half Louis leather heel. 2½ to 7. D-E. Pair............ **$3.79**

FASHION'S VERY NEWEST FANCY

6K109. An Attractive Offering. Women's Stylish Two-Tone Lace Kid Shoes with Neutral Gray Vamp and pearl gray top. Flexible leather sole. Half Louis leather heel. 2½ to 7. D and E. Per pair................. **$3.79**

PROPERTY OF ROGER J. WEINBERG

6K110. Women's Tuxedo Shoe. Black Kid Vamp and Pearl Gray Top. Dome top. 2½ to 7. D and E. Pair............ **$3.79**

6K111. Women's Tuxedo Shoe. Black Kid Vamp and White Kid Top. Dome top. 2½ to 7. D and E. Pair............ **$3.79**

A FAVORITE STYLE IN A SHOE OF QUALITY

6K102. The Vamp of this Stylish Tuxedo Shoe Is Made of Kid in the new Field Mouse shade with champagne kid top. Dome top. Half Louis heel. An exceptional value. 2½ to 7. D and E. Pair................. **$3.79**

6K104. Women's All Bronze Kidskin High Cut Lace Shoe. Goodyear welt sewed soles. Half Louis leather heel. 2½ to 7. D and E. Pair............ **$3.79**

6K108. Women's Ivory Kid High Cut Lace Shoe. Goodyear welt sewed soles. Half Louis leather heel. 2½ to 7. D and E. Pair............ **$3.79**

6K106. Women's Ivory Kid Button Shoe. Goodyear welt sewed soles. Half Louis heel. 2½ to 7. D and E. Pair............ **$3.79**

6K101. A New Fall Pattern in a Patent Leather High Cut Lace Shoe with ivory kid top. Half Louis leather heel. 2½ to 8. D and E. Pair............ **$3.79**

6K100. Women's All Black Kidskin High Cut Lace Shoe. Flexible leather sole. Half Louis heel. 2½ to 8. D and E. Pair............ **$3.79**

Boston Store Chicago

Boston Store Footwear, 1916

450   Fashion & Beauty

The Christmas Charm of "Comfy" Slippers

COMFY slippers make welcome Christmas gifts for every member of the family. The soft COMFY soles make everyone want to wear COMFYS more than ordinary slippers.

The variety of colors and the beautiful finish satisfy the most critical woman. There are colors and color combinations to match her semi-negligee.

COMFYS are a capital gift to make a man forget the early morning chill of cold floors, and lend restfulness to the after-dinner lounge. Just the thing to wear on the way to the bath or while shaving. Convenient, too, for travelling.

Children's slippers are carved with novel designs that make them as fascinating as new toys.

COMFYS are packed in attractive boxes which greatly add to their desirability as Christmas presents.

Send for our new catalog No. 32, illustrating our complete line of COMFYS. Buy COMFY slippers at your dealer's. If he does not sell COMFYS, do not buy ordinary felt slippers, but send your order to us. Enclose price, state size and color desired and give your dealer's name.

We make a complete line of felt shoes and slippers with stiff leather sole and heel. If you are interested in this kind of footwear, ask for our catalog "W."

This scroll trade-mark guarantees you the genuine Daniel Green COMFY with the COMFY cushion sole. This is your protection. Look for it in the slipper.

DANIEL GREEN FELT SHOE COMPANY
74 Lincoln Street
Boston, Massachusetts

"Comfy" Slippers, 1914

A Stylish Shoe That Is Really Comfortable

An enjoyable sensation of elegance and ease is always experienced when a Dr. A. Reed Cushion Shoe is slipped on the foot. Offered in the newest designs and most fashionable shapes, they satisfy the style requirements of the most fastidious.

Dr. A. Reed Cushion Shoes
For Men & Women
The Original and Genuine Cushion Shoes

afford an unequaled degree of comfort. The cushion insole, on which the foot rests as luxuriously as on a velvet rug, absorbs every shock to the body. It keeps the feet from experiencing any extremes of weather and eliminates the discomfort of "breaking in" new shoes.

John Ebberts Shoe Co. and J. P. Smith Shoe Co. are pioneer makers of cushion shoes and exclusive manufacturers of the genuine Dr. A. Reed Cushion Shoes for men and women.

The trade-mark, stamped on the sole of every Dr. A. Reed Cushion Shoe, is your assurance that you are procuring the real article—perfectly made of first-quality leather and materials.

We have a dealer in nearly every city. Write us by his name and a cross-section showing the construction of the genuine Dr. A. Reed Cushion Sole. Address either maker.

JOHN EBBERTS SHOE CO.	J. P. SMITH SHOE CO.
BUFFALO	CHICAGO
Makers of Women's Shoes	Makers of Men's Shoes

Dr. A. Reed Cushion Shoes, 1917

For Girls BUSTER BROWN SHOES For Boys of 2 to 16

Fit For Life's Service

The last shapes the shoe. The shoe shapes the growing foot. The foot consequently assumes the shape of the last.

The Brown Shaping Lasts—upon which Buster Brown Shoes are made—are scientific reproductions, at every age from 2 to 16, of feet correctly developed for endurance.

Buster Brown Shoes therefore properly support and develop the feet through the formative years—insure a graceful carriage—and prevent weak feet, cramped bones, broken arches, and other foot ailments.

Fit your boys and girls for life's service by fitting their feet with Buster Brown Shoes. $3.00, $3.50, $4.00 and up, at all good stores in the United States.

Write today for a free copy of "Training the Growing Feet," the standard authority on correct foot development. Address Brown Shoe Company, Exclusive Manufacturers, St. Louis, U. S. A.

Buster Brown Shoes, 1918

SAFE SHOES

Style 691
This comfortable and dressy Oxford is made of Sorosis kid with front and tip of patent leather. Its heel is 1⅝ inches high.

SOROSIS Safe Shoes

are so fashioned that they cannot injure the feet that wear them. Some shoes are really **dangerous** because they do not conform to natural lines of normal feet but do conform to eccentric lines and oddities of shape that happen to be considered highly fashionable.

The SOROSIS SHOE ESTABLISHMENT

produces many millions of the most intelligently made **Safe Shoes** and it also produces the most distinctly fashionable shoes that are in the market.

Sorosis Stores
New York : James McCreery & Co., 23rd St.
Brooklyn : Cor. Fulton & Hoyt Sts.
Baltimore : 19 Lexington St., W.
Washington : 1213 F St.
Boston : 20 Temple Place & 176 Boylston St.
Chicago : 39 Washington St.
Cincinnati : 6 West Fourth St.
Detroit : Newcomb-Endicott Co.
San Francisco : 216 Post St., & 30 Third St.
Buffalo : H. A. Meldrum Co.
Philadelphia : 1314 Chestnut St.
Pittsburg : Penn Ave. & 5th St. & 214 6th St.

and Departments :
Cleveland : 177 Euclid Ave.
Milwaukee : 93 Wisconsin St.
St. Paul : Field, Schlick & Co.
Denver : 828 16th St.
Hartford : 945 Main St.
Providence : The Shepard Co.
St. Louis : Scruggs, Vandervoort & Barney D. G. Co.
Minneapolis : 712 Nicollet Ave.

London Shops : Regent House, Regent Street, W. ;
59 Westbourne Grove, W. ; 183 Brompton Road, S. W. ;
all large cities in Europe and America.

Sorosis Safe Shoes, 1905

▸ *Luxite Hosiery, 1918*

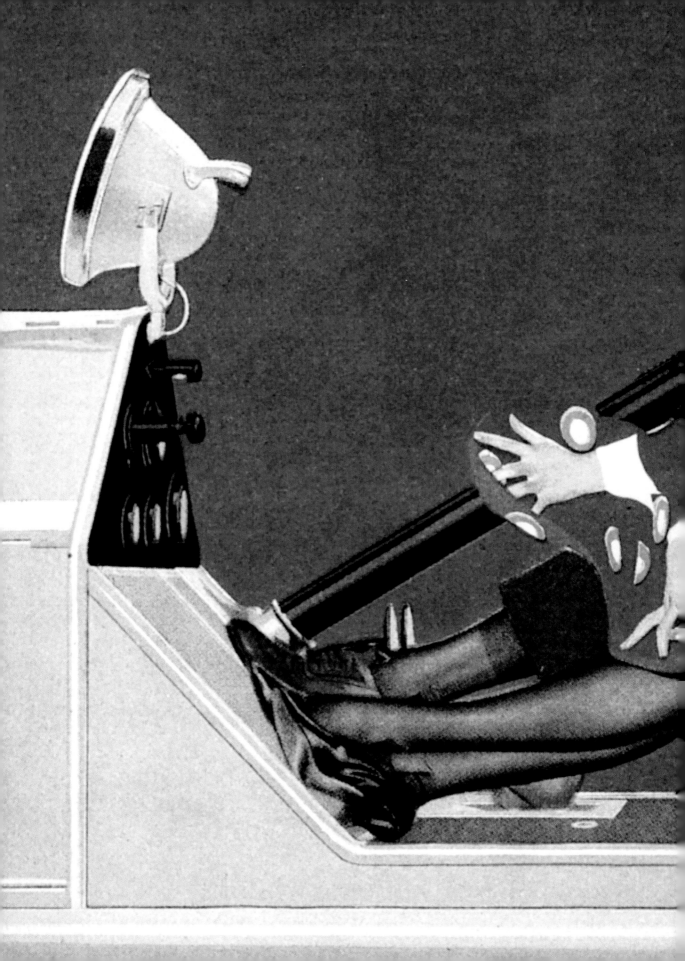

Interesting Booklet
Sent on Request

"You just know she wears them"

McCallum Hosiery Company
Northampton, Mass.

McCallum Hosiery, 1917

▸ American Lady Shoes, 1906

Holeproof Hosiery

—for dress wear

"HOLEPROOF" for men and for women are soft—light weight—stylish—attractive—and perfection in fit.

They are made in twelve colors, ten weights and five grades for men—two colors, two weights and three grades for women.

The best of these grades will grace any ball room. They are sheer, silky and soft as any cotton hose ever made, yet six pairs are guaranteed six months.

Holeproof in Silk for Men and Women—Guaranteed

Holeproof for men may be had in silk at $2 for three pairs guaranteed three months—and in silk for women at $3 for three pairs, guaranteed three months.

Don't judge Holeproof by common guaranteed hosieries. Holeproof is the *original*. Thirty-eight years of hose-making experience go into every pair.

We use only the best Egyptian and Sea Island Cotton, costing an average of seventy cents per pound. Some makers pay only thirty cents. Our yarn is long-fibre, light weight and soft but strong. Cheap yarn is cumbersome, heavy and coarse—so are common guaranteed hosieries.

We spend $55,000 a year just to inspect Holeproof Hose—merely to see that each pair is without a blemish. You can depend on the *genuine* Holeproof—wear them on any occasion and have trim-looking smoothly clad ankles and feet. Dancing pumps cannot wear holes in the heels or the toes.

Are Your Hose Insured?

The genuine bear the trade mark and the signature of Carl Freschl, Pres., shown below. Always look for this identification. If it is not on the toe of each pair the hose are not genuine —no matter who says so.

Prices range from $1.50 up to $6.00 for six pairs, guaranteed six months.

The genuine Holeproof are sold in your town. We'll tell you the dealers' names on request, or ship direct where we have no dealer, charges prepaid on receipt of remittance. Write for free book, "How To Make Your Feet Happy."

HOLEPROOF HOSIERY COMPANY
856 Fourth Street   Milwaukee, Wis.

Carl Freschl Pres

Luxite Hosiery

$\mathcal{T}$HERE is a feeling of luxury and of elegance, a knowledge of being well groomed that comes with the wearing of Luxite Hosiery.

Rich, lustrous and beautiful, the product of finest materials and pure dyes — Luxite is the logical associate of fine clothes.

For men, women and children. Silk, Lusterized Lisle and Cotton. Moderate prices.

Ask for Luxite at your favorite store, or write for descriptive book and price list.

LUXITE TEXTILES, Inc., 629 Fowler St., Milwaukee, Wis.
Makers of High Grade Hosiery Since 1875
New York, Chicago, San Francisco, Liverpool
LUXITE TEXTILES OF CANADA, Limited, London, Ont.

© L. T. Inc.

Luxite Hosiery, ca. 1917

Lord & Taylor

Wholesale Distributors

"ONYX" HOSIERY

Provides the full measure of satisfaction which the experienced purchaser demands—
with the comforting assurance that every hosiery requisite can be easily supplied in the "ONYX" brand—designs—fabrics—styles of highest quality.
These inspire confidence which means the selection of "ONYX"
Hose for all future occasions.   Sold at all leading shops.

Broadway   New York

LOOK FOR THIS
TRADE-MARK
ON EVERY PAIR

LOOK FOR THIS
TRADE-MARK
ON EVERY PAIR

"Onyx" Hosiery, 1907

COLES PHILLIPS

©L. T. Inc.

Hose of Luxite

For Men, Women and Children

HOSIERY, today, is regarded more important to the charm of personal appearance than ever before. Look your best—not on state occasions only—but *always;* that is the modern idea.

Hose of Luxite have the spirit of luxury—yet they are not extravagant. Shapely, shimmering and closely-woven—the product of beautiful materials, pure dyes and specialized methods.

Long wear and elegance are combined in inseparable union.

In Japanese Pure Silk: Men's, 50c per pair; Women's, $1.00, $1.10 and $1.50.

Other styles in Gold-Ray (scientific silk), lisle and cotton. Prices as low as 25c per pair, for Men, Women and Children.

Ask your dealer to supply you. If he cannot do so, write for price list and descriptive booklet today.

LUXITE TEXTILES, Inc., 617 Fowler Street, MILWAUKEE, Wis.

Makers of High-Grade Hosiery Since 1875

New York   Chicago   San Francisco   Liverpool

A beautiful color print of the above painting by Coles Phillips,
size 12x11 inches, will be sent upon receipt of 15 cents in stamps

Luxite Hosiery, 1917

Painted by Coles Phillips for Luxite Textiles, Inc.

© L. T. Inc.

Hose as Shapely as the Curves of the Figure

THE translucent shimmer of Luxite Hosiery half reveals and half conceals. Its texture is so wonderfully soft and silken you can draw a Luxite silk stocking through your finger ring. Luxite launders beautifully because these hose contain no adulterations whatever — nothing but super-fine materials and pure dyes. Naturally Luxite Hosiery wears long and always looks beautiful.

Women's Silk Faced, $1.10; Pure Thread Japanese Silk, $1.30 to $2.25. Other styles 55c upward.
Men's Silk Faced, 65c; Pure Thread Japanese Silk, 85c and $1.10. Other styles 35c up. Children's, 55c up.

LUXITE TEXTILES, Inc., 654 Fowler Street, Milwaukee, Wisconsin

New York   Chicago   San Francisco   *Makers of High Grade Hosiery Since 1875*   Liverpool, England   Sydney, Australia

LUXITE TEXTILES OF CANADA, Limited, London, Ont.

(984)

COLES PHILLIPS

Luxite Hosiery, 1919

Painted by Coles Phillips for Luxite Textiles, Inc.

COLES PHILLIPS

© L. T. Inc.

Luxite Hosiery

For Men, Women and Children

SELDOM does your hosiery escape the attention of others, and if it be this captivating Luxite, wherever you go admiration follows.

Luxite has proved that silk hose will wear splendidly when made as we make Luxite, using the finest Japanese silk thread of many tightly spun strands, and pure dyes that cannot injure either the silk or your feet.

Men's Silk Faced 50c, and Pure Thread Silk 75c and $1.00. Other styles at 35c up. Women's Pure Thread Silk $1.10 to $2.50. Other styles 50c up. Children's 50c per pair and up.

Ask for Luxite Hosiery in the stores. If you cannot conveniently get it, write us for directions and illustrated book and prices.

LUXITE TEXTILES, Inc., 654 Fowler Street, Milwaukee, Wis.
Makers of High Grade Hosiery Since 1875

New York   Chicago   San Francisco   Liverpool, England   Sydney, Australia
LUXITE TEXTILES OF CANADA, Limited, London, Ont.

(975)

Luxite Hosiery, 1918

Created by Bulloz of Paris

COLES PHILLIPS

For description see page 57

Bulloz Of Paris, 1917

▸ *Butterick Dress Patterns, 1906*

Chase Robes will outwear—many times over—other woven fabric robes.

Beautiful—Wonderful fast colorings—original and unique designs.

Comfortable—Shields you like the coat of fur given by Mother Nature.

Sanitary—Not easily soiled—the hair being smooth, does not attract or hold dirt or germs.   Clean—a simple shaking removes dust.

Say "Chase" to your merchant

"A Friend Indeed"

Chase Motor Car Robes, 1917

Kenyon Coats And Suits, ca. 1918

Kleinert's

Millinery for Mermaids

WHAT captivating bits of mermaid millinery are these gaily-bobbing caps and bonnets that enchant feminine hearts with their becomingness.

Fashion's most exclusive bathing beaches are colorful with Kleinert caps, hats and bonnets, in styles to suit every bathing costume.

Insist on the Kleinert name for service.

I. B. KLEINERT RUBBER CO.

719-727 Broadway   New York

Canadian Office:
84 Wellington St., W., Toronto

*Makers of Dress Shields, Bathing Caps,
Hose Supporters, Baby Pants, etc.*

Kleinert's Bathing Caps, 1919

Tom Wye Bathing Suits, ca. 1919

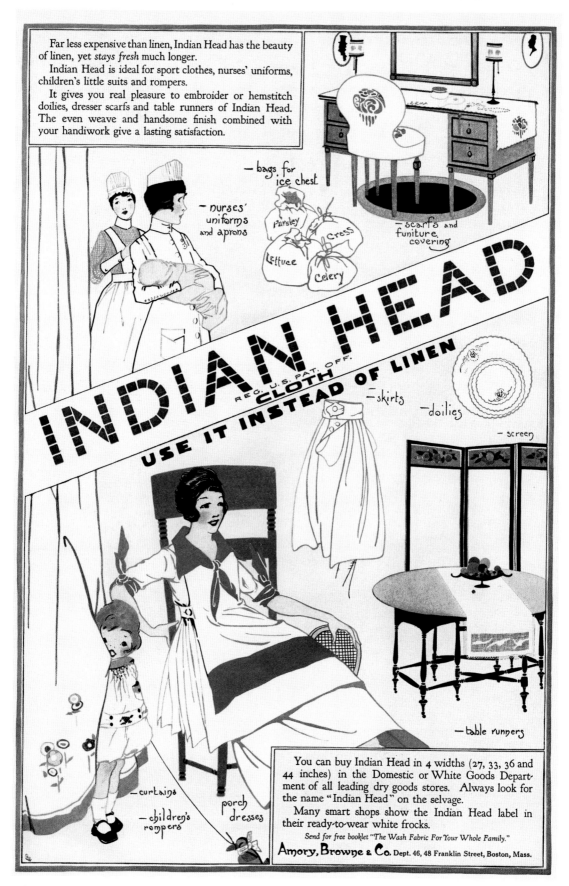

Far less expensive than linen, Indian Head has the beauty of linen, yet *stays fresh* much longer.

Indian Head is ideal for sport clothes, nurses' uniforms, children's little suits and rompers.

It gives you real pleasure to embroider or hemstitch doilies, dresser scarfs and table runners of Indian Head. The even weave and handsome finish combined with your handiwork give a lasting satisfaction.

— bags for ice chest

— nurses' uniforms and aprons

Parsley

Cress

Lettuce

Celery

— scarfs and funiture covering

INDIAN HEAD
REG. U.S. PAT. OFF.
CLOTH
USE IT INSTEAD OF LINEN

— skirts

— doilies

— screen

— table runners

— curtains

— children's rompers

porch dresses

You can buy Indian Head in 4 widths (27, 33, 36 and 44 inches) in the Domestic or White Goods Department of all leading dry goods stores. Always look for the name "Indian Head" on the selvage.

Many smart shops show the Indian Head label in their ready-to-wear white frocks.

Send for free booklet "The Wash Fabric For Your Whole Family."

Amory, Browne & Co. Dept. 46, 48 Franklin Street, Boston, Mass.

Indian Head Fabric, 1918

Vogue Magazine, 1912

Luxite Hosiery, 1919

Naiad Dress Shields, 1912

Boston Store Women's Wear, 1916

Cheney Silks, 1918

Indian Head Fabric, 1918

Kalburnie Zephyr Gingham, 1919

Kilburnie Zephyr Gingham, 1918

Indian Head Fabric, 1918

The Girl in the Picture

is wearing a very smart Tuxedo Sweater with White Vestee. It was designed in the Minerva Studios. It is not one whit more attractive, however, than the many charming and practical suggestions fully described and pictured in the Minerva Knitting Book.

This Manual has been termed "A Masterpiece of Knitting Literature." It contains more than 100 novel and beautiful articles of wear and adornment, with complete and simple instructions for their making.

It is the wonderful loftiness and finish of

MINERVA WORSTED YARNS

that make these designs so appealing — and it is their quality, richness of color and exceptional strength which make MINERVA the invariable choice of women who knit.

MINERVA WORSTED YARNS are scientifically wound on a large ball — its uncoil as smooth and easy as that of silken thread.

Stores that give QUALITY first place carry MINERVA YARNS and the MINERVA KNITTING BOOK. If you cannot obtain them, communicate with us direct. Sales price of the MINERVA KNITTING BOOK, 35 cents — or postpaid by us, 40 cents.

A Bulletin, giving full directions for knitting this fascinating Vestee-Sweater and several other new and fetching designs, will be sent free upon request.

JAMES LEES & SONS CO.
BRIDGEPORT   DEPT. L   PENNA.

Merchants who wish to display MINERVA YARNS this Spring will please communicate at once and request samples. Only a limited number of accounts will be added to our list.

Look for the Trade-Marked Label   It's on the Band of Every Ball

FLATO STUDIO

Minerva Yarns, 1919

Indian Head Fabric, 1919

Fleisher Yarns, 1919

Niagara Maid Underwear, ca. 1908

Rit Fabric Dye, 1919

THE exquisite style and sheer loveliness of the WOLFHEAD UNDERGARMENTS are equalled only by their practical economy. These are days when women have neither time nor money to waste on garments that do not give full service and satisfaction.

WOLFHEAD designs for nightgowns, petticoats, envelope chemise and camisoles embody the most pleasing and most advanced fashion ideas.

They are skilfully cut from superior materials, and trimmed with fine embroideries, imported laces and the daintiest ribbons.

In making them, the most expert and painstaking needlework is employed —you will find no raw edges or careless finishing. And they always fit perfectly. Look for the WOLFHEAD label in every garment.

At the best stores and shops you will find a complete selection of the newest WOLFHEAD styles, at very moderate prices.

If your dealer can not show them to you, write for the name of the nearest store handling them.

THE WOLF COMPANY
Fifth Avenue
New York City

WOLFHEAD
Undergarments

Wolfhead Undergarments, 1918

YOU can feel the very buoyancy and freshness of the Spring in the new WOLFHEAD nightgowns, petticoats, envelopes and camisoles.

The models are graceful and smart. Only fine, firm fabrics are used, which keep their shape through many launderings. For the trimming—there are unusual laces and embroideries, with ribbons of exquisite hues.

Clever needlework and thorough inspection bring every garment to perfection in fit and finish.

You will find a wide variety of WOLFHEAD styles at good shops. Write to us for the name of the dealer nearest you.

Look for the WOLFHEAD label in every garment

THE WOLF COMPANY
Fifth Avenue, New York City

WOLFHEAD
Undergarments

Wolfhead Undergarments, 1919

"Lady Sealpax"

Athletic Underwear for Every Woman

REG. U.S. PAT. OFF.

Poucher

Just as Comfortable as brother's

Lady Sealpax; a better, cooler underwear for women—sold in a cleaner way

LADY SEALPAX is *your* underwear—every woman's underwear—because it really does give you the same "Free as the Air" feeling that "brother" enjoys—and it really does combine luxurious comfort with graceful fit.

Just slip into *Lady Sealpax!* It's a revelation in women's underwear—dainty, sensible, serviceable.

Made of soft, fine fabrics. Drawer just the proper width, athletic armholes, ventilated waistband and elastic backband—all comfort features.

Ask for *Lady Sealpax.* It always comes in a sanitary container (as illustrated)— immaculately fresh and clean. Sold at popular prices.

If your favorite shop does not sell Lady Sealpax write us for descriptive booklet and send your dealer's name.

Sealpax

COPYRIGHT 1918   The Sealpax Company, Baltimore, Md. (also makers of Sealpax Athletic Underwear for Men)

Lady Sealpax Underwear, 1919

Redfern Whalebone Corsets, 1910

Munsingwear Underwear, 1917

W. B. Reduso Corsets, 1911

Warner's Rust-Proof Corsets, 1910

479

Carter's Knit Underwear, 1918

Madewell Underwear, 1919

Crompton Corduroy, 1918

Crompton Corduroy, 1919

Carter's Knit Underwear, 1917

And the winner is...

Too Hot to Handle

The slim body beautiful was not a mainstream concept in the first decades of the twentieth century. The streamlined ideal of the flapper figure had yet to enter the national arena, but there is no doubt that tools like this restrictive rubber garment would hardly encourage lifestyle change. The idea of sweating away pounds while encased in latex may have been revolutionary for the time, but this novelty quickly passed as its more torturous aspects became apparent to consumers.

Extraheißer Gummifummel

Der superschlanke Körper war in den ersten Jahrzehnten des 20. Jahrhunderts noch kein allgemein verbreitetes Schönheitsideal. Die stromlinienförmige Traumfigur des 20er-Jahre-Flapper-Girl war noch nicht auf der überregionalen Bühne aufgetaucht, aber es scheint eindeutig, dass es nicht Hilfsmittel wie dieses beengende Kleidungsstück aus Gummi waren, die zu den Veränderungen im Lebensstil führten. Die Vorstellung, sich eingezwängt in Latex die Pfunde vom Leib zu schwitzen, mag damals revolutionär gewesen sein, doch verschwand dieses Trendprodukt ganz schnell wieder in der Versenkung, als den Käuferinnen der mangelnde Tragekomfort bewusst wurde.

Une vraie torture

Le concept de la minceur comme critère de beauté n'avait pas encore fait son chemin dans l'esprit du public au début du XXe siècle. L'idéal esthétique de la garçonne devait encore faire son apparition sur la scène nationale, mais il ne fait aucun doute que des accessoires comme ces vêtements comprimant en caoutchouc auraient difficilement pu faire accepter un nouveau style de vie. L'idée de maigrir en transpirant engoncé dans du latex était peut-être révolutionnaire pour l'époque, mais cette nouveauté fut rapidement abandonnée lorsque les consommateurs découvrirent le côté douloureux de la chose.

Muertas de calor

Las mujeres de cuerpos estilizados no eran un canon de belleza en las primeras décadas del siglo xx. De hecho, el ideal de las «chicas del charlestón» tardaría en irrumpir en la sociedad estadounidense, pero no cabe duda de que herramientas como esta prenda restrictiva de caucho alentarían ese cambio en el estilo de vida. La idea de quitarse los kilos a base de sudar, enfundadas en látex, tal vez pareciera revolucionaria en la época, pero la novedad no tardó en desaparecer del mercado en cuanto las consumidoras descubrieron que se trataba de una verdadera tortura.

着るにはアツすぎる

20世紀初期、スリムな身体の美しさは主流なコンセプトではなかった。流線型で理想的なフラッパー体型はまだ全国的になっていなかったが、このゴム製衣料品のような拘束的な道具が生活様式の変化を促進することはほとんどなかった。ラテックスに包まれている間に汗をかいて痩せるという考え方はこの時代革命的だったが、あまりにも苦しいことが消費者に明らかになるにつれて、この新製品はすぐに消えてしまった。

FAT-

That part of the body of male or female, opposed to a good figure, uncomfortable, and useless, but which can be easily and speedily

REDUCED BY WEARING

Dr. Jeanne Walter's

Famous Medicated

Rubber Garments

These garments are made either to cover the entire body or any part. The results from their use are quick and they are absolutely safe, being endorsed by leading physicians. Used by Athletes, Jockeys, etc., the world over.

Neck and Chin Bands . $3.00
Chin only $2.00

Also Union Suits, Stockings, Jackets, etc., for the purpose of reducing the flesh anywhere desired. Invaluable to those suffering from rheumatism. Write at once for further particulars.

Dr. JEANNE WALTER, Dept. U.
Inventor and Patentee 45 West 34th St. NEW YORK.

Representatives

Philadelphia, Mrs. Kammerer, 1029 Walnut Street
San Francisco, Adele Millar Co., 166 Geary Street
Chicago, E. Burnham, 138 North State Street.

Dr. Jeanne Walter's Rubber Garments, 1912

Cream Of Wheat, 1910

Cream Of Wheat, 1905

Armour Food Products, 1917 ◀ Cream Of Wheat, 1907

Cream Of Wheat, 1915

Cream Of Wheat, 1909

Cream Of Wheat, 1910

Cream Of Wheat, 1909

Cream Of Wheat, 1912

Cream Of Wheat, 1906

"AH' RECKON AS HOW HE'S DE BES' KNOWN MAN IN DE WORL'"

Painted by Rowland M. Smith for Cream of Wheat Co.

Copyright 1914 by Cream of Wheat Co.

Cream Of Wheat, 1919

Bulwarks of Health.

Ralston Purina foods are real health builders.

They supply, in appetizing form, the wheat elements so essential to growing children.

Ralston—the porridge that the children love.

Purina Branzos, a food laxative. Makes delicious porridge, muffins and bread.

Purina Whole Wheat Flour. Super quality—rich in gluten. Mildly laxative.

Ralston Purina Mills, 810 Gratiot St., St. Louis.

Always sold in checkerboard bags or cartons. Ask your grocer.

PURINA

TRADE MARKS REGISTERED   U.S. PATENT OFFICE

WHOLE WHEAT FLOUR
PURINA MILLS - ST. LOUIS. MO

RALSTON
A BLEND OF
WHEAT
AND
BARLEY
MAKES CHILDREN STURDY

PURINA BRANZOS

Ralston Purina Food Products, 1919

TOM SAWYER, HUCK FINN AND AUNT POLLY.
For particulars inquire of Mark Twain, present address unknown.

Painted by Leslie Thrasher for Cream of Wheat Co.   Copyright 1913 by Cream of Wheat Co.

Cream Of Wheat, 1918

THE THINKER

Men who command great enterprises first master themselves, for food and drink largely define character. **Grape=Nuts** is a master food for thinkers

"There's a Reason"

Adapted from Rodin's Great Masterpiece

Grape-Nuts, 1915

Dicky's Dream

"How happy I'd be, if I lived in a house made of

Post Toasties

Where it rained cream, and the walls fell in."

"The Memory Lingers"

Postum Cereal Company, Limited
Battle Creek, Mich., U. S. A.

Canadian Postum Cereal Co., Ltd.
Windsor, Ontario, Canada.

Post Toasties, ca. 1917

Quaker Cereals, ca. 1902

Ralston Purina Food Products, 1914

Ralston Wheat And Barley, 1919

Shredded Wheat, 1903

▶ *Post Toasties, 1916*

National Oats, 1919

Egg-O-See, 1907

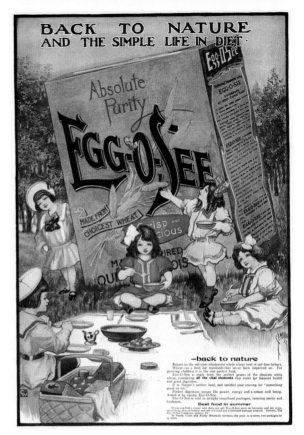

Egg-O-See, ca. 1918

Egg-O-See, ca. 1907

Nestlé, 1901

Sanitas Corn Flakes, 1907

Kellogg's Corn Flakes, 1909

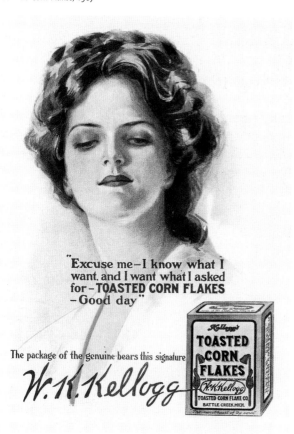

Kellogg's Corn Flakes, 1908

Kellogg's Corn Flakes, 1909

Kellogg's Corn Flakes, 1907

The
Chase

Kellogg's
TOASTED
CORN
FLAKES
H. K. Kellogg
KELLOGG TOASTED CORN FLAKE CO.
BATTLE CREEK, MICH.

"Won its Favor Through its Flavor"—
Made from Selected White Corn
NONE GENUINE WITHOUT THIS SIGNATURE
W. K. Kellogg

Kellogg's Corn Flakes, 1911

▸ *Kellogg's Corn Flakes, 1910*

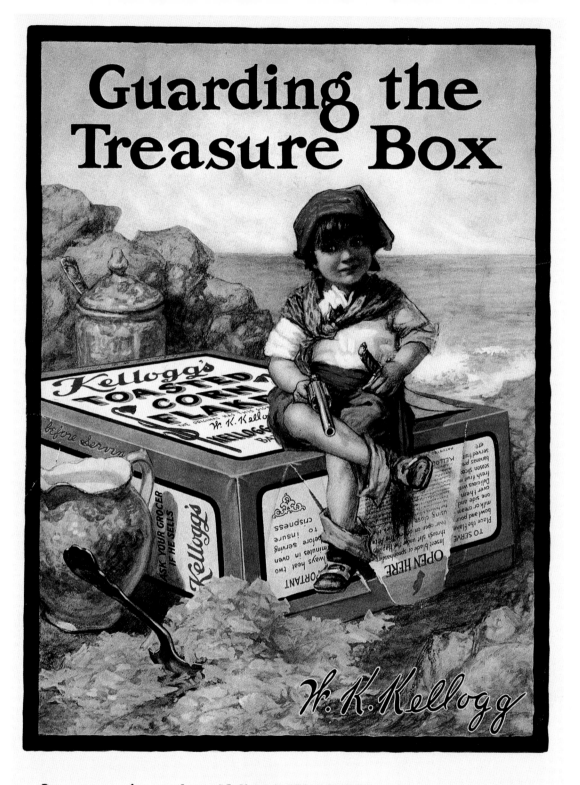

Our reason for packing Kellogg's WAXTITE is best expressed by Dr. Samuel G. Dixon, Commissioner of the Department of Health, State of Pennsylvania: "These paraffined packages are of the greatest value in preserving the health of our people."

Kellogg's Corn Flakes, 1914

Pillsbury's Best Cereal, 1908

Kellogg's Corn Flakes, 1909

Kellogg's Corn Flakes, 1915

Kellogg's Corn Flakes, 1912

The Largest Electric Sign Ever Built

The above photograph shows the monster Kellogg Toasted Corn Flake electric sign on the top of the Mecca Building, at 48th and Broadway, New York.

This sign is 106 feet wide and 80 feet high—the letter "K" in Kellogg's is 66 feet high—the boy's head and the package are 40 feet high.

Eighty tons of structural iron were required for the frame work, making necessary six mammoth trusses to distribute the weight and wind stress over the building.

A mechanical device changes the boy's face and the heading. When he cries the heading reads "I want Kellogg's." He then smiles and the heading reads "I got Kellogg's." The sign portrays a true story told in millions of homes daily.

The immensity of this sign can best be appreciated by the picture above showing the sign in course of construction. Look closely and you will be able to make out eighteen men working on the frame.

W. K. Kellogg

THE ORIGINAL HAS THIS SIGNATURE

Kellogg's Corn Flakes, 1912

Kellogg's Corn Flakes, 1909

Kellogg's Corn Flakes, 1912

Kellogg's Corn Flakes, 1912

Kellogg's Corn Flakes, 1913

Kellogg's Corn Flakes, 1914

Kellogg's Corn Flakes, *1907*

Copyright, 1916, Kellogg Toasted Corn Flake Co.

YOUNG folks with their fresh, unspoiled palates are the real judges of *flavor*. They enjoy the crispness, the wonderful good taste of Kellogg's Toasted Corn Flakes—and they are the ones who keep the imitations away from the table.

The crispness and flavor of Kellogg's are *there*—five million breakfasts a morning—and no telling how many times between meals.

It is a remarkable fact that there is no storage space at Kellogg's. Each day's production is shipped crisp from the ovens in the Kellogg *WAXTITE* package—that keeps the fresh, good flavor in and all other flavors out.

W. K. Kellogg

Kellogg's TOASTED CORN FLAKES

W. K. Kellogg
THE ORIGINAL BEARS THIS SIGNATURE

KELLOGG TOASTED CORN FLAKE CO.
BATTLE CREEK, MICH.
CUBICAL CONTENTS 192 CUBIC INCHES

Kellogg's Corn Flakes, 1916

Every Helping of Kellogg's Proves How Good Corn Flakes Can Be

OVER a thousand-million dishes of Kellogg's Toasted Corn Flakes were eaten last year. No wonder people prefer Kellogg's—the Original. These tender golden flakes are crisp and appetizing, *thin*, delicately toasted, with a flavor tempting to the last spoonful. The right package has this signature:

KRUMBLES is Kellogg's *all-wheat* food. Every single tiny shred is thoroughly toasted.

W.K. Kellogg

Kellogg's Corn Flakes, 1917

Kellogg's Corn Flakes, 1917

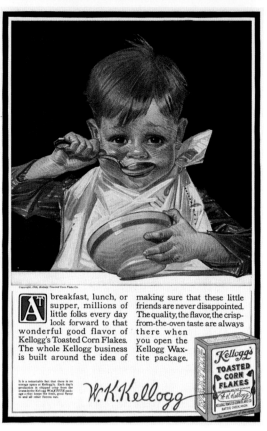

Kellogg's Corn Flakes, 1916

Kellogg's Corn Flakes, 1916

Kellogg's Corn Flakes, 1916

SOMETIMES the liking for Kellogg's Toasted Corn Flakes shows itself very early in life. And the littlest member of the household is the most clamorous of demand!

It's a grand way to get youngsters to take plenty of good top milk. And the tender golden flakes have just the crisp consistency for little teeth to crunch.

When mother says "Corn Flakes" she means *Kellogg's*—and *not* one of the three hundred or more imitations and substitutes.

Baby knows the difference at once—simply refusing to eat flakes that are tasteless and tough.

Remember, *please*, that you don't know Corn Flakes unless you know Kellogg's—the original Toasted Corn Flakes—their goodness insured by our responsibility to over a million homes.

Then too there is the *WAXTITE* package that keeps the fresh, good flavor in—and all other flavors out.

W.K.Kellogg

Kellogg's Corn Flakes, 1915

THERE is a youngster in almost every home who demands Kellogg's Toasted Corn Flakes, with their zestful, appetizing, crisp-from-the-oven taste.

Think of all the homes where they are the best-liked of the cereals—the oftenest repeated—the most called for. Then ask yourself if there is something here that your folks are missing.

Once get accustomed to having the Kellogg Waxtite package handy and you'll see how many breakfasts begin with Kellogg's—how often they are served for the children's supper—between meals—or as a light repast before going to bed.

Folks who have learned the sense of light foods are enjoying these satisfying golden flakes the year around.

And remember, *please*, that you don't know Corn Flakes unless you know *Kellogg's*—the original Toasted Corn Flakes—their goodness insured by our responsibility to over a million homes.

Then too there is the *WAXTITE* package that keeps the fresh, good flavor in—and all other flavors out.

W.K.Kellogg

Kellogg's Corn Flakes, 1915

DO YOU know a little housemother—or a big one—whose appetite is a bit droopy in hot weather?

There's always a refreshing appeal in Kellogg's Toasted Corn Flakes with ripe fruits or berries—a little cold milk poured in at the side of the dish, and sprinkle the berries with powdered sugar —but *not* the golden flakes. All by themselves they have the coaxingest flavor.

There is a thought here for all of us perhaps—breakfast, luncheon, or before going to bed—better than so much meat these summer days.

And remember *please* that you don't know corn flakes unless you know *Kellogg's*—the original Toasted Corn Flakes—with the pride of the maker to keep the delicate process *complete*.

Then too there is the *WAXTITE* package that keeps the fresh, good flavor in—and all other flavors out.

W.K.Kellogg

Kellogg's Corn Flakes, 1915

THE best liked of all the different cereals, and especially so by the youngsters, is Kellogg's Toasted Corn Flakes.

KELLOGG'S IS THE ORIGINAL TOASTED CORN FLAKES.

Imitations change in name and form, but they have never been able to duplicate the delicious Kellogg flavor.

Kellogg's remains as original as ever, light, dainty and appetizing in flavor.

W.K.Kellogg

Kellogg's Corn Flakes, 1916

511

Crystal Domino Sugar, 1906

Crystal Domino Sugar, 1912

Crystal Domino Sugar, 1911

Snowdrift Vegetable Shortening, 1919

Aunt Jemima's Pancake Flour, 1916

Gold Medal Flour, 1917

Gold Medal Flour, 1914

Aunt Jemima Pancake Flour, 1918

Napoleon Flour, ca. 1906

Swans Down Cake Flour, 1917

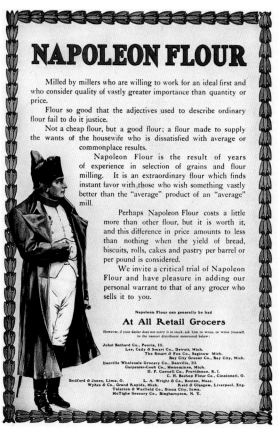

Napoleon Flour, 1908

Occident Flour, 1915

Bread

There is but one answer—one altogether satisfying response, to appetites whetted by sunshine, air and exercise.

Bread!

Of course! Bread with its eye-winning golden-brown crust; its palate-appealing, flaky whiteness; its gratifying and always beneficial refreshment!

In every hour of hunger—indoors or out—bread fills every need of the human system.

Bread is supreme in nutrition; also the most economical of foods.

Eat bread—more bread!

See that your family has plenty of good, nutritious bread on your table today.

A Different Kind of Recipe Book—Free

"Sixty-five Delicious Dishes Made with Bread."—Recipes for plain and fancy combinations of bread and fish, eggs, poultry, vegetables, nuts and fruits. Also tasty and wholesome puddings and pastries easily and quickly made with bread. Ask your baker or grocer for this unique recipe book —free, if you mention this Fleischmann advertisement.

In the United States and Canada, nearly all bakers use

Fleischmann's Yeast

Fleischmann's Yeast, 1919

AND now baby has been raised to a new throne—the proud high-chair; and a whole new world to conquer!

BREAD

His first solid food.

About as impossible to think of raising him without Love as without Bread.

Bread is his start in Life. Show your love by the way you cut the slices, remembering—

—Bread is the one solid food that builds and nourishes without ever taxing his tender digestion.

—Bread is the one food that he loves and need never be denied.

—The one food that unfailingly brings coos and contentment, chubby cheeks and sunshine in your home.

Give him Plenty of Bread.

When you plan your meals today see that bread is given the importance it deserves. Bread is your Best Food —the most delicious and nutritive food you and your family can eat. Prepare your meals so that more bread will be eaten morning, noon and night.

"Sixty-five Delicious Dishes Made with Bread" is a different kind of recipe book of new and wholesome desserts and dishes which are easily and economically made with bread. Your baker or grocer will give you a copy free on request.

In the United States and Canada, nearly all the bakers use

Fleischmann's Yeast

Fleischmann's Yeast, 1919

Her first meal away from home Bread mother made with Yeast Foam

Remember the keen appetite of your school days? Doesn't the memory of "mother's bread" come smacking to your lips again? An eminent authority recommends *homemade* bread and says: "How does the stomach respond to bread and milk and bread and butter? The response is very vigorous and satisfactory, particularly if the stomach in question is that of a hungry school boy or girl."

Use Yeast Foam and Bake at Home

Because it reduces the chances for mistakes through its reliability. *Your mother* probably used Yeast Foam because it has been making a large portion of America's good homemade bread for nearly forty years.

A five-cent package makes *thirty* loaves. Be *sure* to follow the easy directions on every package.

Magic Yeast
        Yeast Foam
Just the same
        Except in name

Magic Yeast is Sold Principally on the Atlantic and Pacific Coasts
Northwestern Yeast Co., Inc., Chicago.

PRICE 5 CENTS
YEAST FOAM
PURITY AND EXCELLENCE
TRADE MARK
PRICE 5 CENTS

Yeast Foam, 1917

Yeast Foam, 1917

Royal Baking Powder, 1904

Fleischmann's Yeast, 1919

Yeast Foam, 1919

Royal Baking Powder, 1906

Royal Baking Powder, 1919

Royal Baking Powder, 1919

Royal Baking Powder, 1919

Royal Baking Powder, 1919

CRYSTAL Domino SUGAR

SOLD ONLY IN 5ᵇ SEALED BOXES!

Imagination could not conceive of a handier and prettier form than that which is presented in "CRYSTAL DOMINO SUGAR". Neither could the most particular people ask for more perfect purity, nor economical people for less waste.

BY GROCERS EVERYWHERE!

Crystal Domino Sugar, 1908

TAPIOCA CREAM

Scald 2 cups milk in double boiler. Add 1½ heaping tablespoons Minute Tapioca; cook 15 minutes. Beat yolks and whites of 2 eggs separately. Divide ⅓ cup sugar putting ½ in the milk, add the rest to yolks with ¼ teaspoon salt. Pour hot mixture slowly into yolks and mix well. Cook in double boiler until it thickens. Flavor with vanilla; pour into pudding dish. Cover with stiffly beaten whites of eggs and brown in oven. Serve cold.

Minute Tapioca

"It's Good for You"

Don't you remember how you hated that phrase except when you saw Minute Tapioca Cream for dessert? Then you knew that, for some mysterious grown-up reason, it meant two big helpings of your favorite dish. Mother knew that each little bit of tapioca was a delicious morsel of health and strength. As each creamy mouthful melted away, the tiny pucker between her eyes only meant she wished that she had made a bigger dish.

Now-a-days we should eat tapioca more than ever. It can be used in so many economical ways to help save the wheat, the sugar, and the fats. Combined with leftovers, cheese, or eggs, it will make the most appetizing lunch or supper dishes. The anxious frown of another generation will be repeated as you wonder if there is enough to go around again.

Minute Gelatine also helps you to plan delightful desserts that are both economical and health giving.

Let us send you the New Minute Conservation Cook Book. Buy Minute Gelatine and Minute Tapioca. You will know them by the Blue Band and the Minute Man.

Minute Tapioca Company, 78 No. Main St., Orange, Mass.

TAPIOCA PRUNE DESSERT

Cook in double boiler 15 minutes 1 pt. milk, 2 heaping tablespoons Minute Tapioca, and pinch salt. Remove from fire; add 1 tablespoon butter, 2 tablespoons sugar, yolks of two eggs. Pour into buttered pan and bake for ½ hr. in moderate oven. Spread over Tapioca 1 cup prunes steamed until tender and rubbed through a sieve. Pile on top of prunes whites of two eggs beaten with 2 tablespoons sugar. Brown in oven. Serve hot or cold with milk or cream.

No Soaking Always Ready to Cook

Minute Tapioca

MINUTE TAPIOCA CO. ORANGE, MASS

APRICOT ICE CREAM

Soak over night ¼-lb. dried apricots in 1 qt. cold water. Cook until soft (in same water) and rub through a sieve. Boil 1 cup sugar in 2 cups water for 15 minutes and add to the apricots. (This will keep several days.) Mix together one envelope Minute Gelatine, ⅓ cup sugar, pinch soda, pinch salt and dissolve in 1 cup of hot milk. Set in cold place. When beginning to jell, whip until double in bulk, then add gradually 1 cup milk. Beat into the apricots and freeze.

MINUTE TAPIOCA COMPANY
78 North Main Street, Orange, Mass.

Please send me your Conservation Cook Book, which gives new and economical receipts for Minute Tapioca and Minute Gelatine.

Name_____

Address_____

Grocer's Name_____

Minute Tapioca, 1918

525

Royal Baking Powder, 1919

Pillsbury's Health Bran, 1918

Wesson Oil, 1918

Wesson Oil, 1918

Argo Corn Starch, 1919

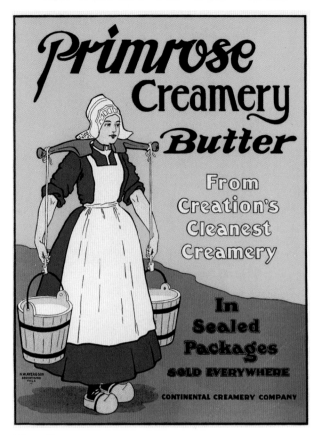

Primrose Butter, 1903

Borden's Milk Products, 1918

Borden's Evaporated Milk, 1919

Baker's Cocoa, 1906

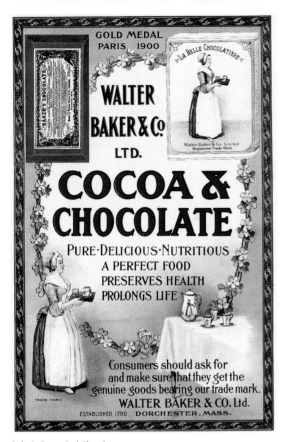

Baker's Cocoa And Chocolate, 1901

Baker's Cocoa, 1906

Baker's Cocoa, 1901

Baker's Cocoa, 1911

Necco And Hub Wafers, 1913

Nut Tootsie Rolls, 1919

Nut Tootsie Rolls, 1919

Nut Tootsie Rolls, 1919

Life Savers Candy, 1917

Life Savers Candy, 1917

Cracker Jack, 1919

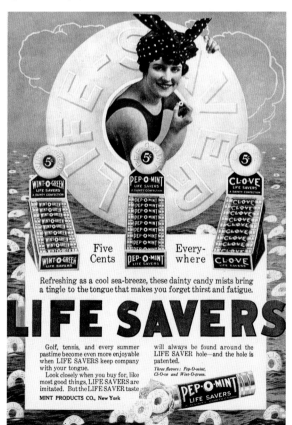

Life Savers Candy, 1916

Peter's Chocolate, 1911   ▸ *Life Savers Candy, 1919*

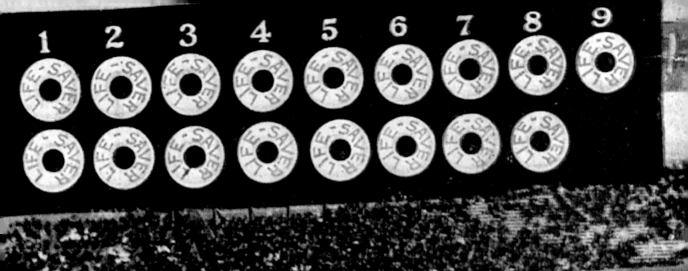

VERs are a Hit with Everyone

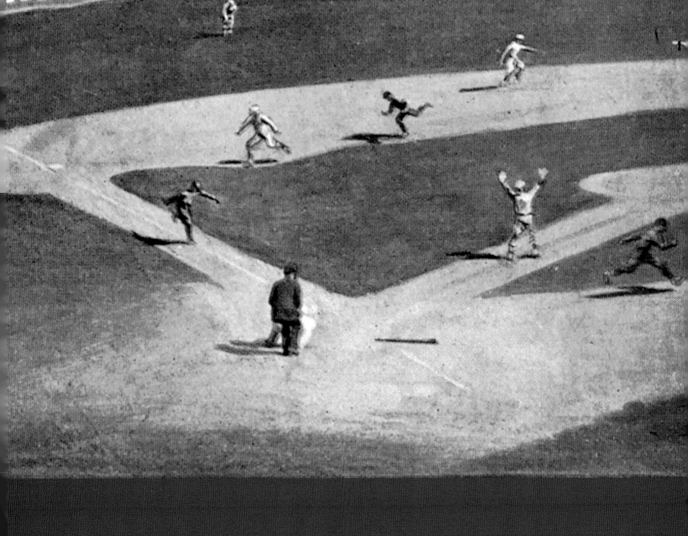

ADAMS CALIFORNIA FRUIT CHEWING GUM

RUTH ROLAND says: Ripe, red cherries and Adams California Fruit Gum I think are equally delicious. I love them both.

Adams California Fruit Gum, 1919

Adams California Fruit Gum, 1919

ADAMS CALIFORNIA FRUIT CHEWING GUM

WITH THE FRUITY FLAVOR

EVELYN CONWAY (whose beauty thrills the crowds at the Dillingham-Ziegfeld "Cocoanut Grove") declares: "I can think of no more delightful way to satisfy one's craving for the taste of fruit than to chew Adams California Fruit Gum."

Evelyn Conway

Adams California Fruit Gum, 1913

ADAMS CALIFORNIA FRUIT CHEWING GUM
WITH THE FRUITY FLAVOR

MARION DAVIES, appearing in "Oh, Boy!"
at the Princess Theatre, New York, says:
"All of California's Fruits combined could
not be more delightful than the flavor of
Adams California Fruit Gum. It is delicious."

Marion Davies

Adams California Fruit Gum, 1917

Wrigley's Spearmint Gum, 1913

Charms Fruit Candy, 1919

Triscuit Biscuits, 1903

Wrigley's Spearmint Gum, 1911

Zu Zu Ginger Snaps, 1904

Adams California Fruit Gum, 1919

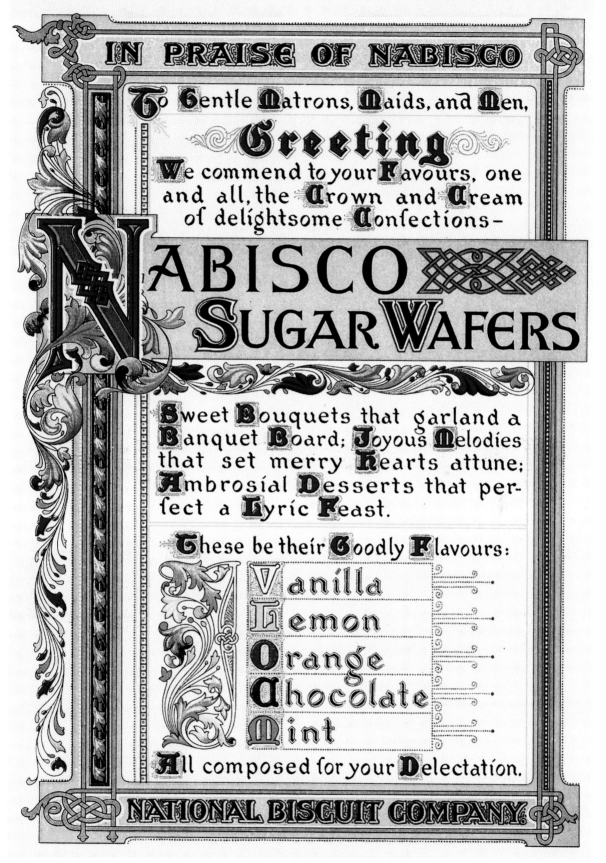

Nabisco Sugar Wafers, 1904

Sweet Temptation

Knows no more alluring charm than Nabisco Sugar Wafers. A dessert confection sometimes called a fairy sandwich because of its airy lightness and exquisite composition. Deliciously flavored with Lemon, Orange, Chocolate, Vanilla and Mint, to please the fanciful desire and afford the hostess opportunity for many original conceptions in the serving of dessert. To know the possibilities of

NABISCO SUGAR WAFERS

serve them in your favorite flavor with sherbet, ice cream or fruit, with coffee, tea or any other beverage.

NATIONAL BISCUIT COMPANY

Nabisco Sugar Wafers, 1904

Veribest Canned Meats, 1904

Armour Food Products, 1917

Council Canned Meats, 1919

Underwood Canned Meats, 1906

Beech-Nut Bacon, 1916

MORRIS

Supreme
Ham

For dinner—there's nothing more delicious than a Supreme Ham, baked and seasoned with cloves. Serve it to your guests at the meal you want remembered. Its tenderness and fine, mild flavor are the result of our Supreme cure. All Morris Supreme foods are delicious; they belong in your market basket.

MORRIS & COMPANY

Morris Ham, 1919

WILSON'S
Certified
HAM

THIS picture is from an actual photograph. It shows the *quality* that is "Certified" in these hams.

We can *certify* it because we select the hams, give them our slow, mild cure and smoke them to the last touch of perfection in flavor.

"CERTIFIED" quality means hams that cook better, slice in tender, tempting style—wafer-thin or as thick as you like—and have a flavor that is unapproachable.

We shall be glad to send you free a copy of "Wilson's Meat Cookery"—our book showing how to buy and cook meats economically.

Address Wilson & Co., Dept. 1234, Chicago

This mark **WILSON & CO.** *your guarantee*"

The Wilson label protects your table

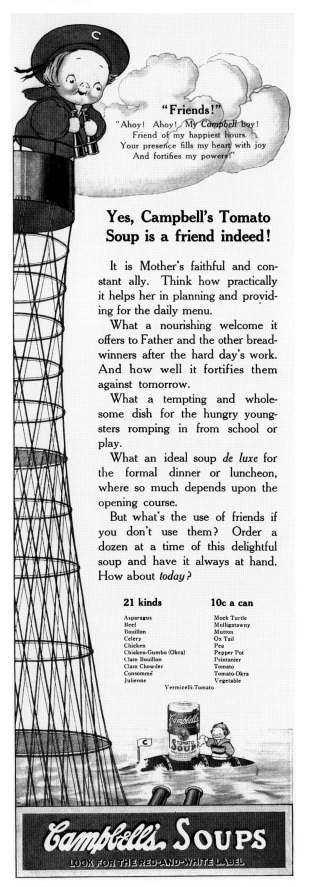

"Friends!"

"Ahoy! Ahoy! My *Campbell* boy!
Friend of my happiest hours.
Your presence fills my heart with joy
And fortifies my powers!"

Yes, Campbell's Tomato Soup is a friend indeed!

It is Mother's faithful and constant ally. Think how practically it helps her in planning and providing for the daily menu.

What a nourishing welcome it offers to Father and the other breadwinners after the hard day's work. And how well it fortifies them against tomorrow.

What a tempting and wholesome dish for the hungry youngsters romping in from school or play.

What an ideal soup *de luxe* for the formal dinner or luncheon, where so much depends upon the opening course.

But what's the use of friends if you don't use them? Order a dozen at a time of this delightful soup and have it always at hand. How about *today*?

21 kinds	10c a can
Asparagus	Mock Turtle
Beef	Mulligatawny
Bouillon	Mutton
Celery	Ox Tail
Chicken	Pea
Chicken-Gumbo (Okra)	Pepper Pot
Clam Bouillon	Printanier
Clam Chowder	Tomato
Consommé	Tomato-Okra
Julienne	Vegetable
	Vermicelli-Tomato

Campbell's SOUPS

LOOK FOR THE RED-AND-WHITE LABEL

Campbell's Soups, 1915

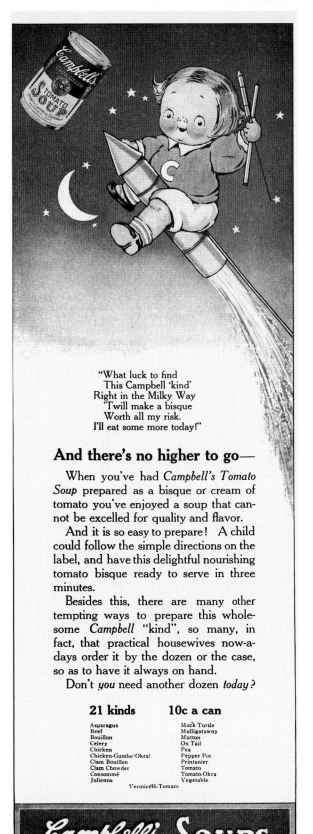

"What luck to find
This Campbell 'kind'
Right in the Milky Way
'Twill make a bisque
Worth all my risk.
I'll eat some more today!"

And there's no higher to go—

When you've had *Campbell's Tomato Soup* prepared as a bisque or cream of tomato you've enjoyed a soup that cannot be excelled for quality and flavor.

And it is so easy to prepare! A child could follow the simple directions on the label, and have this delightful nourishing tomato bisque ready to serve in three minutes.

Besides this, there are many other tempting ways to prepare this wholesome *Campbell* "kind", so many, in fact, that practical housewives now-a-days order it by the dozen or the case, so as to have it always on hand.

Don't *you* need another dozen *today*?

21 kinds	10c a can
Asparagus	Mock Turtle
Beef	Mulligatawny
Bouillon	Mutton
Celery	Ox Tail
Chicken	Pea
Chicken-Gumbo (Okra)	Pepper Pot
Clam Bouillon	Printanier
Clam Chowder	Tomato
Consommé	Tomato-Okra
Julienne	Vegetable
	Vermicelli-Tomato

Campbell's SOUPS

LOOK FOR THE RED-AND-WHITE LABEL

Campbell's Soups, 1915

Get some fun out of life

Don't let the everlasting three-meals-a-day problem tie you down to constant drudgery.

When you think of dinner think of

Campbell's Tomato Soup

It is a nourishing wholesome appetizer which makes a "go" of any dinner, hearty or light.

Have it for the children's luncheon and your own when you are tired or busy. Have it for the family supper or the emergency meal at any time.

Prepare it as a plain tomato bouillon or a rich cream of tomato—or in any of the various tempting ways in which it is so easily prepared. It calls for only three minutes time and no trouble whatever. Why not order a dozen *today?*

Your money back if not satisfied.

21 kinds   10c a can

Asparagus	Clam Chowder	Pea
Beef	Consommé	Pepper Pot
Bouillon	Julienne	Printanier
Celery	Mock Turtle	Tomato
Chicken	Mulligatawny	Tomato-Okra
Chicken-Gumbo (Okra)	Mutton	Vegetable
Clam Bouillon	Ox Tail	Vermicelli - Tomato

Campbell's Soups, 1915

A new leaf

Turn it over today! If you eat soup only once in a while on some special occasion, make it a point from now on to enjoy it once a day at least. Get the full and regular benefit of

Campbell's Vegetable Soup

This is one of the best liked and oftenest used of all the Campbell "kinds."

Extremely nourishing as well as palatable, this tempting soup contains such wholesome vegetables as carrots, white potatoes, sweet potatoes, "baby" lima beans, small peas, tender corn, barley, green okra, tomatoes, and other choice vegetables, beside "alphabet" macaroni, celery and parsley—all combined in a strong concentrated stock made from selected beef.

This soup is more than a mere dinner course. It is a substantial, satisfying dish for the family meals at any time. Why not order a supply from your grocer *today?*

Your money back if not satisfied.

21 kinds   10c a can

Campbell's Soups, 1915

Some New Ideas

Shouts of "Oh, Good-e-e-e!" and clapping of hands greet mamma's appearance with a big dish of Jell-O for Bobbie and Jack.

It is a plain dish of Strawberry Jell-O, made and served without sugar or cream—but perfectly delicious.

Substantial dishes that are good to eat and generally made without any trimmings or garnishments, are very popular just now. Probably the Bavarian creams made as follows are the most satisfactory:

Dissolve a package of Lemon Jell-O in half a pint of boiling water and add half a pint of the juice from a can of pineapple. When cold and still liquid whip to consistency of whipped cream and add a cup of shredded or chopped pineapple.

Either fresh or canned fruit of almost any other kind can be used in making these Bavarian creams. Canned peaches and peach juice are particularly good.

JELL-O

The whipped Jell-O takes the place of whipped cream in these dishes, and no eggs are used in them. Anybody can make them.

In every case of sickness or convalescence there is a period when feeding is a most important factor, and often it is found that Jell-O is the one particular dish which satisfies the craving for something refreshing and revives the weakened appetite. It is relished when nothing else is.

The Jell-O Book contains a special recipe for whipping Jell-O, which is a simple process. If you have not already received a copy of this book we shall be glad to send you one if you will give us your name and address.

Jell-O is put up in six pure fruit flavors: Strawberry, Raspberry, Lemon, Orange, Cherry, Chocolate, and is sold by all grocers, 2 packages for **25** cents.

THE GENESEE PURE FOOD COMPANY,
Le Roy, N. Y., and Bridgeburg, Ont.

Jell-O, 1918

FREE

BEAUTIFULLY illustrated Corn Products Cook Book of 68 pages containing more than a hundred valuable recipes for candies of all kinds, cakes and pastry of every variety, sauces, and salad dressings.

All recipes originated by leading professional cooks and endorsed by Domestic Science Experts. Every housewife should possess a copy of this book—sent free. *Write today.*

Corn Products Refining Co.
DEPT. 10
P. O. Box 161, New York

Make Your Christmas Candy at Home with Karo

THE variety of wholesome candies so easily made with Karo syrup gives a really intelligent solution of the Christmas candy problem.

It's lots of fun for the children themselves to make it, and Karo always insures success.

Christmas candies cost more than ever this year. It is worth your while to let the children make Karo candies at home. It is as good as can be bought, and *at a fraction of the cost* of good store candy.

"Mine's Best"

"Oh, I know mine is best," Dorothy says. "Just *taste* it, Bobbie !"

And Bobbie says, "It's good, but mine's best."

For Dorothy's party mamma has made up six lovely dishes of

JELL-O

each of a different flavor, and all so good that three little girls and three little boys hold one opinion: "Mine's best."

Children know what is good to eat. Who ever heard of a child that did not like Jell-O, or ever saw two youngsters who could agree as to which flavor was best—all being so good?

The Jell-O Book tells how to make many new desserts and salads in the easy Jell-O way, which cuts out work and worry and most of the expense. A copy of the book will be mailed free to any woman who will send us her name and address.

Jell-O is put up in six pure fruit flavors: Strawberry, Raspberry, Lemon, Orange, Cherry, Chocolate, and is sold two for 25 cents.

THE GENESEE PURE FOOD COMPANY
Le Roy, N. Y., and Bridgeburg, Ont.

Jell-O, 1912

Full Measure and Highest Quality

When you buy syrup, be sure it comes in Log Cabin Cans—then it is Towle's Log Cabin Syrup—the purest, sweetest and most perfectly flavored of table syrups.

Towle's Log Cabin Syrups are guaranteed always the same in flavor and of full measure and highest quality. You can use Towle's Log Cabin Syrups year after year with absolute certainty that you will always have the same quality and flavor this year that you have had in years past and will have in the years to come.

Towle's Log Cabin Maple Syrup
Towle's Log Cabin Cane and Maple Syrup
Towle's Log Cabin Pen-o-che Syrup

are all put up in genuine Log Cabin Cans in pints, quarts and gallon sizes. Each syrup is distinct in quality and flavor. Towle has made syrups for more than a quarter of a century and the Towle name and reputation is in itself a guarantee of excellence.

Try Towle's Log Cabin Syrup on your own table. You will like it, your family will like it, your children will like it better than any other syrup you have ever used.

If your grocer does not sell Towle's Log Cabin Syrups, go to one who does.

To every reader of this advertisement, who will send us 10c in coin or stamps we will forward immediately by mail, postage paid, a handsome silver-plated teaspoon as shown in this advertisement, which is actual size of spoon you will receive. There is a tag on every Log Cabin Can which can be used by you to secure more spoons.

Send for the little books, "From Camp to Table" and "Pen-o-che Secrets." They are both valuable and will furnish you a great fund of dessert and candy making pleasure during the long winter evenings.

The Towle Maple Syrup Company
Custer Street, St. Paul, Minn

This Cut Actual Size

Towle's Log Cabin Syrups, 1908

They Wanted JELL-O

Do you remember the dreadful disappointment it used to be in the old days at home when mother brought on for dessert some baked apples or pie-plant pie, or something else that was "common," and you wanted shortcake or pudding ?

Now the little folks want

JELL-O

It is not always best to give the children what they want, but no mistake can be made in giving them JELL-O for dessert. It is good for them.

Every child loves JELL-O, which is so delicious and refreshing, so full of nutriment, so pure and wholesome, so economical and so easily prepared, that there is no reason why the little tots or anybody else should be disappointed in dessert. The whole family like it just as well as the youngest member.

A JELL-O dessert costs ten cents and can be made in a minute. It sounds almost too good to be true, but it isn't.
All grocers sell it in seven flavors.
Illustrated Recipe Book free on request.

The Genesee Pure Food Co., Le Roy, N.Y., and Bridgeburg, Can.

Jell-O, 1910

"Which ?" says Joan, *"Choose it quick."*
"Bo!, I guess," says chubby Dick.

Ask any small boy to choose between a dish of strawberry ice cream and one of vanilla, or between two different dishes of Jell-O, and he will certainly feel like answering as Dick did.

JELL-O

More different kinds of good things to eat are made of Jell-O than of anything else. The Jell-O Book explains the newest and easiest ways of making them—dozens of different ways of making desserts and salads. This Jell-O Book will be sent to you free if you will send us your name and address.

Grocers and general storekeepers everywhere sell Jell-O, two packages for 25 cents, in all the different pure fruit flavors: Strawberry, Raspberry, Lemon, Orange, Cherry, Chocolate.

THE GENESEE PURE FOOD COMPANY
Le Roy, N. Y., and Bridgeburg, Ont.

Jell-O, 1919

JELL-O

America's Most Famous Dessert

Two Perfect Things.

As the welcome valentine combines just enough sentiment with beauty, so the perfect dessert has just enough flavor, is just sweet enough or tart enough, and just substantial enough.

Ask any well-informed woman what dessert possesses these qualities and she will tell you

JELL-O

A Jell-O dessert can be made in a minute. The package of Jell-O to make it costs only 10 cents at any grocer's.

There are seven delightful Jell-O flavors: Strawberry, Raspberry, Lemon, Orange, Cherry, Peach, Chocolate.

The splendid recipe book, "Desserts of the World," illustrated in ten colors and gold, will be sent free to all who write and ask us for it.

The Genesee Pure Food Co.,   **Le Roy, N. Y., and Bridgeburg, Can.**

Jell-O, 1912

Snider's Catsup, 1915

Snider's Catsup, 1915

Snider's Catsup, 1916

Snider's Food Products, 1914

Blue Ribbon Peaches, 1919

Baker's Coconut, 1919

Blue Label, 1903

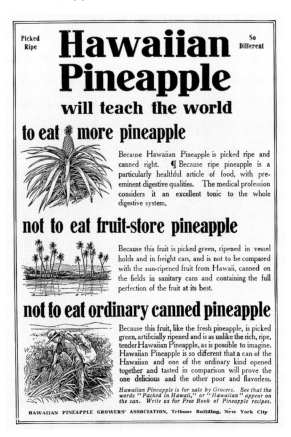

Hawaiian Pineapple Growers' Association, 1909

Sunkist

Iced Orange Juice

Thin, tender Orange *Slices*
Fresh, cool, juicy *Orange Salads*
Dainty, luscious *Orange-Desserts*

—what is more delicious, especially in summer, and what is better for you as a summer food, or drink?

Sunkist Orange Juice is famous for its flavor.

Sunkist Oranges cost no more than ordinary kinds. Dealers everywhere sell Sunkist Oranges and Lemons.

Be sure to get the large Sunkist Orange Juice Extractor—10c from dealers or 16c by mail east of Missouri river, 15c from dealers or 24c by mail west of Missouri river, 24c by mail to Canada.

CALIFORNIA FRUIT GROWERS EXCHANGE Co-operative Non-profit
Eastern Headquarters, Dept. B-21, 139 N. Clark St., CHICAGO, ILL.

Sunkist Oranges, 1916

Sunkist

VALENCIA ORANGES

Far More than just "delicious"

Oranges—what do they mean *to you?*

To millions, they mean more than merely *flavor.*

True, no fruit is more delicious. And because that lusciousness is the thing that is immediately sensed in *eating* oranges, they have become known to many thousands as "good" simply because they *taste* good.

But there's more good in them than that—there's the good that oranges *do;* think of their *food-value,* their *healthfulness* and *purity.* Every *physician* knows oranges for *these* qualities—that's why tiny babies are fed *orange* juice.

If you *like* oranges, and they are so *good for* you—for your family, for your children—they should be served *more often* in your home. Fact is, why not every day, at every meal? We'll tell you how to make scores of tempting salads and desserts.

You can depend on this brand, *Sunkist. Sunkist Valencia Oranges are delicious now.* Only California's *selected* oranges are marketed as Sunkist—*luscious, juicy, sweet, clean* oranges. Glove-picked, scrubbed with brushes, wrapped in *sanitary tissue.*

Remember—Sunkist oranges are a *fresh-picked fruit the year 'round*—as fresh and good in *summer* as in winter.

Both Sunkist oranges and lemons are sold by first-class dealers everywhere. Ask *your* dealer for Sunkist Valencia Oranges.

California Fruit Growers Exchange (Co-operative—Non-profit)
Eastern Headquarters, Dept. B44, 139 N. Clark Street, Chicago

Sunkist Oranges, 1916

Del Monte Canned Fruits And Vegetables, 1918

Libby's Food Products, 1919

Del Monte Canned Fruits And Vegetables, 1919

Sunkist Oranges, 1918

Sunkist Lemons, 1919

Sunkist Lemons, 1916

Eatmor Cranberries, 1919

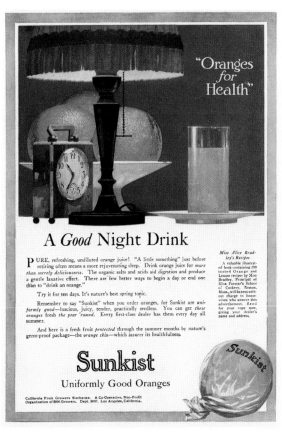

Sunkist Oranges, 1917

To make appetites glad —
every day in the year

There's a DEL MONTE
variety for every menu
need — an appeal that
always tempts.

CALIFORNIA PACKING CORPORATION
San Francisco, California

Send for our free Recipe Book

Del·Monte
BRAND
QUALITY
REG. U.S.   PAT. OFF.
CANNED FRUITS
& VEGETABLES

Del Monte Canned Fruits And Vegetables, 1919

Let Nature Mix Yours

WHEN you want a luscious, cooling drink this summer, simply squeeze the juice from an orange.

Nature has mixed this refreshment for you as only Nature can.

She has made it delicious.

She has combined in it invaluable, natural salts and acids that man has never imitated—elements that the system needs, particularly in summer.

This pure, delicious beverage comes to you sealed in Nature's germ proof package—the orange skin.

The salts and acids of the orange are natural digestants also. So pure orange juice—a delightful appetizer and a refreshing drink—is valuable *at meals* for important dietetic reasons.

Use orange juice, therefore, as your summer drink. "Drink an Orange" at breakfast, lunch and dinner.

New Ideas for Hostesses in Free Book

We have issued a new book of recipes showing scores of ways to use orange juice in tempting beverages. The recipes are by Alice Bradley, Principal of Miss Farmer's School of Cookery, Boston.

There are zestful appetizers, juleps, fizzes, frappés, punches, "cups" and other attractive things to serve when you entertain.

This new book is called "Sunkist New-Day Drinks." Send a post card for a copy.

Sunkist Marmalade

Made of the rich, pure juice and yellow part of the peel of fresh ripe fruit from California Groves. A little lemon or grapefruit juice, and pure sugar are added —nothing else.

Made the home way, in small quantities, by expert women cooks.

Ask your dealer for it. It has the real "home taste."

Sunkist

Uniformly Good Oranges

Always use *Sunkist* Oranges for their rich, *full-flavored* juice. Sunkist Oranges are ripened on the tree and picked fresh daily in California, all year 'round. First-class dealers are supplied with these fresh oranges all summer.

"Drink an Orange"

CALIFORNIA FRUIT GROWERS EXCHANGE
A Non-profit, Co-operative Organization of 8,500 Growers
Dept. H-11, Los Angeles, Cal.
Also Distributors of Sunkist Marmalade and Sunkist (California) Lemons

Sunkist Oranges, 1919

Meat from Wheat

The Biggest Food Value in America for **10¢**

Making big men out of little men

Nature and outdoors make big men. The men closest to Nature draw most from her strength.

Golden Age Americanized Macaroni is Nature's richest bounty, its most wholesome food in purest form—the stuff that men are made of—the food for Young America.

W.S.S.
WAR SAVINGS STAMPS
ISSUED BY THE
UNITED STATES
GOVERNMENT

Write for Miss Yackey's Calorie Cook Book—it's free. Gives 52 recipes for preparing macaroni, spaghetti and noodles in delightful ways. Special calorie charts and guide providing proper diet for children, growing youths, invalids, convalescents and athletes.

The Cleveland Macaroni Company   Cleveland, Ohio, U. S. A.
Modern Macaroni Makers

Golden Age Macaroni, 1919

King's Dehydrated Vegetables, 1919

Golden Age Macaroni, 1919

Golden Age Macaroni, 1919

Planters Peanuts, 1919

Beech-Nut Peanut Butter, 1919

Beech-Nut Peanut Butter, 1917

Beech-Nut Peanut Butter, 1918

Beech-Nut Peanut Butter, 1918

Game's Over, But There's More Fun Coming

IT'S coming in these Beech-Nut Peanut Butter sandwiches—the kind he likes best in the whole world. Beech-Nut just naturally fits in with the joy of football and boy-scouting and tree-climbing and the thousand other kinds of outdooring every healthy youngster—boy or girl—loves.

Why not give *your* youngsters some?

Slice up your wheat loaf and spread Beech-Nut Peanut Butter thick. Every Beech-Nut Peanut Butter sandwich you make contains the same amount of Strength, Heat and Energy as a brimming glass of full cream milk.

Nourishment is what mother likes to think about when she makes the sandwiches. And when the child eats them, he or she thinks about the irresistible peanut *flavor*—so tempting, so good, so perfectly satisfying that sweets "aren't in it".

Send the children to the grocer's *now* for a jar of Beech-Nut Peanut Butter. They won't loiter on *this* errand.

*Ask your Grocer about the Superior
Quality of Beech-Nut Peanut Butter*

BEECH-NUT PACKING COMPANY, CANAJOHARIE, NEW YORK

Beech-Nut Peanut Butter, 1917

DRINK
Coca-Cola
TRADE MARK REGISTERED
DELICIOUS REFRESHING
DRINK
Coca-Cola
COOLING
REFRESHING

It relieves fatigue and excitement, and induces a spirit of thorough, restful satisfaction as delightful to the senses as *Coca-Cola* is to the sense of taste.

Sold at all founts and carbonated in bottles.

Coca-Cola, 1906 ◂ *Coca-Cola, 1906*

Coca-Cola, 1907

Coca-Cola, 1916

Coca-Cola, 1917

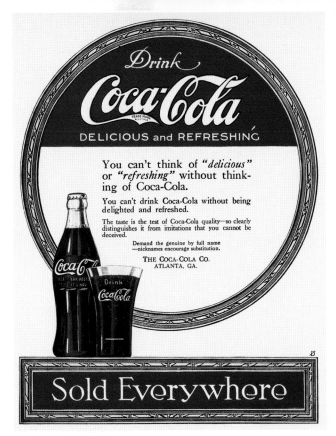

Coca-Cola, 1919

Coca-Cola, 1917

Coca-Cola, 1914

Coca-Cola, 1916

Coca-Cola, 1914

Coca-Cola, 1917

White Rock Bottled Water, 1907

White Rock Bottled Water, 1910

White Rock Bottled Water, 1910

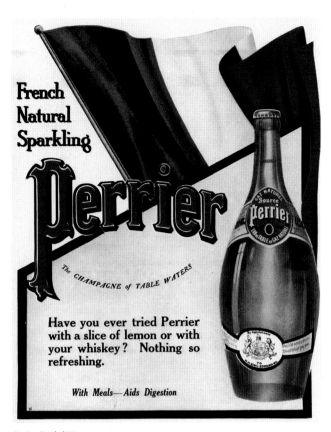

Perrier Bottled Water, 1909

Hiawatha Bottled Water, 1907

Clysmic Bottled Water, 1915

Phez Loganberry Juice, 1919

Clicquot Club Ginger Ale, 1918

Runkel's Cocoa, 1919

Red Wing Grape Juice, 1916

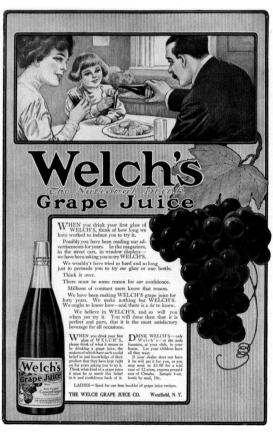

Welch's Grape Juice, 1911

Just say "Hires"

and get the genuine

Hires is Nature's drink—made from roots, barks, herbs, berries --and pure cane sugar. Made pure and kept up to the Hires standard for 50 years, despite the high cost of the best ingredients. Yet you pay no more for genuine Hires than for artificial imitations.

In bottles, or at fountains

THE CHARLES E. HIRES CO.
Philadelphia

Hires

Hires Rootbeer, 1919

A Compliment to Your Guests

Sheboygan will always anticipate your guests' desire for refreshment. Their memory of its deliciousness will prove a compliment to your judgment in serving it.

It is a rare combination of fruit flavors—syrup and aqua—spiced with imported Jamaica ginger, which delicately imparts that favored tang and nip without the bite.

For an outing — chilled bottles can be kept cold by wrapping separately in paper.

Your Grocer or Druggist will supply you. Served at leading fountains—cafes, hotels, clubs and dining cars.

Sheboygan Beverage Company, Sheboygan, Wis.

Makers of Ginger Ale, Sarsaparilla, Root Beer, Lemon Soda, Cream Soda and Orange Phosphate. Bottlers of Sheboygan Mineral Water.

★ For occasions and all occasions

Sheboygan
GINGER ALE

Soda Fountain

Picnic

Kiddies

Sheboygan Ginger Ale, 1919

Clicquot Club Ginger Ale, 1917

▶ Postum, 1911

JAFFEE

The Rational Meal-Time Drink For Every Meal

YOU will like your hot steaming cup of Jaffee at breakfast. You'll like its appetizing color. You'll like its rich, distinctive flavor, a flavor *all its own.*

Perhaps, like many people who cannot drink coffee, you will find that Jaffee shortly will become your favorite drink. In all events, you and the whole family will take keen pleasure in its flavor, and in the confidence of Jaffee's harmless wholesomeness.

You will like it so well that you will not throw out the Jaffee left from breakfast, but will pour it off and set it aside to cool. Then at luncheon or dinner you will serve delicious *iced* Jaffee—another delightful drink.

WHAT JAFFEE IS:

Jaffee is the result of long study and experiment. It is made wholly from blended fruits and cereals. It contains no coffee, caffeine or other stimulant. It is not an imitation of coffee.

The same minute care which has made Beech-Nut Bacon, Beech-Nut Peanut Butter, Beech-Nut Conserves and Condiments standards of food purity and flavor is Jaffee's *guarantee* of flavor.

Jaffee is highly economical—100 cups for 30c. Saves sugar—requires but ½ the usual sweetening. Order a package from your grocer today.

BEECH-NUT PACKING COMPANY, CANAJOHARIE, N. Y.
"Foods of Finest Flavor"

Beech-Nut Jaffee, 1918

G. Washington's Coffee, 1919

Don't take anybody's word for it. But if you're a coffee drinker, and feel as though something is wrong with your nerves, *Quit Coffee* and use

POSTUM

You'll know more after a couple of weeks about the effects of coffee, than you can learn from reading in a couple of years.

"There's a Reason" for POSTUM

Postum, 1919

Postum, 1912

Which Face Represents Your Feelings?

Cover the right half of this picture and see a man with whom coffee disagrees. Cover the left half and see — there's health and comfort in

POSTUM

Postum, 1918

And the winner is...

Beer Babies

The ingredients of this nutritious extract are not revealed in the advertisement, but one has to wonder what potent formula could both soothe the nerves and strengthen the lacteal glands of expectant mothers — when it was manufactured by a brewery. During an era when traces of cocaine were routinely added to sodas, one hopes a bit of Pabst brew didn't spill into the tonic. Then again, that would explain why their extract "... insures quiet, peaceful sleep."

Bierflaschen-Babys

Die Inhaltsstoffe dieses nahrhaften Saftes werden in der Anzeige nicht verraten, aber man darf sich fragen, welch hochwirksame Formel wohl gleichzeitig die Nerven beruhigen und die Milchdrüsen werdender Mütter anregen konnte – angesichts der Tatsache, dass er von einer Brauerei hergestellt wurde. Man kann nur hoffen, dass in dieser Ära, in der Limonaden regelmäßig Kokainspuren beigemischt wurden, nichts vom Pabst-Bier mit in das Tonikum geraten war. Das würde allerdings erklären, warum das Extrakt für „seligen Schlummer" sorgte.

Les bébés de la bière

Les ingrédients de cet extrait nutritif ne sont pas mentionnés dans l'annonce, mais on peut se demander quel genre de recette efficace pouvait à la fois calmer les nerfs et favoriser le fonctionnement des glandes mammaires chez la future mère – quand on sait que le produit était fabriqué dans une brasserie. A l'époque où l'on trouvait des traces de cocaïne dans les boissons gazeuses, il faut espérer que la préparation de Pabst n'avait pas débordé dans le fortifiant. Toutefois, cela pourrait expliquer pourquoi cet extrait « procure un sommeil calme et paisible ».

Bebés «cebados»

Los ingredientes de este nutritivo extracto no se desvelan en el anuncio, pero uno se plantea qué potente fórmula fabricada en una cervecería podía calmar los nervios y al mismo tiempo fortalecer las glándulas lácteas de las madres en estado de buena esperanza. En una época en la que se añadían motas de cocaína a las gaseosas, no sería de extrañar que se echaran unas gotitas de cerveza Pabst en esta agua tónica ... cosa que explicaría por qué este extracto «garantiza un sueño plácido».

ビールベイビー

広告ではこの栄養たっぷりのエキスの材料は明らかにされていないが、醸造所で製造される際に、どんな効能ある処方によって妊婦の神経を安らげ、さらに乳腺を強くすることができるのかと不思議に思わずにはいられない。少量のコカインが日常的にソーダ水に加えられていたこの時代、Pabstの醸造酒がほんのちょっぴり強壮薬を入れなかったことを願うものである。が一方では、それでこそ彼等の精製物が「穏やかで平和な眠りをお約束」するのであるが。

The Joys of Motherhood

are increased ten-fold when both mother and babe enjoy perfect health. Called upon to bear a double burden, the expectant mother must have additional nourishment not supplied by ordinary foods.

Pabst Extract
The "Best" Tonic

prepares the way for happy, healthy motherhood. It is both a *tonic* and a *food* —highly concentrated and pleasant to the taste. Soothes the nerves, strengthens the lacteal glands, invigorates mind and body and insures quiet, peaceful sleep.

Order a Dozen From Your Druggist

Insist Upon It Being "Pabst"

FREE BOOKLET, "Health Darts," tells all uses and benefits of Pabst Extract. Write for it.

PABST EXTRACT CO.
Milwaukee, Wis.

Pabst Extract, 1913

Northern Pacific Railway, 1900

Chicago Great Western Railway, 1902

Southern Pacific Steamships, 1910 ◄ *Chicago Great Western Railway, 1901*

Southern Pacific Steamships, 1910

California

THE OLD AND THE NEW WAY

The NEW way is by the SOUTHERN PACIFIC, Sunset Route Express Trains, equipped with latest Pullman Drawing-Room Sleepers, Combination Library, Observation and Buffet Cars, Dining and Chair Cars, a veritable "Hotel on Wheels" with clean Motive Power, Oil-Burning Locomotives, no dirt, dust or cinders, traversing the sugar plantations and rice fields of quaint Louisiana, the historic cities of the great State of Texas, through the interesting states of Arizona and New Mexico, on to the "Road of a Thousand Wonders," to the Garden of the World, the "Italy of America," CALIFORNIA. Connections made at San Francisco with magnificent new steamers of the Pacific Mail Steamship Company for Honolulu, China, Japan, Philippines and Round the World. For all information apply to any agent of

Southern Pacific

NEW YORK, N. Y.   BALTIMORE, MD.
349 Broadway   Baltimore, and Hanover Sts.
1 Broadway

CHICAGO, ILL.   LOS ANGELES, CAL.
120 Jackson Boulevard   600 South Spring St.

ATLANTA, GA.   NEW ORLEANS, LA.
124 Peachtree St.   Magazine and Natchez Sts.

BOSTON, MASS.   PHILADELPHIA, PA.
170 Washington St.   632 Chestnut St.

CINCINNATI, OHIO   SAN FRANCISCO, CAL.
53 East Fourth St.   Ferry Building

HOUSTON, TEXAS   SYRACUSE, N. Y.
Main and Franklin Sts.   212 West Washington St.

HAMBURG, GERMANY
"Amerikahaus," Ferdinand Strasse

Southern Pacific Railway, 1907

Southern Pacific Railway, 1904

Santa Fe Railroad, 1916

New York Central Rail Lines, 1912

Overland Limited Railway, 1907

Union Pacific And Southern Pacific Railway, 1908

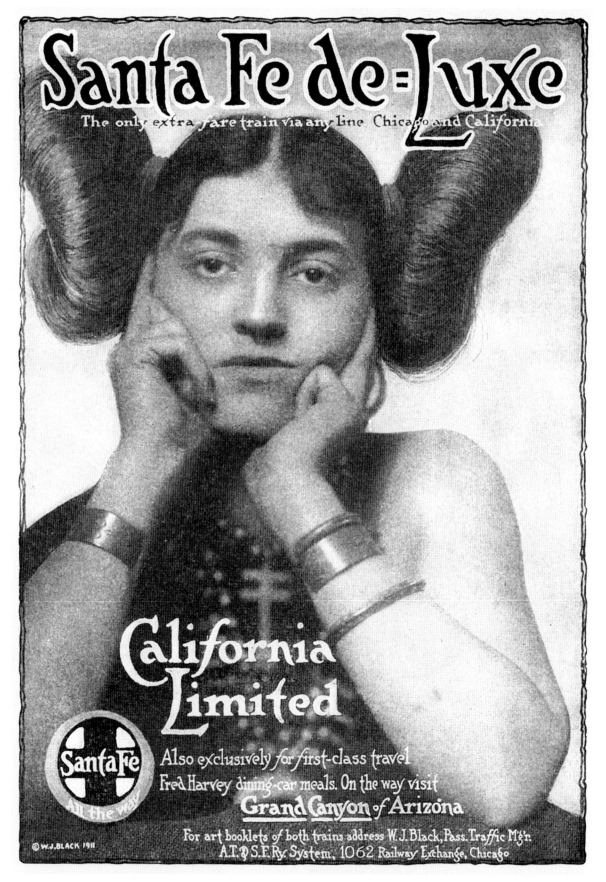

Santa Fe Railroad, 1911

NORTHERN PACIFIC

YELLOWSTONE PARK LINE

GRAND CANYON OF THE YELLOWSTONE

NEW CANYON HOTEL

PLENTY OF SPORT

OLD FAITHFUL GEYSER

EMIGRANT PEAK AND GARDINER RIVER

PLAN NOW FOR NEXT SUMMER'S TRIP TO YELLOWSTONE NATIONAL PARK

The place of all places where you can most profitably spend next summer's vacation is America's Only Geyserland—the nation's largest, oldest and most unique playground. Health, education and recreation are afforded by a sojourn, even though it be brief, in this Wonderland. Geysers, cataracts, canyons, beasts, birds, fish—nature's lavish spread of scenery— her wonderful collection of phenomena—as here enjoyed have no equal elsewhere. Through service to Gardiner, Montana, the original entrance to Yellowstone Park via the Northern Pacific provides a trip of supreme pleasure. Famous dining car meals. Write today for illustrated literature about Yellowstone Park and the trip over the Northern Pacific.

A. M. CLELAND, General Passenger Agent, ST. PAUL.

Northern Pacific Railway

New York Office: 1244 Broadway   Chicago Office: 144 So. Clark St.

Northern Pacific Railway, 1913

Pennsylvania Railroad, 1916

Northern Pacific Railway, 1903

Union Pacific Railway, 1911

Santa Fe Railroad, 1902

Southern Pacific Railway, 1910

The Rock Island Lines
8000 Miles of Modern Railroad

Winter is Only a Name in Golden California

—only a word used to designate a season of the year.

Don't risk the cold weather with its dangers and discomforts.

Take the most enjoyable vacation of your whole life and escape the blizzards and the cold.

Take the "GOLDEN STATE LIMITED" to the balmy land of sea and sunshine—where mountains merge with meadows—where lakes and lagoons lie sparkling under sapphire skies—where springs flow their crystal waters into splendid streams—where fruits and flowers are abundant the whole year through—and where health and happiness await you with a warm welcome.

This semi-tropic land is less than three days from Chicago and St. Louis by the magnificent

"GOLDEN STATE LIMITED"
VIA ROCK ISLAND LINES

New all-steel Pullman equipment—entire train, baggage to observation car, through between Chicago and Los Angeles without change—every luxury of modern travel—for first-class passengers exclusively.

Leaves Chicago 9:00 p. m.
" St. Louis 10:30 p. m. } Kansas City 11:05 a. m. Arrives Los Angeles 3:30 p. m. third day.

THE DIRECT ROUTE OF LOWEST ALTITUDES

The most comfortable and interesting route to California.

The Californian—a second transcontinental train via the *Golden State Route*—modern equipment—excellent service. Reservations, tickets and descriptive booklets about the "Golden State Limited" and "The Californian" from

L. M. ALLEN, Passenger Traffic Manager
Room 278, La Salle Station, Chicago

Rock Island

Rock Island Rail Lines, 1915

Southern Pacific Water And Rail Lines, 1910

The Cleveland And Buffalo Transit Co., 1905

Niagara River Steamship Line, ca. 1904

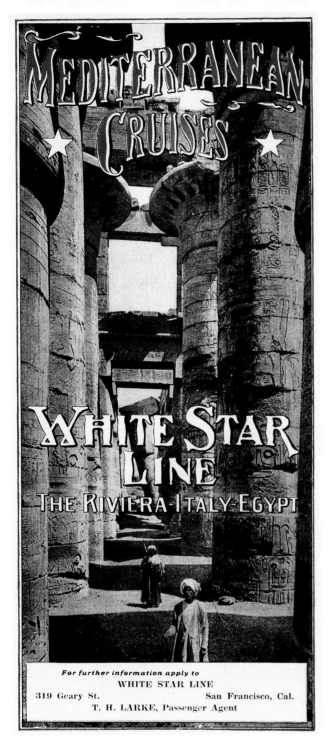

White Star Cruise Line, 1913

Florida East Coast, 1913

Santa Fe Railroad, 1916

California Is Calling You

Sunny skies and shining seas. Blooming flowers and ripening fruits. Invigorating air that's a joy to breathe. All the outdoor sports you can think of. Every form of indoor enjoyment. These are among the infinite fascinations that await you in the land of perpetual sunshine. The *ideal* way, the *shortest* way to go there is by the new, daily, extra fare

OVERLAND LIMITED
Only 64½ hours between
Chicago and San Francisco
Saves a Business Day en Route

Overland Limited is the only exclusively first-class train between Chicago and San Francisco, and the only daily extra fare train between Chicago and California. Extra fare $10.00, and you will agree it is worth more. *Minimum* extra fare for *maximum* extra comforts.

Leaves Chicago from the new Chicago & North Western Passenger Terminal daily at 7.00 p.m., arriving San Francisco 9.30 a. m., third day. The short running time is accomplished by the elimination of stops.

Chicago & North Western
Union Pacific — Southern Pacific

Extra Heavy Steel Rails. Thoroughly Ballasted Roadbed. Automatic Electric Block Safety Signals All the Way. 1473 Miles Double Track.

Direct Route to California Expositions, 1915

For Tickets, Reservations and Full Particulars,
apply to nearest representative, or

J. B. DeFRIEST, Gen'l Eastern Agt.
287 Broadway, New York, N. Y.
H. A. GROSS, Gen'l Agt. Pas. Dept.,   W. G. NEIMYER, Gen'l Agt.
148 South Clark Street, Chicago, Ill.   55 West Jackson Blvd., Chicago, Ill.

On this superior train you have at your command the comforts, conveniences and personal service of the highest class hotel, club or modern home.

Maid, Manicurist, Valet, Barber, Stenographer, News Bulletins, Shower Baths. Library, Buffet, Club and Observation Cars.

All Steel, All New Up-to-the-minute Equipment.

Overland Limited Railway, 1915

Royal Palm Train, 1913

THE GREAT LAKES OF AMERICA

"In all the world no trip like this."

NORTHERN STEAMSHIP CO.

From Buffalo to Chicago or Duluth

SEASON OPENS JUNE 21st

EUROPEAN OR AMERICAN PLAN
(American Plan includes all expenses in one ticket)

Connecting at Duluth with the

GREAT NORTHERN RAILWAY

"THE COMFORTABLE WAY" *to the*

LEWIS & CLARK EXPOSITION

A perfect combination of Lake Voyage and Overland Travel

For full particulars, literature, etc., write to

F. I. WHITNEY, P. T. M.
Great Northern Ry.
St. Paul, Minn.

W. M. LOWRIE, G. P. A.
Northern S. S. Co.
Buffalo, N. Y.

SEAMAN

Northern Steamship Co., 1905

Glenwood Hotel, 1903

Santa Fe Railroad, 1916

Southern California Real Estate Investment Co., 1906

Atlantic City, New Jersey, 1905　▸ Hotel St. Francis, 1904

San Diego

California's Great Exposition Celebrating the Opening of the Panama Canal
California's Christmas Gift

IT is a big idea in gifts, and rather unusual, but one in which all the peoples of the world may participate; one which comes to a full realization on the stroke of midnight at New Year's Eve and lasts until another New Year's Eve in 1916.

The greater part of the United States and Canada—and if you insist, the Northern hemisphere of the old world—is buried today under snow and ice, or soon will be. The song birds are gone, the flowers are gone and the balmy days are gone.

But on the Pacific Coast, near Old Mexico, lies a city where the birds are singing, where roses are in bloom and the oranges are ripe, where snow never comes in and where it is always June. This is San Diego, the Mecca of those who wish comfort and health and happiness—it is the land where one truly lives.

To this land came Spanish sailors and Spanish soldiers and Spanish settlers in the centuries which have passed, and from their life sprang the traditions which still rule their arts and architecture and romance.

And in that Spanish atmosphere of mission and cathedral, of quiet patio and gay fiesta, has been built San Diego's Exposition Beautiful.

THE PLAZA AÚ

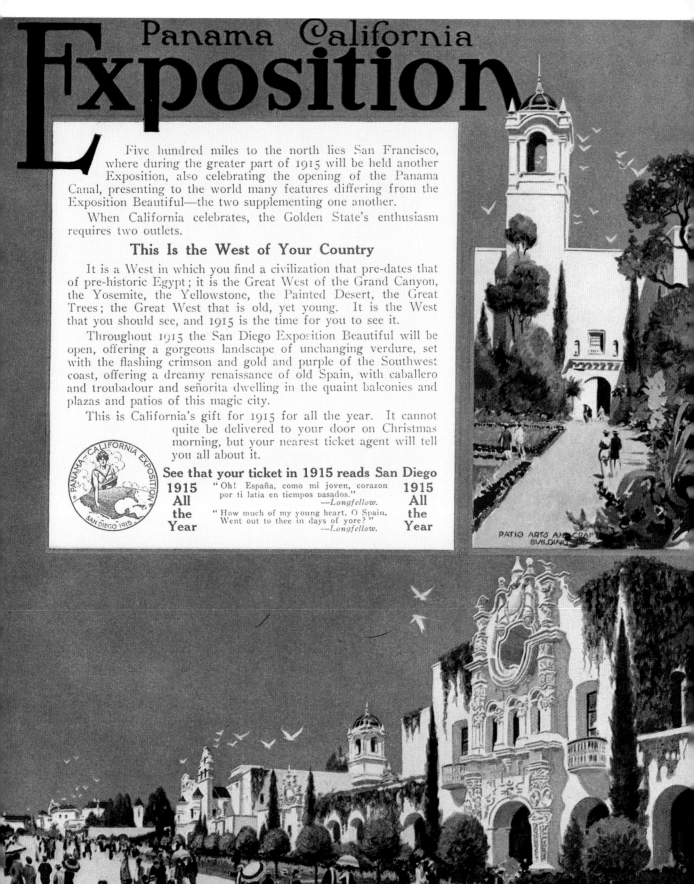

Panama California
Exposition

Five hundred miles to the north lies San Francisco, where during the greater part of 1915 will be held another Exposition, also celebrating the opening of the Panama Canal, presenting to the world many features differing from the Exposition Beautiful—the two supplementing one another.

When California celebrates, the Golden State's enthusiasm requires two outlets.

This Is the West of Your Country

It is a West in which you find a civilization that pre-dates that of pre-historic Egypt; it is the Great West of the Grand Canyon, the Yosemite, the Yellowstone, the Painted Desert, the Great Trees; the Great West that is old, yet young. It is the West that you should see, and 1915 is the time for you to see it.

Throughout 1915 the San Diego Exposition Beautiful will be open, offering a gorgeous landscape of unchanging verdure, set with the flashing crimson and gold and purple of the Southwest coast, offering a dreamy renaissance of old Spain, with caballero and troubadour and señorita dwelling in the quaint balconies and plazas and patios of this magic city.

This is California's gift for 1915 for all the year. It cannot quite be delivered to your door on Christmas morning, but your nearest ticket agent will tell you all about it.

See that your ticket in 1915 reads San Diego

1915
All
the
Year

"Oh! España, como mi joven, corazon
por ti latia en tiempos pasados."
—*Longfellow.*

"How much of my young heart, O Spain,
Went out to thee in days of yore?"
—*Longfellow.*

1915
All
the
Year

PATIO ARTS AND CRAFTS BUILDING

IT APPEARS TODAY.

HAWAII
PLEASURELAND
For The TOURIST

A Trip Exceeding All Anticipation

YOUR enjoyment of fascinating Honolulu and the "Isles of Peace" depends largely upon **the route you travel.**

For the traveler who desires a fast, safe trip—with every comfort and luxury—the new de luxe service offered by the floating

"Palace of the Pacific"—S. S. GREAT NORTHERN

should prove attractive.

This trip will prove a realization of your fondest travel dreams—the delightful ocean voyage on this $3,000,000 triple turbiner—the tropical climate, picturesque scenery, and natural wonders all combining to make it a trip never to be forgotten.

VOLCANO KILAUEA—"HOME OF ETERNAL FIRE"

Stop is made at Hilo, affording passengers opportunity of seeing the world-famous Volcano Kilauea both by day and by night.

Mail the coupon below and let us give you full details of a trip to the "Paradise of the Pacific" via the "Palace of the Pacific."

H. A. JACKSON, General Traffic Manager, SAN FRANCISCO

H. A. JACKSON, General Traffic Manager,
Great Northern Pacific S. S. Co., San Francisco.

Please send me your free information and descriptive literature on the Hawaiian Islands.

Name...

Address..

City...State..................

SAILINGS
From San Francisco
Nov. 7, 27; Dec. 15; Jan. 4, 23; Feb. 12; Mar. 5, 23.
From Los Angeles
One Day Later.

Fares on Application

Only Four Days
From The Mainland

Panama-California International Exposition, 1914 ◄ *Great Northern Pacific Steamship Co., 1916*

Southern Pacific Steamships, 1903

Southern Pacific Steamships, 1907

Pacific Mail Steamship Co., 1906

CLARK'S 14th ANNUAL CRUISE to the **MEDITERRANEAN** and the **ORIENT** FEBRUARY 8th 1912

The White Star S.S. ARABIC (16,000 TONS) similar in type to the BALTIC, CEDRIC and CELTIC, one of the largest and steadiest ships in the World.

SPECIAL FEATURES:
MADEIRA, CADIZ.
SEVILLE (ALHAMBRA)
MALTA, ATHENS,
CONSTANTINOPLE,
19 DAYS IN PALESTINE & EGYPT.
4 DAYS IN ROME MONTE CARLO ETC. ETC.

BY THE SPECIALLY CHARTERED
WHITE STAR S.S. ARABIC
February 8th to April 19th 1912.
A TOUR OF 71 DAYS
COSTING ONLY $400.00 AND UP.
IF INTERESTED SEND FOR ILLUSTRATED PROGRAM.

NO OVERCROWDING
FIRST CLASS THROUGHOUT
INCLUDING
SHORE EXCURSIONS, GUIDES.
FEES, HOTELS, DRIVES ETC.

HOMEWARD OCEAN TICKETS GOOD ON THE S.S. ADRIATIC, BALTIC, CELTIC, CEDRIC, ETC.

For further particulars apply to H. B. RICE CO., 609 South Spring St., Los Angeles, Cal.

Clark's Cruise Line, 1912

"ONE HUNDRED GOLDEN HOURS AT SEA"

Magnificent New 10,000 Ton Steamships, with Luxurious Accommodations
Suites, Staterooms, Baths, Promenade Decks, Unsurpassed Cuisine

Southern Pacific Passenger Steamships
"CREOLE" "MOMUS" "ANTILLES" "PROTEUS" "COMUS"

Weekly in Both Directions between

NEW YORK AND NEW ORLEANS
A Delightful Ocean Trip Summer or Winter

Connections at New Orleans with

SUNSET ROUTE
Trains of Superior Equipment to and from Points in

LOUISIANA, TEXAS, NEW AND OLD MEXICO, ARIZONA, CALIFORNIA, OREGON

Superior Service All the Way

Send for Copy "A Hundred Golden Hours At Sea" Free

L. H. NUTTING, G. P. A., 366 Broadway, New York
Or Any Southern Pacific Agent

Southern Pacific Steamships, 1908

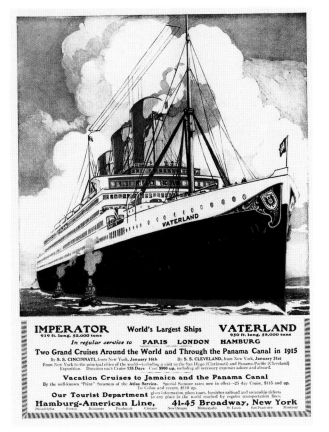

IMPERATOR World's Largest Ships **VATERLAND**
919 ft. long, 52,000 tons   950 ft. long, 58,000 tons
In regular service to PARIS LONDON HAMBURG
Two Grand Cruises Around the World and Through the Panama Canal in 1915
By S. S. CINCINNATI, from New York, January 16th   By S. S. CLEVELAND, from New York, January 31st
From New York to the principal cities of the world—including a visit to the San Diego (Cincinnati) and Panama-Pacific (Cleveland)
Exposition. Duration each Cruise 135 Days Cost $900 up, including all necessary expenses ashore and aboard.
Vacation Cruises to Jamaica and the Panama Canal
By the well-known "Prinz" Steamers of the Atlas Service. Special Summer rates now in effect—25 day Cruise, $115 and up.
To Colon and return, $110 up.
Our Tourist Department gives information, plans tours, furnishes railroad and steamship tickets
to any place in the world reached by regular transportation lines.
Hamburg-American Line, 41-45 Broadway, New York
Philadelphia   Boston   Baltimore   Pittsburgh   Chicago   New Orleans   Minneapolis   St. Louis   San Francisco   Montreal

Hamburg-American Cruise Line, 1914

Austrian Lloyd Cruise Line, 1912

THE TRANS-ATLANTIC SERVICES OF THE

NORTH GERMAN LLOYD, BREMEN.

Imperial MAIL SERVICES to CHINA. JAPAN and AUSTRALIA.

LUXURY, COMFORT, SAFETY, SPEED

OELRICHS & CO., General Agents - - - - 5 BROADWAY, NEW YORK

Oelrichs & Co., 1909

▸ *United Fruit Company Steamship Service, 1912*

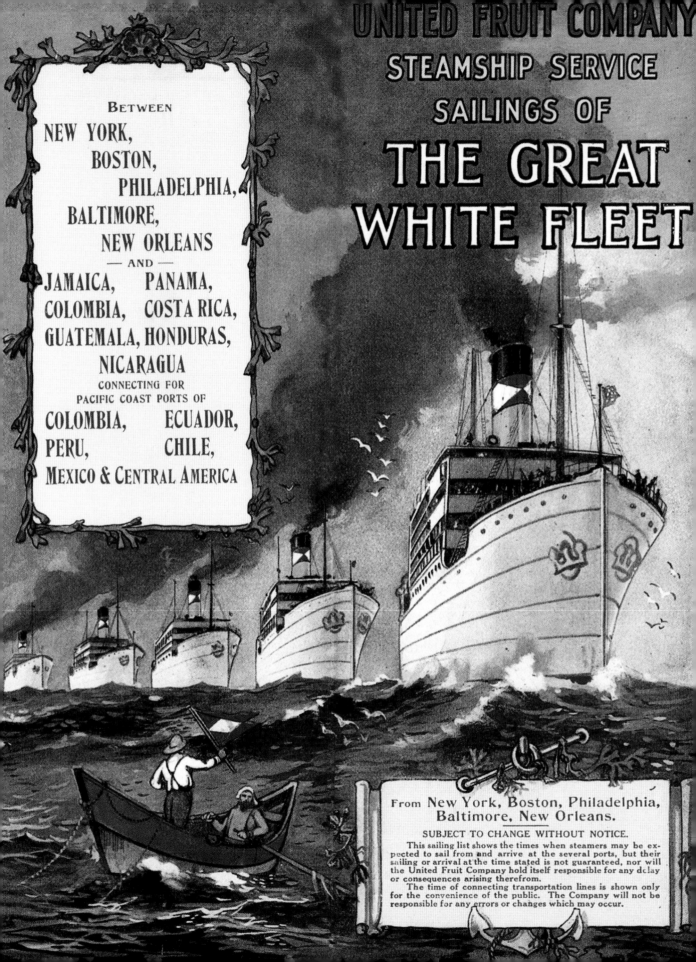

Cunard Cruise Line, ca. 1914

HAMBURG-AMERICAN LINE
CRUISES

In Service next May, S.S. Imperator
World's Largest Ship

ORIENT From New York, January 28, 1913
by S.S. Cincinnati (17,000 tons),
80 days, $325 and up.

WEST INDIES 8 Cruises during January, February, March
and April by S.S. Moltke and S.S. Victoria Luise.

AROUND THE WORLD
Sixth Cruise sailing from San Francisco by
S.S. Cleveland (17,000 tons), duration
including all necessary

Write for booklet stating Cruise

Hamburg-American Line
41-45 Broadway   New York

Hamburg-American Cruise Line, 1912

▸ *Southern Pacific Steamships, 1907*

Hamburg-American Cruise Line, 1911

▶ Cunard Cruise Line, 1911

BIRCH-FIELD & Co.

THE GREAT WHITE FLEET

"—there she lies

*white as a swan—
our home for two weeks"*

—and such a home; all the staterooms are outside rooms, de luxe and en suite; there are baths in plenty; spacious decks; meals that tempt the appetite. Courteous service; restful ease.

Havana, the beautiful; Jamaica, "Land of Smiling Summer;" the Panama Canal; the romantic byways of the Spanish Main—you can enjoy them all in the wonderful ships of the GREAT WHITE FLEET, built especially for tropical travel.

Sailings of GREAT WHITE FLEET Ships from New York and New Orleans every Wednesday, Thursday and Saturday.

Cruises from 17 to 22 days to

CUBA, JAMAICA, PANAMA CANAL, COLOMBIAN PORTS, CENTRAL and SOUTH AMERICA

Liberal stopover privileges granted.

Ships sailing from New York on Wednesdays and on all days from New Orleans are American-plan service; fare includes meals and berth. Cruises de luxe from New York, sailings every Saturday on the palatial new steamers, Pastores, Tenadores and Calamares. A la carte service on these ships only. Pay for what you eat.

OFFICES FOR INFORMATION

Long Wharf, Boston; 630 Common Street, New Orleans; 1955 Continental and Commercial Bank Building, Chicago, or any ticket or tourist agent; or write

**PASSENGER DEPARTMENT
UNITED FRUIT COMPANY STEAMSHIP SERVICE
17 Battery Place, New York**

for folders, sailing list and full information.

Write for our new book —edition de luxe—

The Story of a la Carte

A historic gem, in which is related in Ancient Medieval and Modern times what people ate at Sea—and how. A story of sea dining, from 4,500 B.C. to date.

SAILING UNDER THE AMERICAN FLAG

UNITED FRUIT COMPANY STEAMSHIP SERVICE

United Fruit Company Steamship Service, 1914

United Fruit Company Steamship Service, 1916

SOUTH AMERICA

LAMPORT & HOLT LINE

Lamport & Holt Cruise Line, ca. 1912

▶ *White Star Cruise Line, 1913*

VENICE

And the winner is...

Southern Hospitality

In less enlightened times, racial stereotypes were used extensively to promote a range of products and services. The Plant System, which offered train service to Florida, established a regional image with this trio of happy, barefoot, Black boys atop a crate. The carefree appearance was what the public expected in the South, but the reality African Americans experienced was far from that. Needless to say, these boys could never have set foot inside the fine resorts of the Sunshine State.

Gastfreundschaft in den Südstaaten

In der weniger multikulturell aufgeklärten „guten alten Zeit" wurden rassistische Vorurteile in großem Umfang benutzt, um jede Menge Produkte und Dienstleistungen anzupreisen. Das „Plant System", das eine Zugverbindung nach Florida unterhielt, gab sich mit dem Bild dieses Trios glücklicher, barfüßiger schwarzer Jungen auf einer Kiste ein regional geprägtes Image. Schwarze hatten munter und sorglos zu sein, auch wenn die Lebensrealität der Afroamerikaner ganz anders aussah. Dass diese Jungs keinen Fuß in eines der feinen Hotels im *Sunshine State* setzen durften, versteht sich von selbst.

L'hospitalité du Sud

A une époque moins civilisée, les stéréotypes raciaux étaient abondamment utilisés dans la publicité pour proposer produits et services. *Plant System*, qui offrait un service de trains pour la Floride, s'était créé une image typique de la région avec ce trio de joyeux petits Noirs aux pied nus, assis sur une caisse. Dans l'esprit du public, le Sud était associé à une certaine idée de désinvolture, ce qui était très loin de la réalité quotidienne des Afros-américains. Inutile de dire que ces gamins n'auraient jamais pu mettre les pieds dans les luxueuses résidences de l'Etat du soleil.

Hospitalidad sureña

En tiempos menos progresistas, los estereotipos raciales se usaban con profusión para promocionar una serie de productos y servicios. La excursión Plant System, que ofrecía un servicio de trenes hasta Florida, invitaba a descubrir «la vida en las plantaciones» y vendía la región con la imagen de este trío de alegres muchachos negros con los pies descalzos sentados en un cajón de madera. El aspecto descuidado era lo que el público esperaba encontrar en el Sur, pero la realidad que experimentaban los afroamericanos era bien distinta. Sobra decir que a aquellos muchachos no se les habría permitido poner un pie en los complejos vacacionales de lujo del Estado del Sol.

南のおもてなし

啓蒙が進んでいなかった頃、商品やサービスの範囲を拡大するために人種的な手段が常套的に使われていた。フロリダへ運行する列車会社 Plant System は、この木箱に乗って幸せそうな裸足の黒人の男の子3人組によって地域イメージを確立した。のんきな風采は人々が南部に期待しているものを表しているが、現実のアフリカ系アメリカ人の体験はそれから程遠いものだった。言うまでもなく、この男の子達はサンシャイン・ステート（訳者注：フロリダ州の異名）の美しいリゾートの中へは足を踏み入れたことも無かった。

The Plant System Railroads And Steamboats, 1900

Index

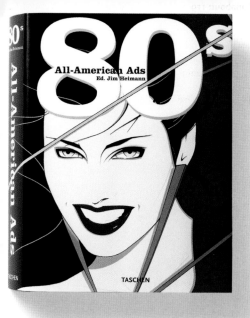

ALL-AMERICAN ADS OF THE 80s
Steven Heller, Ed. Jim Heimann / Flexi-cover,
format: 19.6 x 25.5 cm (7.7 x 10 in.), 608 pp.
**ONLY € 29.99 / $ 39.99
£ 19.99 / ¥ 5.900**

Where's the beef?

Pushing products in the Reagan years

With the cold war ebbing, crime and inflation at record levels, and movie star-turned-President Ronald Reagan launching a Star Wars of his own, the 1980s did not seem likely to become one of the most outrageous, flamboyant, and prosperous decades of the 20th century. The "greed is good" mantra on Wall Street spawned the power-dressing, exercise-obsessed "Me Generation" of Yuppies—high on cash, cocaine, and Calvins. The art world enjoyed the influx of capital; computers and video games ruled in the office and at home; and the Rubik's Cube craze swept the nation.

Leg warmers were big, shoulder pads were bigger and hair was biggest of all. Whether your heart warms nostalgically at the memory of E.T., marathon Trivial Pursuit sessions, and The Cosby Show; if you think Knight Rider, Alf, and break dancing are totally awesome; or Tiffany, baggy acid wash jeans, and Cabbage Patch Kids make you wanna scream, "gag me with a spoon," this book's for you. To all those who still hear the echoes of "I want my MTV": *All-American Ads of the 80s* will leave you ready to reach out and touch someone. So just do it!

The editor:

Jim Heimann is a resident of Los Angeles, a graphic designer, writer, historian, and instructor at Art Center College of Design in Pasadena, California. He is the author of numerous books on architecture, popular culture, and Hollywood history, and serves as a consultant to the entertainment industry.

ALSO AVAILABLE

ALL-AMERICAN ADS OF THE 20s
Steven Heller, Ed. Jim Heimann /
Flexi-cover, 640 pp.

ALL-AMERICAN ADS OF THE 30s
Steven Heller, Ed. Jim Heimann /
Flexi-cover, 768 pp.

ALL-AMERICAN ADS OF THE 40s
W.R. Wilkerson III, Ed. Jim Heimann /
Flexi-cover, 768 pp.

ALL-AMERICAN ADS OF THE 50s
Ed. Jim Heimann / Flexi-cover, 928 pp.

ALL-AMERICAN ADS OF THE 60s
Steven Heller, Ed. Jim Heimann /
Flexi-cover, 960 pp.

ALL-AMERICAN ADS OF THE 70s
Steven Heller, Ed. Jim Heimann /
Flexi-cover, 704 pp.

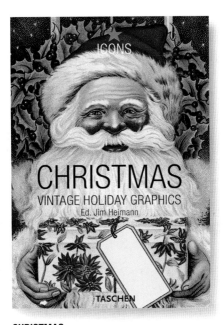
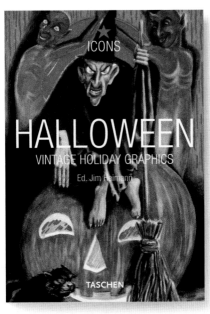
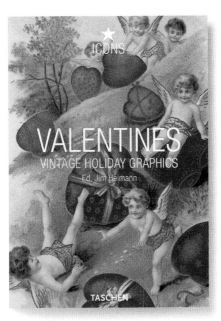

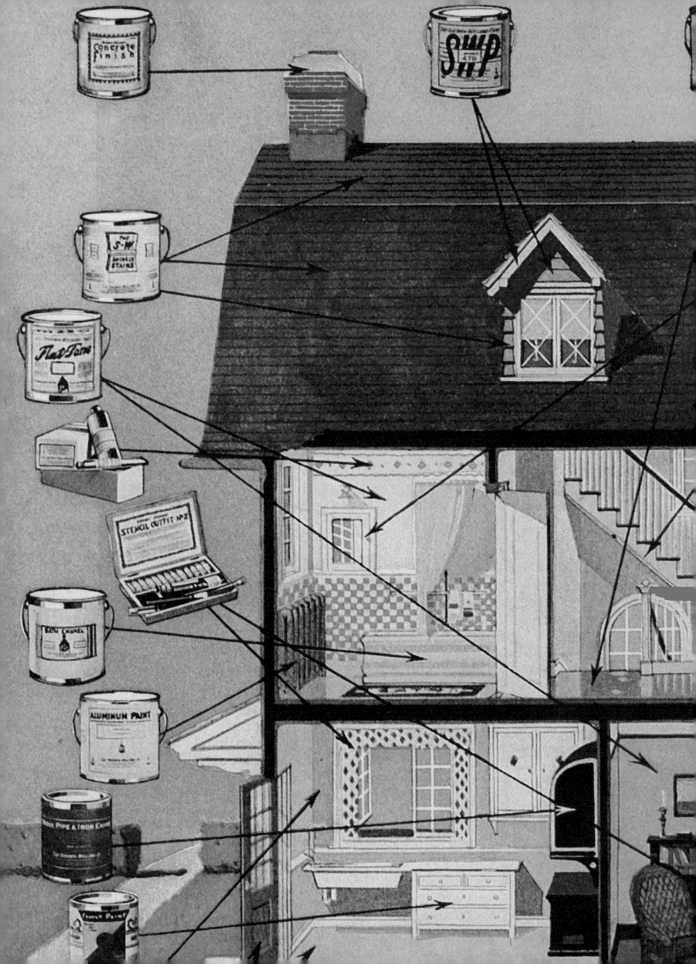